T3-BSB-787

UNDERSTANDING VIOLENCE AND ABUSE

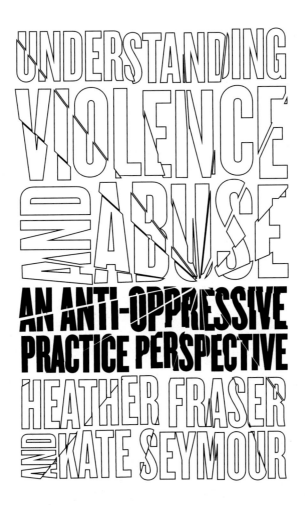

UNDERSTANDING VIOLENCE AND ABUSE

AN ANTI-OPPRESSIVE PRACTICE PERSPECTIVE

HEATHER FRASER AND KATE SEYMOUR

FERNWOOD PUBLISHING
HALIFAX & WINNIPEG

BRESCIA UNIVERSITY
COLLEGE LIBRARY

Copyright © 2017 Heather Fraser and Kate Seymour

All rights reserved. No part of this book may be reproduced or transmitted in any form by any means without permission in writing from the publisher, except by a reviewer, who may quote brief passages in a review.

Editing: Jessica Antony
Cover design: John van der Woude
Printed and bound in Canada

Published by Fernwood Publishing
32 Oceanvista Lane, Black Point, Nova Scotia, B0J 1B0
and 748 Broadway Avenue, Winnipeg, Manitoba, R3G 0X3
www.fernwoodpublishing.ca

Fernwood Publishing Company Limited gratefully acknowledges the financial support of the Government of Canada, the Manitoba Department of Culture, Heritage and Tourism under the Manitoba Publishers Marketing Assistance Program and the Province of Manitoba, through the Book Publishing Tax Credit, for our publishing program. We are pleased to work in partnership with the Province of Nova Scotia to develop and promote our creative industries for the benefit of all Nova Scotians. We acknowledge the support of the Canada Council for the Arts, which last year invested $153 million to bring the arts to Canadians throughout the country.

Library and Archives Canada Cataloguing in Publication

Fraser, Heather, 1965-, author
Understanding violence and abuse: an anti-oppressive
practice perspective / Heather Fraser and Kate Seymour.

Includes bibliographical references and index.
ISBN 978-1-55266-887-0 (softcover)

1. Violence—Case studies. 2. Offenses against the
person—Case studies. I. Seymour, Kate, 1968–, author
II. Title.

HM886.F73 2017   303.6   C2017-903174-0

CONTENTS

ACKNOWLEDGEMENTS

From Heather: Thanks to Jessica Antony at Fernwood Publishing for her work on the project. Thanks also to Flinders University for providing support for the project, and to Professor Bob Pease, for originally suggesting we write this. To Nik Taylor, thank you for your friendship and support, but also your feedback on this project. To my partner Bruce and companion animals, Gus, Murray, Alice, Sunny and Charli, thanks for supporting me in the beautiful ways that you do.

From Kate: For my sister, JRS, physically not here but with me always, and my dear, tender-hearted mum, WSS, who loves us both; it was and always will be just the three of us. To my funny, sweet and very loud children, Rosa Joanna and Archer George, and their father Reg: thank you, my heart is full.

Part I

CONCEPTUALIZING VIOLENCE AND ABUSE

I. INTRODUCTION AND OVERVIEW

- **Why focus on violence and abuse?**
- **Why understand violence and abuse FROM an anti-oppressive practice (AOP) perspective?**
- **How is this book organized?**

Global statistics of violence and abuse — inclusive of neglect and deprivation — are staggering. The World Health Organization (2013) estimates that as many as 38 percent of all murders of women across the world are committed by intimate partners. In Canada, there were 516 homicides in 2014 (see <http://www.statcan.gc.ca/tables-tableaux/sum-som/l01/cst01/legal12a-eng.htm>). Between 2004 and 2014, the number of Canadian soldiers killed in combat in Afghanistan was 138, a number eclipsed by the 160 returned soldiers who committed suicide during this same period (Campion-Smith 2014). In 2015 in the United States, gun violence accounted for 53,151 incidents and 13,402 deaths <http://www.gunviolencearchive.org/past-tolls>. In the U.S. during 2015, police killed 1134 people, with young Black men the most likely target (Guardian 2015). Yet, in the popular imagination, it is random strangers who commit violence in dark alleys, old warehouses and unlit car parks. Less often do we recognize family members abusing their "loved ones" at home, people being killed by police and individuals so desperate that they take their own lives. These are just some of the many twists in the public and private stories told about violence and abuse.

From an anti-oppressive practice (AOP) perspective, a great variety of violence and abuse are recognized and responded to, not just those committed by "bad" or "mad" individuals. A major goal of this book is to shift the conversation about violence and abuse to connect large-scale violence and systemic abuse with those perpetrated by individuals, including those known to victims/survivors. To use Walton's (2011) phrase, we need to stop "spinning our wheels" to look at safety in the context of oppression, privilege and diversity. We need to consider "normative cruelties," that is, cruelties produced in everyday life, often unnoticed and, as a consequence, neglected (Ringrose and Renold 2010).

We have been writing this book during a time of rapid global economic, social and environmental change; a time where we are experiencing the effects of climate change and ongoing violence across but also within borders (see Ife 2012, 2016). Welfare austerity and more punitive approaches to asylum seekers and people living in poverty are occurring in increasingly more countries (see Mendes 2008). While this makes our work harder, it is even more reason to engage with violence and abuse from an AOP perspective — because it takes into account not only interpersonal (and intrapersonal) factors and experiences, but also those relating to collectives, social symbols, structures and cultures.

Recent decades have brought new rounds of public disclosures of violence and abuse, with calls to "put intimate partner violence on your radar" (Collett and Bennett 2015), to hold perpetrators accountable and to connect the dots between social attitudes that devalue people and actions that degrade and/or violate. Beyond family homes we have witnessed truth commissions (see Androff 2010), inquiries into deaths in custody and institutional [negligent] responses to sexual abuse (see Fater and Mullaney 2000). Around the world religious institutions are being exposed for their refusal to support victims/survivors of abuse and instead collude with, if not hide, perpetrators (see for instance, the Historical Institutional Abuse Inquiry (2014) in Northern Ireland). Laws have also been introduced to prosecute child sex tourists who exploit children overseas (see Hodgson 1993). Previously untouchable entertainers such as Jimmy Saville and Rolf Harris have been charged as criminals (see Middleton, Stavropoulos, Dorahy, et al. 2014). We are now more aware of the sexual abuse perpetrated against boys and men (see Easton 2013) and the institutional failures to hold perpetrators to account.

Recognition of the link between human and animal abuse is occurring, albeit in some countries more than others, and has resulted in policies and programs that directly address human and animal experiences of violence and try to prevent it (see National Link Coalition 2016). At the local community level, new programs have been instituted at schools to prevent bullying, including the bullying of gay, lesbian, bisexual and transgendered students (Ryan and Rivers 2003). However, at the same time, neoliberalism, welfare austerity and more punitive approaches to health, welfare and education are being adopted across the world and are making life much harder for many, especially people living in poverty (see Mendes 2008).

New laws, policies and programs are usually the result of decades of campaigning to first recognize and then redress violence and abuse that has not, until now, been publicly addressed. Those promoting gender equality and non-violence know that not all forms of violence and abuse are equally recognized (see Connell 2014; Fater and Mullaney 2000; Flood 2001; Pease 2011). Some violence and abuse can go unnoticed, even encouraged and legitimated in laws and customs, in turn producing crises of public confidence in authority sources such as the state, the media and the church (Veenema, Goodwin, Clifton and Corley 2015). Consider, for instance, that rape in marriage was not a crime in South Australia until 1976; that domestic violence was not a crime in Bangladesh until 2010; and that marrying girls under the age of eighteen was legal in Kenya until 2014 (see <http://www.girlsnotbrides.org/child-marriage/kenya/>). In thirty-one states in the U.S., familial child sex offenders are still legally entitled to visitation and custody rights with their child victims (see <http://www.thewire.com/national/2012/08/31-states-grant-rapists-custody-and-visitation-rights/56118/>).

Indigenous communities in Australia, New Zealand, Canada and elsewhere continue to struggle for equality, against poverty and staggeringly high incarceration rates, linked to past and present systemic violence committed against them (see Baines 2006; Brown and Strega 2005; Dominelli and Campling 2002). With other people of colour and discredited religious and cultural identities, younger Black men are at risk of violence, especially from other men on the streets and in prisons.

Violence and abuse can occur inside institutions, including those with great prestige. Under the cover of respectability, in such places as "nice" homes, churches and schools, trusted authorities including fathers, mothers, priests and teachers commit abuse and violence (see Jewkes 2002; Phillips and Vandenbroek 2014). For victims/survivors and their loved ones, violence and abuse is shocking and often life changing, catapulting subjects into new identities and futures (see Bass and Davis 2002; Veenema, Thornton and Corley 2015). It is a necessary but obvious point to make that violence and abuse can be fatal. For the people (and animals) who die as a result of violence or abuse, there is obviously no future, other than the grief family members and friends will feel and the memories they carry of the victims' lives. The emotional, spiritual and psychological effects for individuals, groups and communities are important to understand. Attending to the structural context and political underpinnings — social, cultural, economic and environmental — of violence and abuse is equally critical. The key contribution of this book is to bring together the personal and the political in order to expand the ways in which we think about and respond to violence and abuse.

While the scale, extent and variety of violence and abuse makes our work harder, it is even more reason to conceptualize and respond to violence and abuse from an AOP perspective. Throughout this book we argue that unfair advantage, not just disadvantage, needs to be recognized to avoid unwittingly reinscribing deficiency and inferiority onto the oppressed. The oppressed are so because of the perpetuation of unfair systems of privilege; they are two sides of the same coin. Like oppression, privileges so often get explained away through appeals to hyper-individualism, discourses undergirded by old-fashioned notions of pulling yourself up by your bootstraps and associated clichés such as "you can make it if you only try hard enough." Thinking about who gets to voice which experiences and which experiences and groups lie silent, dormant, unheard, is an expression of this. While structural inequalities need to be challenged, practical tasks are also necessary to ensure that the needs of individuals and families are met. Practical support to rebuild lives can involve any number of activities including advocating, lobbying and mobilizing for changes that address inequalities. However, because this book is about understanding violence and abuse from an AOP perspective, we resist the inclination to prematurely problem solve and offer solutions. We are aware that policy alone cannot solve the extensive and varied problems of abuse and violence. There is more on this later.

ABOUT US, YOUR AUTHORS

Co-authoring this book are two women whose interest in violence and abuse is not just academic and professional, but also personal and political. Throughout the process of writing this book we have forged a sense of solidarity and renewed sense of purpose for fighting violence and abuse, in all its forms, especially those that seem too hard, big, complex, entrenched and infinite. Yet, we never set out with this explicit intention. It happened more organically after the team initially meant to write this book had fallen away. Since the two of us are both social work academics in neighbouring offices on the same campus, we thought, why not write it together?

Looking back there are many reasons for not coming together to write, not least our theoretical differences, which we were yet to come up close with. One of us is a more orthodox structural/materialist feminist, perhaps reflecting her experience as a women's advocate in domestic violence, focusing specifically on the rights of women and children. The other is more post-structural, perhaps reflecting her experience in corrections, working closely with men. To the uninitiated it might sound odd, but these differences are not automatically bridged, even through our shared experiences of white and middle-class privilege.

The process of writing this book has been painful, as much as it's been intellectually stimulating. Emotionally, it is intense being immersed in so many interconnected questions about violence and abuse and their seemingly infinite varieties. The ambitious nature of our attempts to connect so many varieties of violence and abuse gave us regular pause for thought. Reading about the effects of so many forms of violence and abuse, in so many contexts, can hurt. That is the price of empathy — feeling others' pain.

In a society that loves to both individualize experience and group people into heroes and villains, it requires discipline to take a different path. The simplistic and, largely, unthinking tendency to cast people as good or evil, innocent or guilty, worthy or unworthy, is indeed seductive, especially during periods of great uncertainty and fear. It can be comforting to feel that we know, straight away, who needs rescuing and who needs to be condemned. Refusing to fall into this trap is essential to anti-oppressive practice, not least because so many of the supposed villains are unfairly held responsible for the violence others perpetrate against themselves and children. The non-abusive parent (of whom most are mothers) is often held responsible for "failing to protect" their children, a concept and public policy initiative that has swept much of the Western world and holds mostly women unfairly to account for their male partners' violence (see Carlton, Krane, Lapierre, et al. 2013).

This book is as much a product of our friendship and solidarity as it is cognition. Over the course of the last two years we have gotten to know, trust and respect each other. This has allowed us to share more risky emotions and thoughts, further strengthening our connection. Looking back, we can see that this book was possible because of our preparedness to talk about our shared purpose but also our many differences. We hope that the book is stronger for it.

Heather Fraser was born in Australia and has been a social work academic for twenty years. Heather's practice experience relates predominantly to women and children, particularly in areas related to abuse. Before becoming an academic she worked with young people experiencing homelessness as a result of neglect and/or abuse, then as a hospital social worker, a women's policy and information officer, a needle exchange worker and, after this, a community social worker in Bethnal Green, London. She has been a feminist for decades and teaches from an AOP perspective. Among other publications, Heather is the author of the (2008) book, *In the Name of Love, Women's Narratives of Love and Abuse,* and the co-author of *Neoliberalization, Universities and the Public Intellectual: Species, Gender and Class and the Production of Knowledge* (Fraser and Taylor 2016). With Nik Taylor, she is also working on a new book, *Rescuing Me, Rescuing You: Companion Animals and Domestic Violence* (forthcoming 2018).

Kate Seymour is an Australian social work academic with a background in criminology, as well as direct practice experience in the areas of child protection and adult offending. Her research interests and expertise relates to the mobilization of discourses of gender, masculinities and violence in the policies and practices of violence prevention and intervention. She is a skilled qualitative researcher and has established a growing reputation for her contribution to the critical study of masculinities and men's violence.

THE WAY THE BOOK IS ORGANIZED

As our title suggests, our overarching aim is to understand violence and abuse from an AOP perspective. This is ambitious enough. Future work can contribute by both identifying more definitive AOP interventions and exploring alternative economic systems, whether these be global, national and/or local. Here, though, we are interested in opening up discussion and raising critical questions about violence and abuse, rather than prescribing "best practices."

The book is organized into three parts, nine chapters and some closing comments. For explanatory purposes, we have mapped out our ideas about how to approach violence and abuse from an AOP perspective, moving from the conceptualization of violence and abuse to the recognition of and responses to violence and abuse. In practice, these three activities do not occur in a neat, linear fashion, but rather overlap and feed back into each other. Throughout we draw on a range of examples and case studies. In this our aim has been to reach widely; as Australian authors, however, we do acknowledge a distinctly Australian "flavour."

Part 1 focuses on how we are conceptualizing violence and abuse. In it we define key terms, discuss different ways of studying violence and abuse and how seemingly innocent terms such as "vulnerability" and "resilience" have deeply political implications. Our discussion of AOP principles is designed to show the connections between AOP ideas and practices, especially those relevant to violence and abuse.

Part 2 recognizes violence and abuse through the dual lens of privilege and oppression. Our aim here is to concentrate on the often ignored violence and abuse associated with class oppression, street violence, white privilege, war and Islamophobia. The shame attached to the experience of abuse in intimate relationships will also be considered, and examples drawn from a wide range of countries will be explored.

Part 3 focuses more explicitly on AOP responses to violence and abuse through modalities of practice relating to law and social policy, international aid, community organizing and group work, then individual and therapeutic interventions. Interlacing these discussions are many examples, but also practice notes derived from large bodies of violence and abuse research now available.

Chapter by Chapter Overview

Chapter 1 provides an overview of violence and abuse from an AOP perspective. We discuss why a theoretical perspective is important, both for conceptualizing violence and abuse within broader social and cultural contexts and taking account of dominant and subordinate discourses.

In Chapter 2, we make the argument that how we name, frame and define violence and abuse reveals a great deal about those doing the defining. The policy and practice interventions that follow impact on all members of society and not just those identified as violators and the violated. Violence and abuse that is ignored, unnamed and/or trivialized is equally revealing, reflecting broader assumptions regarding what is "normal" and "acceptable." This chapter provides critical context for the content and complex detail that follows.

The AOP practice principles relevant to understanding violence and abuse are examined in Chapter 3. Our approach is deliberately broad as we seek to explore practice principles that allow professionals to consider structural — and not just individual — responses to violence and abuse. We argue that the production and negotiation of group identities are critical to the ways in which victims and perpetrators relate to both their immediate and globalized environments. In so doing, we show how risk management and other related concepts, such as resilience, can take on distinctly different, and perhaps unintended, meanings in the "real world."

Chapter 4 maps the interrelationships between the social structures of class, "race," culture and ethnicity and experiences of violence and abuse. Race and class privilege are discussed, as well as the cumulative and continuing effects of colonization. Rather than inspecting Other groups and trying to learn how "they" operate, the approach we advocate here is that AOP workers, first and foremost, maintain a critically reflexive stance concerning their socio-cultural location and all that this means. We acknowledge that this is potentially confronting work, especially for those who have not already inspected their (unearned) social privileges.

Chapter 5 explores the interconnections between gender and violence within the context of globally and locally structured power relations. We discuss the significant implications of sex, gender and sexuality as dominant discourses for understanding both patterns and experiences of abuse and violence. The issues explored here include violence against women, men's diverse experiences of/ with violence and abuse and the importance of homophobia and transphobia with respect to violence against lesbian, gay, bisexual, transsexual and transgender, intersex and queer (collectively LGBTIQ) people in particular.

Ability and age are the organizing themes for Chapter 6. Attention is shared across a range of fields, including child abuse, elder abuse and disablism. We show how ageism can be perpetrated against older and younger people. We note that violence and abuse prevent many younger and older people from being able to live in their family homes. Using a range of international statistics and case studies, we show that abuse can also happen behind the closed doors of "care." Many disabled people, like some elderly people and the very young, have little or no control over who dispenses care to them and how. The challenges and barriers confronting disabled people in residential settings — whether "home" or institution — enable abuse perpetrated by caregivers to continue over protracted periods of time without detection. Recognizing the structural burden of care in (Westernised) society and the general undervaluing of the caregiving role nonetheless provides important context. Attention must also be given to those caregivers abused by the people they care for, and/or their relatives.

Legal and social policy responses are the focus of Chapter 7. Countries such as Canada, Australia and England are signatories to United Nations Conventions and Declarations, as well as in agreement with other international regulatory bodies associated with human rights and responsibilities. Collectively, these policy commitments and aspirations envisage a world where violence and abuse does not cast a shadow over (so many) peoples' lives. However, from an AOP point of view, such agreements constitute only one of several necessary responses. Considering a range of international examples, we explore the ways in which social policies have been applied to causes of violence and abuse, not just their symptoms. We note that law reform and criminal proceedings are important elements of the overall suite of responses to address violence and abuse from an AOP perspective. State-sanctioned military interventions conducted in the name of protecting vulnerable groups are discussed and case studies are provided to highlight the complexities associated with "protectionist" legislation.

Chapter 8 considers social movements and community responses to violence and abuse. Feminist, pro-feminist, queer and child-rights perspectives are prominent as we consider how social movements (new and old) and specific communities have organized to lobby for or re-orchestrate responses to particular forms of violence and abuse. Trade union responses to violence and abuse in and beyond workplaces are considered, along with disability activism and LGBTIQ-inspired responses to violence and abuse. We note how lobbying for changes to laws and social policies has been a staple of anti-violence work across identity groups in addition to promoting social and cultural attitudinal changes and the provision of immediate and direct support to those affected by violence or abuse. Highlighting the broad array of responses to violence and abuse is a key goal of their chapter in order to emphasise the various points of alliance relevant to AOP practitioners.

Chapter 9 showcases individual and therapeutic responses to violence. While individual and therapeutic responses to violence and abuse are not the only focus of AOP perspectives, they are still very important. People whose lives are affected by violence are likely to have needs that require both immediate and longer term professional attention. They/we have the right to be treated with dignity, respect and sensitivity. For victims and survivors of abuse, self-determination is a social work value and aspiration that cannot be over-emphasized in the "helping process." Feminist, queer, Black and disabled rights approaches to programs and services for victims, survivors, perpetrators and people designated as "at risk" are given space because they have much to offer practitioners in relation to egalitarian practice (also see Ife 2016). Narrative, strengths-based, psychoanalytic and cognitive-behavioural approaches that are used in conjunction with AOP principles will also be considered.

A note of caution: working in the area of violence and abuse is demanding and can be both emotionally intense and intellectually stimulating. Studying violence and abuse from an AOP perspective can evoke strong and sometimes unexpected emotions. It runs the risk of "triggering," "restimulating" or "activating" painful emotions from the past, even flashbacks of the moments of threat or attack (see Bass and Davis 2002). If this applies to you, take care. Even if it does not, take care and be kind to yourself. If you feel confronted, shocked or distressed, draw on social supports. We need this support if we are to progress a critical understanding of, and responses to, violence and abuse in the future.

2. DEFINITIONS AND TERMINOLOGY

- **What words and images come to mind when you think of violence and abuse?**
- **How are violence and vulnerability connected?**
- **How do we distinguish between forms of violence as either necessary and legitimate or unacceptable and illegitimate?**

This chapter considers the ways in which abuse and violence are talked about in the public domain. It is common, for example, to hear about the problems associated with violence in Indigenous communities, violence against women and children, family violence, bullying and school violence, cyber bullying and so on. Talk of alcohol-related violence, gang violence, street violence, terrorism, suicide bombings, child abuse, self-defence, public brawls, road rage, school shootings, punch-ups, home invasions, aggression and "stranger danger" is increasingly commonplace. Each constitutes abuse and violence, but what else do they have in common? What distinguishes one "kind" of violence from another? Why might some violences be punished, others treated and others ignored? Why are some considered understandable in the circumstances and not others? In other words, is violence — in and of itself — the problem? Or does it depend on who is involved and where it occurs? We spend time thinking through these issues because they are crucial to understanding violence and abuse from an AOP perspective.

DEFINING VIOLENCE AND ABUSE: AN AOP PERSPECTIVE

Often assumed to be and talked about as self-evident, violence is actually a "remarkably 'slippery' concept" (Hume 2007: 149). As the questions above suggest, violence both means different things to different people and is understood in very different ways depending on the context and people involved. We all carry images in our mind — images of abuse and violence, both legitimate and illegitimate — and these "come out" in the ways that we talk about violence (Liebling and Stanko 2001: 428). This is likely to be so regardless of how much we know, whether anecdotally, experientially or academically, as professionals, researchers or "ordinary" people.

It is possible to find accounts claiming to have captured the meaning, parameters and defining characteristics of violence and abuse. Such definitions, however, are invariably transitory and illusory, offering little more than snapshots of constant motion. While extensive literature exists across a range of disciplines and theoretical perspectives that offers authoritative explanations of violence and abuse, it generally starts from the assumption that violence is a distinct phenomenon — in Deleuze's (1994) terms, a "ready-made" problem. In other words, abuse and violence are assumed to be problems that are universally understood, with logical and self-evident explanations and rational, actionable solutions. As Deleuze (1994: 158) explains it:

> We are led to believe that the activity of thinking, along with the truth and falsehood in relation to that activity, begins only with the search for solutions, that both of these concern only solutions … the master sets a problem, our task is to solve it, and the result is accredited true or false by a powerful authority.

Rather than approaching violence and abuse as pre-existing "things" to be examined or explained, in this book we are more interested in the ways that these have been conceptualized, explained and, most importantly, problematized. Our aim is *not* to provide definitive or expert accounts of violence and abuse; instead we offer a framework and set of principles for thinking critically about abuse and violence as constructs, albeit with very real impacts for individuals, families, communities and societies. For some readers, this will be very challenging as the call to solve or at least confidently address problems can be strong and lingering on conceptualizations may feel frustrating: *yes, yes, but tell us what to do!* We resist falling into this trap of prematurely solving and emphasizing "doing" over "thinking" because we believe that it is critical to properly understand the very precepts underlying the construction of violence and abuse.

To talk about violence and abuse as constructs is not to say that they are not "real." Rather it is to recognize that their "definitions and its meanings are continually contested" (Liebling and Stanko 2001: 424). As Stanko (2003: 3) observed, the concepts of violence, and to a somewhat lesser extent abuse, are profoundly ambiguous, noting that, "what violence means is and will always be fluid, not fixed." Improving the ways in which we respond to violence requires that we think differently: reviewing what is "known," examining the assumptions upon which this is based, identifying the gaps, asking new questions and suggesting new connections. To this end, this book seeks to complexify — not simplify — what is known about abuse and violence by proposing different questions and new "parameters, and dilemmas" (Lee 2001: 46).

Why Theories Matter

Theories matter because they shape how we understand the world (Dalrymple and Burke 2006; Mullaly 2007; Pease 2011; Payne 2014). Intentionally or otherwise, all sentient beings operate from theories they form about the world. To manage the world around us we make assumptions, sometimes knowingly and other times without conscious thought. Even if we are not aware of or able to articulate how we have arrived at our conclusions, we are still forming and using concepts, ideas and beliefs. When we string these ideas together we are using theories; attempts to define — in this case abuse and violence — our theoretical preferences are inevitably reflected.

Many popularly adopted intervention methods in health, welfare and education disaggregate people from their circumstances and contexts. This is evident, for instance, when attention is given *only* to individual cognitive, behavioural and/or personality "deficits" and not to the material and social circumstances that give rise to violence. Such approaches also overlook the ways in which systems and structures are, themselves, abusive (see Morley, Macfarlane and Ablett 2014). Law and order politics, characterized by talk of "getting tough" on crime and criminals, for instance, reflects a particular theoretical stance, reducing violence to illegal acts and thereby disregarding the power relations in which abuse and violence are embedded. An individualistic focus on offender responsibility also underpins other so-called tough policies, such as those associated with "zero tolerance" and the "war on drugs" (see Wodak 2015), as well as border control, anti-immigration and the "war on terror." By divorcing offending individuals from their context — instead emphasizing certain "problem" traits and character deficits — governments are able to justify bold and draconian actions.

A critical awareness of theory is essential for anti-oppressive practitioners (and students), across all modes, fields and disciplines of practice, to ensure informed approaches to decisions about what to do, who should be assisted, by whom and for how long (see McLaughlin 2005; Rush and Keenan 2014). AOP theories matter not just to (student and practicing) social workers (Rush and Keenan 2014), but also (student and practicing) nurses (Hutchison 2015), teachers (Ngo and Kumashiro 2014), doctors and other health professionals, community and personal workers (Baines and Edwards 2015) — including those providing support to refugees (Lacroix, Baffoe and Liguori 2015) — urban and social planners and many more. When people declare themselves to be "atheoretical" (without theory), they are denying their organization of ideas into action. When they declare themselves to be "apolitical" or "neutral," they are denying their exercise and experience of power, including their involvement in relationships of authority (see Dalrymple and Burke 2006; Dominelli 1996). Often, declarations of atheoretical neutrality are done in the name of objectivity and are rewarded by systems and people that prefer to underplay, if not ignore, power relations (Brown and Strega 2005; Dominelli 1996).

As anti-oppressive students and practitioners we cannot purport to be working for non-violence while ignoring contexts and power differentials (Allan, Pease and Briskman 2009; Baines 2006; Brown and Strega 2005; Sakamoto and Pitner 2005). We cannot ignore the ways in which whole groups, not just individuals, get sub-ordinated. We cannot default to hyper-individual perspectives of social problems (see McDonald 2005; Morley, Macfarlane and Ablett 2014; Mullaly 2007) or rush to dominantly approved solutions. Rather than a direct expression of personality, violence reflects the complex interactions of social context, social positioning, roles and expectations (see Dominelli and Campling 2002). Accordingly, we must be ever-alert to the tendency to oversimplify complex phenomena by, for example, condemning perpetrators of violence as sick, mad and/or evil, and advocating harsh, punitive responses.

Social problems relate to social environments and affect social groups; while they impact on individuals, their origins lie in structural conditions that affect some segments of the population much more than, or instead of, others (Morley et al. 2014; Mullaly 2007). Social problems are complex, multiple and intersecting; the experience of social disadvantage snowballs so that problems are rarely one issue, instead requiring coordinated and multi-dimensional solutions. Recognizing patterns of injustice does not, however, mean losing sight of the specificities of contexts and individual circumstances; nor of individual's suffering. The interplay of person-in-environment, or individual-in-society, remains crucial. In practice, this means privileging social justice over charity, valuing the uniqueness of individuals but also their connections to others (near and far), appreciating the importance of self-determination and placing rights, not just responsibilities, at the centre of our thinking.

AOP takes account of the four domains of: a) the intrapersonal (within the self); b) the interpersonal (such as families, groups, work/classmates); c) the cultural (including community based ways of living); and d) the structural (laws, economies, social institutions). Focusing on the manifestation of violence and abuse in each of these intersecting and overlapping domains helps us to avoid fixating on just one part of the equation. In the absence of attention to structural, cultural and systemic factors, individual and interpersonal interventions can become merely band-aids. We must therefore ask ourselves, what circumstances might have brought particular abuse or violence to bear? What are the conditions that enable — even encourage — domination and the violence of some against certain others (see Flood 2001; Pease 2011)?

Talking about Violence

The language that we choose to use shines light on some things while obscuring others. For instance, rather than asking why a particular *man beats his wife*, we may instead first consider how men are collectively positioned in society and how they are treated by the legal, employment and education systems as the context for understanding men who violate their partners. The words "man beat his wife" are placed in italics because they are used so often, to the point of becoming almost a cliché, reiterating men's agency (or personal power) and assumptions about women's subordinate passivity. At the same time, the overuse of such terms side-lines if not eclipses the many other forms of violence and abuse that people and animals experience unrelated to heterosexual coupledom.

It is difficult to use or even think about the word violence in a neutral manner because it is such a loaded term. That there are so many ways of referencing violence attests to this, each evoking different ideas and images of good and evil, intentionality and innocence, blame and morality and so on. Liebling and Stanko (2001: 426) describe *violence talk* as a "contemporary form of moral discourse, steeped in contradictory notions of what kinds of ... violence are normal, acceptable, illegal and abnormal." In this sense, it is both highly personal — in that our ideas and imagery of violence are likely to come out in the ways that we talk about violence — and inseparable from our own identity and experiences. When violence becomes public is it opened up to discussions where it can be "ascribed a whole new range of meanings ... [including] ... individually and socially approved rationalisations" (Hume 2007: 151).

This attention to ways of speaking and thinking about violence amounts to a focus on the discourses of violence. The term "discourse" is often used in reference to language or, more commonly, communication and debate. Here — and, again, following Foucault — it refers to bodies of social knowledge. Discourses, as explained by Willig (2001: 107) make available "certain ways-of-seeing and certain ways-of-being" that are inextricably connected to "wider social processes of legitimation and power"; that is, to what can be said and what can be thought. Ways of naming and responding to violence affirm both what and who is recognized and recognizable as violent and/or violence. This acknowledges that, as observed by Stanko (2003: 12), "not all violence is condemned; not all forms of violence are punished; [and] not all forms of violence receive widespread disapproval." A focus on discourses and problematizations provides a framework for thinking critically about the ways in which certain violences, and not others, are constructed as contemporary social problems.

We cannot stress enough that approaching abuse and violence as constructs, rather than empirically and self-evidently "real," is a crucial starting point for anti-oppressive perspectives. To talk about constructs, as compared to universal facts, acknowledges that what we generally think of as "reality, knowledge, thought, facts, texts, selves, and so on" (Bruffee 1986: 774) are generated within particular contexts (historical, societal and so forth) by "communities of like-minded peers" (774). In this respect, recognizing that the social world is constructed, that "meanings are made, definitions produced and interpretations propounded" (Clarke and Cochrane 1998: 29), represents the very essence of hope in the implication that things can be different, that other constructions are possible. Instead of approaching knowledge as something that can be pinned down, like a butterfly pinned to a specimen board, our AOP attention is drawn to the "contingency of those of our social practices that we wrongly come to regard as inevitable" (Boghossian 2001: 3).

PROBLEMATIZING VIOLENCE AND ABUSE

From an AOP perspective, violence and abuse are terms that need to be problematized. "Problematization," a rather clumsy word, represents a critical re-visioning of the ways in which we have become accustomed to see, know and understand the social world. As used here, it derives from Michel Foucault's work on the counter-history(ies) of ideas, most notably in relation to the dominance of particular bodies of knowledge and ways of knowing. In short, Foucault emphasized that while some forms of knowledge are "endowed with the status of the one-and-only reason," these can only ever be, merely, "*one* possible form among others" (cited in McHoul and Grace 1993: 9, emphasis in original). A problematizing approach is one that focuses on "how and to what extent it might be possible to think differently" (Foucault 1985: 9), by turning "something that is commonly seen as natural ... into something problematic" (Sandberg and Alvesson 2011: 32).

A problematizing approach is especially valuable for rethinking what we think we know about violence. Foucault's (2007: 138) concern with "making things more fragile" enables us to see that "what appears obvious to us" — in this case, violence, "is not at all so obvious" (139). In other words, what violence *means* is far from self-evident and this is particularly so when we consider those violences that come to be seen as so-called problem violences. Focusing on the problematization of violence, therefore, directs our attention to both the ways in which we speak about and conceptualize violence and the representations of violence as understandable in certain circumstances and not in others (Morgan 1987).

From an AOP perspective, "making things more fragile" involves challenging stereotypical assumptions about violence and abuse. New questions need to be asked and assumptions re-examined when these are represented as primarily the manifestations of the problems presented by particular groups of people, in particular areas, from whom other groups need to be protected and/or as indicative of (public) disorder. It is easy (or easier), though not terribly useful, to point to the violence and aberrant behaviour of others, especially marginalized Others such as young, racialized, working-class men. Individual and societal responses to violence are, however, inevitably bound up with power relations, structural hierarchies, social division and the perpetuation of privilege. It is important that we take the time to fully appreciate these connections.

Professional "Knowers" and Expertise

What we claim to know about violence connects to the broader parameters of "social knowledge, cultural legacies [and] institutional support" (Stanko 2003: 11). These shape the meanings we attribute to violence; in short, to whether this is "legitimised or condemned" (Stanko 2003: 11). Examining the discursive resources — or knowledges — that are drawn upon in constructing certain violences as *problem* violence means taking a critical view of expert knowledge and the notion of expertise. This is to recognize the power relations associated with so-called expert knowledges and professional knowers/knowing. Rose (1999: xi), for example, argues that expertise is, essentially, a "mode of authority" because it performs an exclusionary function in determining who is able to speak authoritatively about an issue. In this respect, focusing on the role of expert knowledges in constructing, producing and demarcating "truth" enables us to think more critically about the ways in which violence is thought about, positioned, divided up and claimed by different disciplinary and professional groups. In other words, it refers to the ways in which "certain persons, things or forms of conduct come to be seen as problematic" (Rose 1999: xi).

In his focus on "the authorities who define phenomena as problems," Rose (1999: xi) encourages us to think carefully about the ways in which "certain persons, things or forms of conduct come to be seen as problematic." Which criteria are used? How might such an assessment be made? Where is the line in the sand? It is in this sense that paying attention to prevailing discourses of truth, to those knowledges that have come to be accepted as truth, is such a critical task. To the extent that these enable "processes of objectification" (Grenier 2007: 426) — of dividing up people and acts in such a way that these are seen as representing ab/normality, deviance and so on — it is clear that the application of expertise, as the ability to classify and diagnose, certify and label, is immensely powerful.

In taking seriously Foucault's questioning of truth and how this can be told, we must ask not what is violence — as if this is possible to answer once and for all — but rather what violences mean and how these meanings have come about. A focus on the "how" rather than the "what" is vital. We need to ask critical questions such as, "by what techniques, [and] according to what regularities and conditions, is it possible for something to *count* as the truth about sickness, life?" (McHoul and Grace 1993: 25). What do we know as the truth about violence?

An AOP perspective recognizes that expertise and hierarchies of difference are interconnected. Expert knowledges can be understood as constituting, both "forms of authority and practical techniques" (Rose 1999: ii). Similarly, realms of intervention — that is, the accepted range of treatment and therapies — may be divided along disciplinary lines, each associated with distinct domains of knowledge, authority and expertise. Professions, including psychology, social work and health practitioners, are able to shape the truth by "controlling who has the expertise to speak about an issue [and] in what context" (Breckenridge 1999: 14). Limitations as to "who may be allowed to speak ... legitimately of certain issues" (Breckenridge 1999: 14) are evident, for example, in the positioning of violence as distinct from domestic violence — commonly understood as gendered violence — and the related demarcation of expertise and authority. As discussed later in this book, the naming of some violences enables these to be divided off, as representing a certain kind of problem and requiring particular types of intervention.

IDENTITY, DIFFERENCE, VIOLENCE AND VULNERABILITY

Just as the ways that we talk about violence and abuse vary, so too do the ways in which we respond to them. Violence may — or may not — be seen as significant, as of concern, as requiring treatment or punishment and so on. For example, in differentiating violence — "generic violence," for lack of a better term — from domestic violence, which is often understood as gendered violence, generic violence has been claimed as the territory of a particular professional group and area of expertise, namely psychology. These are not straightforward categories though; violences are further divided up in accordance with ideas — expert knowledge — about severity, risk and dangerousness. Put simply, the perpetration of violence, depending on the circumstances, such as the do-er and the knower, might be variously seen as mad, bad or very bad with implications for how this is understood, explained and responded to. Responses, then, might range from specialized psychological assessment and intervention, to punishment emphasizing deterrence, to more low-key interventions (such as anger management courses), to nothing at all.

Mason (2006: 175) argues that violence "makes a 'statement'" that marks the "bodies of its victims with signs of vulnerability." Vulnerability, then, like violence, is an embodied concept and, as such, is inseparable from societal context and positioning. The social hierarchies of identity and difference — gender, sexuality, age, dis/ability, race and ethnicity — are then "translated into vulnerability through the body" (Hollander 2001: 105). Ideas about who we should fear, as observed by Day (2008: 84–85) for example, are critical to the construction of race privilege, serving to "maintain and justify exclusion," discrimination and inequality. Thinking critically about notions of vulnerability and risk is important because it focuses our attention on questions concerning who is deemed worthy of, or in need of, protection; which violences are, and are not, deemed problematic; what safety means and how this is constructed differently for different groups in society and so on.

It is not enough to ask what violence *is*. Even assuming that it is possible to answer such a question, if we do not have an understanding of the hows and the whys — the ways in which violences are conceptualized and categorized and with what effects — we will be unable to see violence as anything but an individual problem; more specifically, as a problem *of* individuals. This is evident also in the tendency to frame violence, particularly criminal violence, as a problem of, or in relation to, particular groups (youth, Indigenous peoples, gangs) and settings (licensed premises, rural communities, public areas). In this sense, violence in and of itself seems less important than the circumstances in which it occurs, these enabling it to be named and framed as something to do with young people, alcohol and other drug use, licensing regulations, "cultural difference" and so on. We hear about violence in Indigenous communities, violence against women and children, school violence and bullying, alcohol-related violence, road rage, gang violence and so on as if these are distinct and unrelated phenomena. Violence is, therefore, depicted as a manifestation of the problems presented by particular groups of people, in particular areas (rural/urban), from whom other groups need to be protected and who are indicative of (public) disorder.

It is vital that we pay attention to the ways in which certain violences are constructed as *problem* violence. Asking different questions of and about violence highlights issues relating to the separation of acceptable (that is, "normal" or understandable) and unacceptable (problem) violences; of appropriate ("boys will be boys") and unfair ("pick on someone your own size") violences; as well as the demarcation of violences as public or private, legitimated/officially sanctioned or illegal/criminal and so on. Such designations and distinctions signify who is implicated in relation to violence — as perpetrator or victim, as risky or at risk, as safe or vulnerable. Partitioning off behaviours as representing particular types of problems and particular types of people (such as "violent offenders") and the territory of some professional groups and not others, perpetuates stigmatization and societal division while also closing down cross-disciplinary discussion and collaboration.

TERMINOLOGIES OF VIOLENCE

Terminology, or the ways in which we name and refer to things, is important to inspect because in deciding to use particular terms and not others, we signify our position in relation to both the nature of violence and "who is doing what to whom" (Jones 2004: 87). This is not to say that we always do so knowingly or intentionally. Rather, it is to recognize the broader politics and power relations associated with not only who and what is "implicated in the experience[s] of violence" (Evans 2008: 63), but also who is able to authoritatively speak of this. Definitions of violence often reflect "several, sometimes overlapping standpoints: the violated, the violator, those dealing with violence and those who analyse violence" (Hearn and McKie 2010: 138) and the status given to "any one of these perspectives" is indicative of the wider context of power relations.

Naming (terminology) reflects the framing and conceptualizing of violence and abuse. For example, naming violence as a "breakdown in the social order" — as something that has "gone wrong" or someone who has "done wrong" — shifts the focus away from inequities embedded in current societal structures and arrangements (Horton 2011). Terminologies of violence have practical implications. Because the choice of terms used by a particular agency, organization or researcher reflects what is understood as constituting violence (what violence is), this will impact on what is — and is not — counted. No matter how scientific the methods, measurements of violence are not free from politics. What is seen as the size or extent of the so-called problem relates directly to terminology and definitions, which in practice often exclude, ignore or underplay some forms of violence. For example, measures of violence commonly focus upon *physical* acts of violence. In this context, the term "abuse" is often used to distinguish non-physical from physical acts of violence, unhelpfully reinforcing both fixed ideas about violence and the ambiguity of abuse. This is further reflected in the reliance on statistical data regarding the incidence and impacts of physical and sexual violence for a range of purposes including as a measure of the effectiveness of policy and interventions.

The presumption that violence is physical violence has important implications, in particular for the recognition and visibility of diverse experiences of abuse and violence. In Australia, for example, the Personal Safety Survey, conducted by the Australian Bureau of Statistics (ABS) every four years, is the central source for the national measurement and monitoring of domestic violence. The ABS definition of "couple" includes only people who are living together as "resident[s] in the same household." Similarly, their definition of "partner violence" explicitly excludes "violence experienced by persons in an intimate relationship which *does not* involve living together" and "violence" here is limited to the "occurrence, attempt or threat of either physical or sexual assault" (ABS 2013a). It is clear that data collected on the basis of these definitions could not, and does not, reflect the actual occurrence and experience of domestic/partner violence in Australia. Nonetheless, as a quantitative representation of the problem of domestic violence in Australia, it is this data that will drive policy and funding decisions.

A FRAMEWORK FOR UNDERSTANDING VIOLENCE AND ABUSE

As discussed earlier in this chapter, there are many difficulties associated with defining violence and abuse and finding meaningful terminology to use. As a way forward we offer the following framework as a useful way of thinking about and distinguishing between forms or dimensions of violence. Here we draw upon Galtung's (1990) notion of a "violence triangle" as a way of depicting the relationships between categories of violence.

Galtung drew a distinction between "direct," "structural" and "cultural" violence, emphasizing the interactional complexities that enable, embed and perpetuate violence. Direct violences are visible and commonly recognizable; they are acts or events of violence, including interpersonal violence, meaning violence between individuals, a term generally used to refer to that between people who are known to one another; and/or collective violence, which describes the "use of violence by people who identify themselves as members of a group — whether this group is transitory or has a more permanent identity — against another group or set of individuals, in order to achieve political, economic or social objectives" (WHO 2002: 5). Examples include gang warfare, civil conflicts, state and group terrorism, rape as a weapon of war and the large-scale displacement of people from their homelands.

Figure 1: Direct, structural and cultural violences

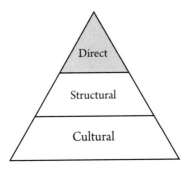

Structural violence refers to "social arrangements" that are "embedded in the political and economic organization of our social world" (Farmer et al. 2006: 1686), which advantage some individuals and groups and not others via, for example, access to goods, resources and opportunities including political power/agency, education, health care and legal status.

Galtung described cultural violence as those aspects of culture, including religions, ideology, language, dominant knowledge and so on, that are "used to justify or legitimise direct or structural violence" (Galtung 1990: 291). Cultural violence, he argued, enables us to see "exploitation and/or repression as normal and natural" (295) or, indeed, to not see it all. As depicted in Figure 2, direct, structural and cultural violences are interconnected and coexist:

In Galtung's explanation, cultural violence is *internalized* and structural violence is *institutionalized* and, in this sense, structural violence makes cultural violence "transparent" (295).

Symbolic violence is also a useful addition to our working framework. It fits within and across structural and cultural violence. The concept of symbolic violence highlights violence that "is exercised upon a social agent with his or her complicity" (Bourdieu and Wacquant 2002: 167), including ideas about value, worth and distinction (such as ways of eating, dressing, talking, good taste and so on) that function as social markers and, therefore, to exclude. Gender norms and class relations are especially relevant here.

With Galtung (1990), we are proposing a paradigm shift in the way violence and abuse is viewed, classified, treated and, in many other ways, ignored. Making this shift requires us to move away from individually focused, behaviourally oriented conceptualizations of violence and abuse. We share Greenleaf and Williams' (2009: 5) criticism of "the entrenched intrapsychic perspective" that underpins so many policies, programs and services, over-emphasizing personality traits and

Figure 2: Galtung's (1990) "violence triangle," depicting the relationship between "categories" of violence

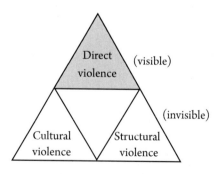

disorders at the expense of societal context. We also share their view that, "when problems are environmentally based, solutions should be so as well" (Greenleaf and Williams 2009: 5). This paradigm shift requires attention to both theory and practice, connecting the political with the personal. Although it is tempting to focus only on the personal dimensions of violence and abuse, ignoring the theoretical and the political is not a viable position for anti-oppressive practitioners (also see Dalrymple and Burke 2006; Dominelli 1996; Dominelli and Campling 2002).

Well-being and safety require more than the absence of violence and abuse (Ife 2012, 2016; McDonald 2005). For all of us — humans and (other) animals — to flourish, we need nutritious food, clean air and water, protective shelter and other material resources (Ife 2012, 2016). Irrespective of our differences, we share basic needs and rights. However, rather than fairly negotiated — even appreciated in their own right — differences based on class, race/ethnicity, gender, sexuality, ability, age and species form hierarchical divisions, separating groups from each other. Instead of encouraging cooperation and interdependence, groups are often pitted against one another, to compete for power, resources and status (also see Coker and Macquoid 2015).

Examples of:		
Direct violence (events and acts)	Structural violence (systems and processes)	Cultural violence (ongoing and enduring)
Physical force Aggression Killing, injury Rape, sexual assault/ abuse Verbal violence (abuse, humiliation and so on) Detention and imprisonment Disease, chronic ill-health, death	Social/political/ economic systems Exploitation and domination Inequality Privilege Marginalization and discrimination Social differentiation and division	Dominant histories and stories Beliefs and assumptions Attitudes and prejudice Religions Positivism/empiricism What we see as natural, normal/what we don't see at all
Environmental damage (deforestation, global warming, resource depletion and so on)	Industrial activity, pollution	Economic growth, commercialization Ideology re: human mastery of/over (and notions of progress, for example)
Violence directed at wildlife Violence directed at farmed and incarcerated animals	Culling, habitat clearing and scientific testing on animals for unsustainable human needs and profits	Speciesism, and the ongoing assumptions that humans are free to use animals however they choose

Taking an AOP perspective means being oriented towards rights and well-being. This challenges the idea that service users — clients, patients, students — should be "deserving" and grateful for the charity with which they have been provided (see Mendes 2003; Mullaly 2007; Hamm 2001). It means taking a critical stance towards systems that atomize individuals from their communities and disaggregate their body parts and functions, evident, for instance, when a medical model of health is adopted without regard for social, structural and other public health considerations (Greenleaf and Williams 2009). Across fields of practice and professional borders, it means looking at the systems that cause, perpetuate and/or claim to address social problems, not just the people immediately affected (see Baines 2006; Brown and Strega 2005; Mendes 2003; Morley et al. 2014). It involves noticing the unnoticed acts and the invisible perpetrators. It means paying attention to legitimized violence as well as the violences that are un(der)reported and left largely unpunished.

CONCLUSION

The aim of this chapter has been to stimulate — and perhaps unsettle — your thinking about violence and abuse and orient you to the chapters that follow. Liebling and Stanko (2001: 427) explore the complexity of issues associated with taking "a stance on violence." Indeed, they argue that it is impossible to study/research violence *without* taking a stance, one way or the other, whether we acknowledge this or not. Challenging your usual ways of thinking, or "stepping out of the discourse" as Smith (2003: 154) puts it, can be both confronting and uncomfortable. It can be frustrating for people who prefer to do rather than think and reflect, to take the time to work through these conceptual complexities. We believe it is worth the effort, though, because adopting a critical and reflective stance, as the basis of an anti-oppressive approach, offers the potential for transformative change.

3. AOP KEY CONCEPTS AND PRACTICE PRINCIPLES

- How does intersectionality relate to AOP?

- Why care about poverty?

- Should AOP workers promote peace and non-violence?

At the start of this book we explained why violence and abuse are important concerns for anti-oppressive students and practitioners in all fields of the helping professions — social work, nursing, health and medicine, education and so on. Effectively, we argued that AOP workers focus on violence and abuse not just because of the sheer extent and impact of violence and abuse, but also because so many other forms of violence and abuse are still ignored, underestimated and, in some cases, legitimated.

We have designed this book to help people studying and working across field, mode and occupation to think about violence and abuse from an AOP perspective. Making connections in and between the different forms of violence and abuse is part of AOP work (Fraser and Craik 2009). We have already discussed the importance of language, especially language used to represent different forms of violence and abuse. Our attention to language continues in this chapter through our exploration of key anti-oppressive concepts and practice principles.

AOP key concepts and practice principles relevant to violence and abuse are the focus for discussion in this chapter. Based on our research and practice experience, we offer guidelines for *praxis,* that is, the interplay or interaction of theory and practice (see Ife 2012; Mullaly 2010; Payne 2007). The practice principles discussed here include: 1) connecting violence and abuse to power and social (in) justice; 2) analyzing the effects of privilege and oppression; 3) having courage and fostering critical consciousness; 4) advocating peace and non-violence; 5) working with others in alliances and across borders; and 6) carefully incorporating other approaches into AOP work. We emphasize practice principles that allow the consideration of collective, not just individual, responses to violence and abuse.

Under the final practice principle, we discuss the possibilities for incorporating other approaches, theories and frameworks with AOP. We argue that, while there is considerable scope to do so, AOP workers must be cautious in order to avoid the inconsistencies and incompatibilities that can occur when perspectives with different underlying values and principles are brought together in an ad hoc and depoliticized fashion. To be anti-oppressive is to hold power relations central to our analyses. This stands in stark contrast to most popular, dominant (and often organizationally endorsed) approaches to practice that individualize social problems and, by implication (if not intention), ignore the contexts in which individuals, families and communities live.

PRINCIPLE I:
CONNECTING VIOLENCE AND ABUSE TO POWER AND SOCIAL (IN)JUSTICE

As explored throughout this book, recognizing intersecting privileges and oppressions are central to anti-oppressive work (Mattsson 2014). Developing our own critical consciousness (see Ife 2012; Sakamoto and Pitner 2005) and that of others should accompany the practical assistance that we provide. In this view, human rights such as freedom of movement and freedom of expression are not just abstract concepts but bodily rights and lived experiences, affecting individuals and families as well as whole communities and societies (Ife 2012, 2016). As such, it is worth spending time contemplating these, including when we are in conversations with others affected by violence and abuse.

Power, control and inequality are central AOP themes of violence and abuse. To quote the Newfoundland and Labrador Violence Prevention Unit (2015), "The roots of all forms of violence are founded in the many types of inequality which continue to exist and grow in society." As discussed in the previous chapter, violence and abuse may be directed at the self, other individuals and collectives and is embedded in structures and cultures. This includes the systematic discrimination of members of socially devalued (or oppressed) groups, not just the most obvious forms of interpersonal violence and abuse.

Our Working Definitions of Violence and Abuse

Violence and abuse are terms that are hard to capture not just because they overlap, but also because they are used in so many different ways (also see Nerenberg 2000). For violence and abuse alike, disputes occur over definitions, causes, effects, responses, prevention plans and interventions. In Chapter 2 we raised critical questions about the use of language and the ways in which different discourses influence how violence and abuse is defined, understood and responded to. We understand violence and abuse as concepts that are distinct but overlap. *Violence* often involves the swift use or threat of force for the purposes of control, destruction, damage and/or intimidation and dominance, in relation to which there is a high likelihood that harm will be inflicted. However, violence includes not only physical but also *non-physical* threats and other methods of domination. The effects of violence are generally immediate and may also be ongoing. Examples of violence include but are not limited to: fights and physical combat; physical, sexual, psychological or spiritual assault by a person/s known or unknown; being robbed at knife or gunpoint; kidnapping/abduction; police or armies firing on protesters; extortion; police harassment of ethnic minorities; policing practices such as the use of body searches; vigilante group behaviour; murder, attempted murder and threats of murder; deliberate poisoning; and so on.

Our definition of *violence* is deliberately broad, emphasizing the use of force to dominate and control others. This force and control is often injurious to those who are subordinated and whose rights to safety and freedom are violated. Importantly, violence may — or may not — contain physical force. The World Health Organization (WHO) (2016a) definition of violence stresses intentionality and familiarity with the assailant/s. *Intentionality* speaks to doing something on purpose, such as robbing a person at gunpoint rather than accidentally knocking them over with a car. *Familiarity* speaks to whether the assailants and victims are personally known to each other, as is the case in domestic violence, most child abuse cases and elder abuse (see Johnson 2015).

In its plural version, *violences* refers to multiple expressions of violence; it is a reminder that not all violence is the same nor should be treated the same. As awkward as it might seem, the term violences captures the many possible manifestations of violence — the range of people and social groups impacted, the variety of contexts and the range of outcomes and implications. It calls for attention to the ways in which some violences are rendered problematic while others escape scrutiny or penalty.

Abuse involves the misuse of power and authority, the misuse of privileges and/or the neglect of responsibility for dependants. Emotional, psychological, sexual, financial, religious and physical forms of abuse are all possible. Abuse can also involve more persuasive, emotionally manipulative and exploitative ways of controlling and dominating. Some forms of abuse, including sexual abuse, do not involve direct force or physical violence but grooming and conscription. The negative effects of abuse may or may not be immediately obvious but are often apparent over time. Tactics of abuse are many and varied and often escalate over months or years. Abuse may stay secret for long periods of time, particularly when victims perceive that they will be blamed for being abused (see Herman 2013). Examples of abuse include, but are not limited to: conscription to war; financial abuse by sexual intimates; psychological abuse of children; mistreatment of elders; sexual abuse by clergy as well as the collusion of the churches to hide and/or deny this abuse (Skold and Swain 2015).

The terms violence and abuse, then, have many meanings. *Violence* involves domination and control injurious to violated parties, in which force, or the threat of force, may be used to ensure victims' compliance. Crucially, not all violences are treated equally; some are rendered problematic while others escape scrutiny or penalty. *Abuse* may involve being exploited, discredited, demeaned or deliberately hurt or injured, and may be repeated over extended periods of time. Abuse can be intentional or reflect a disregard of the needs, rights and interests of other people. Systemic abuse, for example, affects whole groups. Regardless of form and defini-tion, though, violence and abuse profoundly impact on the health and well-being of groups and individuals (see Veenema et al. 2015).

Being Anti-Oppressive

AOP perspectives include a body of ideas and practices concerned with power and the interplay of injustice and inequality at the macro (large-scale), mezzo (mid-scale) and micro (personal) levels of life, whether in welfare, health, education or other fields of practice (Ferguson and Lavalette 2006; McLaughlin 2005, 2015; Mullaly 2010). In social work, AOP perspectives are informed by and overlap with human and animal rights perspectives, as well as green, feminist and anti-racist perspectives (see Dominelli 2012a; Ife 2012), emancipatory perspectives (Tew 2006; Powell 2001) and critical, structural and post-modern perspectives that work with the concepts of power, privilege and oppression (Mullaly 2010).

What makes us anti-oppressive practitioners is that we recognize and work with power relations rather than deny or ignore them (Adams, Dominelli and Payne 2009; McLaughlin 2005, 2015). Power relations are recognized as central to all human interactions, affecting all communication, not just those formally designated as political (Baines 2011; Strier and Binyamin 2009). When we speak of *power* we mean not just having power (as a possession), but exercising power and agency in groups, not just as individuals (see Powell 2001). We understand that power may be expressed positively or negatively (see Tew 2006); that control and domina-tion may be part of power relations, but that power can also mean pushing for the recognition of rights, and/or subordinates pushing back against the dominant (McLaughlin 2005, 2015).

Oppression is a key concept in AOP because it allows us to conceptualize the unfair, cruel exercise of authority over members of devalued social groups subject to negative stereotypes and other processes of inferiorization (Ferguson and Lavalette 2006; Mullaly 2010; Nzira and Williams 2009). Oppression is a term meaningfully applied to members of devalued social groups; groups that are subject to negative stereotypes, including those of a sexual variety (Baines 2011). While non-human animals are not usually included in AOP, there is a push to address this omission and recognize speciesism, or the assumed superiority of humans over all (other) animals (Fraser and Taylor 2017).

Oppression is not a random or individual experience, nor the distorted perceptions of the overly "dramatic," "sensitive" or "emotional." It is also not a term meaningfully applied to all individuals who experience frustrations, limits or pain (Mullaly 2010). Oppressed populations are those likely to be subject to denied opportunities, restricted social, economic and cultural participation, marginalization, exploitation and violence (Mullaly 2010; Young 2009). In Australia, for example, oppressed persons are identified with the following categories: female, working class, Black, Indigenous, "ethnic," Muslim, homosexual, bisexual or transgendered, old or very young, and/or the disabled, whether physically, mentally and/or intellectually (Pease 2009). Oppression can occur on multiple levels, for instance, in relation to gender, sexuality, class, race, age and/or disability (Ferguson and Lavalette 2006; Mullaly 2010; Pease 2009). It also occurs, often with fatal consequences, in relation to species (Fraser and Taylor 2016).

Privilege refers to rights, benefits and immunity given to particular groups (Mullaly 2010). Often privileges are unfair and unequally distributed to members of overvalued groups, that is, groups whose members are assumed to be natural leaders and decision makers, irrespective of their demonstrated leadership abilities (Pease 2010). Examples of unearned gender and sexual privilege have been based on *patriarchy*, which literally means "the law of the [heterosexual] father" and is expressed through social systems that automatically privilege white, male, able-bodied authority and leadership (Fraser 2008; Pease 2010). The extent of human privilege over (other) animals is so extensive we often do not even think of, or reference, other animals in our discussions of violence and abuse.

PRINCIPLE 2:
ANALYZING THE INTERLOCKING EFFECTS OF PRIVILEGE AND OPPRESSION

Taking an AOP approach means thinking about how violence and abuse affects groups and communities, not just individuals and families. It means thinking about the many causes and effects of violence and abuse, including those that give rise to violent environments. Consider the following news report, for example:

Police were called to more than 18,000 domestic violence incidents in

South Australia in just one year, figures released for the first time reveal. Almost one in four police taskings in 2014–2015 were in the Elizabeth Police Local Service Area, which encompasses several [chronically impoverished] suburbs. (Holderhead and Novak 2016: 1)

The suburb of Elizabeth in South Australia has been declared Australia's "fourth most violent location" (Cornish 2014), with high alcohol use and high rates of domestic and street violence. Regions such as Elizabeth have experienced the near death of manufacturing, steep rises in unemployment and poverty, serious mental and physical health problems and drug and other addiction problems (including the use of the drug "ice," a form of methamphetamine). The extent and impact of these problems have been evidenced in "burden of disease" studies that measure the number of years lost to illness/disease by residential postcode (see AIHW 2011).

From an AOP perspective, we are careful not to conflate people with the social problems they are facing. Instead of rushing to conclusions — that there is something inherently wrong with the people who live in the Elizabeth region — we see the bigger picture, the wider contexts of power relations and domination both locally and globally (Ferguson and Lavalette 2006). We do so without losing sight of the effects of privilege and oppression on real people, recognizing that societal structures play out in and through our bodies in a range of settings, from the workplace to the privacy of the home, from popular culture and the media to social systems and services.

Intersecting Oppression and Privilege

Intersectionality is a concept AOP advocates use to refer to the interlocking and connected nature of experiences of discrimination, disadvantage, privilege and oppression, related to people's gender, class, race/ethnicity, sexuality, age, ability and religion, but also the assumed superiority of humans over the environment and other species. Intersectionality speaks to McDonald and Coleman's (1999) concern with the multiple nature of oppression. It counters ideas that oppressions should be placed in a hierarchy, and by implication involve the pitting of oppressed groups against each other. To this we add the multiple and intersecting effects of privilege, whether it be in the form or white privilege, male privilege, able-bodied and/or age-related privilege, middle- or upper-class privilege (see Pease 2010) and/ or through the privileges automatically attributed to humans over all other animals.

There are good arguments for AOP students and workers to be concerned about *speciesism,* or the assumed superiority of humans over all other animals, who are ranked, usually in accordance with their use-value to humans (see Legge 2016; Ryan 2014; Taylor et al. 2016). In *The War Against Animals,* Wadiwel (2015) notes how sentience and other forms of argument to argue for animals' value plays into liberal and pro-capitalist assumptions — that we must work hard to convince others of animals' intrinsic value. A different view is that we challenge the terms of reference that dispute human use-value systems. Use-value, both human and non-human, dominate intrinsic value claims. Since the main goal for capitalism is to chase profits, and in turn, reduce labour costs, animals face life and death problems associated with use-value (Noske 1997). Their mistreatment and slaughter, while so often hidden and denied by humans, cannot be — and should not be — denied (see Legge 2016; Ryan 2014).

Oppression and privilege based on (human) ethnicity and race are important concerns for AOP workers. As a term, *ethnicity* refers to shared values, norms and social practices used to construct a group identity, with "race" often used to signify biological differences in skin colour and other superficial characteristics (Morley, Macfarlane and Ablett 2014). *Racism* refers to the practices of inferiorization used against subordinated ethnic groups. Racist assumptions are often made that race and ethnicity are fixed, predetermined and self-evident. From an AOP perspective, however, concepts such as race and ethnicity are taken to be social constructions of difference rather than biologically determined, stable categories (see Chapter 4). This is why we refer to "racialized persons" — people whose race and ethnicity have been cast as different, as Other.

Evidence of the social constructedness of race can be seen in the changing nature of racial classifications over time, and across the world. For instance, thoracic medical researchers, Braun, Wolfgang and Dickersin (2013) confront this very issue when they try to make sense of the many studies showing that non-white people, as a group, have significantly compromised lung functioning. The difficulty they faced in trying to ascertain the risk of lung pathology by racial demographic was that the ways in which race and ethnicity are understood, defined and categorized across the world both vary enormously and change over time (Braun, Wolfgang and Dickersin 2013). It is for this reason that scholars such as Dominelli refer to 'race' in single quotation marks, indicating the changing political nature of the term.

The Ongoing Race to Colonize

The processes of *colonization* (that is, the economic, political and cultural processes used by a dominant nation to control another nation) have historically produced dramatically different outcomes for those on either side of the colonizer/colonized (see Allan, Briskman and Pease 2009). *Neocolonialism* simply means new forms of colonization, such as the growing domination of multinational corporations who control most of the world's economies, including various global industries, including but not limited to: agriculture and land ownership, banking, insurance, health care and pharmaceuticals.

Related to neocolonialism is *neoliberalism,* which means the modified use and revival of past liberal ideas based on individual rights and interests in deregulated "free market" capitalism that advances private business practices, not government intervention, wherever possible (Fraser and Taylor 2016). When we speak of *neoliberalization* we are referring to the processes associated with, and justified by, liberal political economic theories, advocating for the economic goals to be prioritized over all others, including the rights of private interests to own and control what were public utilities (such as health, education and welfare). "New public management" has been used to marketize the deregulation and privatization of public institutions, public health, education and welfare. It was originally conceptualized by Hood (1991) to describe the application of private enterprise approaches to organizing and evaluating public institutions.

Part of neoliberalism is *corporatism,* which refers to the rise of professional and industrial, private corporate power and influence and infiltration of corporate values and practices in public life (see Fraser and Taylor 2016). Corporatized public health, welfare and education services are predominantly provided to people ranked lower on the social class hierarchy. *Social class* (often just referred to as class) speaks to people's income, status and wealth (or lack of) that influence health, well-being and life chances (Ferguson and Lavalette 2006; Lenski 1966). The *ruling elite* is the class of people with the most wealth and status in society, and who hold the most prominent and privileged positions of power. Sometimes the ruling elite are referred to as the 1% of the population who own most of the world's resources, leaving the 99% to share the leftovers. Because the ruling elite operate across national and state borders, Phillips and Soeiro (2012) describe this 1% as the transnational, corporate ruling elite.

In Commonwealth countries such as Australia, New Zealand and Canada, as elsewhere, the ruling elite head up corporations, generating profits that allow them to form the *super rich.* These are high net-worth individuals with multi-million-dollar liquid assets; the upper echelons of the upper class (see for example, Beaverstock, Hubbard and Short 2004). From a Marxist perspective, these individuals are the ruling elite who control, if not own, most of the means of production, including the production of news (see Lenski 1966). Most members of the ruling elite/super rich yield significant corporate power, and many are part of an active business lobbying system that advocates hard for the interests of big business (see Haseler 2000). Most members of the super rich are white, able bodied and male, and able to side-step criticisms of being greedy by participating in "corporate responsibility" programs (see Drucker 1984). These funds are then used for philanthropic work, which can provide important forms of assistance, but not usually for people stigmatized as low class, unworthy or undeserving.

Below the super rich are members of the *upper class,* who also enjoy considerable (class-based) privileges beyond those attached to property ownership. For instance,

Roth-Douquet and Schaeffer (2006) note how few members of the upper class in the United States go to war. Below the upper class is the *middle class,* which is a broad, middle-ranked socioeconomic category often applied to small business people, managers and other professionals, and their families. Some highly sought after trades people, especially those who run private business, may be symbolically and culturally classified as working class but may have incomes that put them in a middle-class bracket.

Under the middle class are the *working class/es,* a broad reference for the social status attributed to skilled trades and service workers. Negative uses of the term working class often means it stands not just for being low or unskilled, but also unrefined. *Low socio-economic status* (LSES) is a classification of people whose access to decent income, education and occupational status is limited if not denied; the term often overlaps with but is not the same as "working class." Across the world working-class people often find that liveable wages, decent working conditions, paid sick leave, health insurance and enough money to buy good quality food is out of their reach. Those who live in *chronic poverty,* that is, having insufficient income and other resources to adequately meet their daily needs, are the people living below the poverty line, many of whom are women.

Conventional Constructions of Gender and Ability/Disability
Gender refers to the socially constructed roles and characteristics designated masculine or feminine, which are traditionally placed in opposition to each other. Gender is different from the concept of sex, which is first assigned at birth; or the concept of *sexuality,* which develops over the life course. *Transgender* means going beyond the poles of masculinity and femininity and having a gender identity that does not conform to heteronormativity.

Heteronormativity is the institutionalization of heterosexuality and marginalization of other sexualities. *Cisgenderism* is a term with dual meanings. The more neutral version of cisgenderism refers to people whose gender aligns with the genitalia with which they were born; that is, people who are not transgendered. However, it can also be used to refer to the oppression of transgendered people by assuming that birth genitalia will and should define adult gender identities.

As a concept, *disability,* has traditionally referred to a condition that serves to limit, or handicap a person. Today, disability is understood not to be fixed or self-evident but reflective of different interpretations and contexts, including those that unfairly limit the development of potential of people living with disabilities (see Grönvik 2009). In the West, and increasingly in developing countries, people with disabilities have been de-institutionalized, not always with improved outcomes in health and well-being. Our definition of disability is informed by the World Health Organization, who defines it as: "impairments, activity limitations, and participation restrictions" including problems in "body function or structure," difficulties completing tasks and/or participating in desired activities (WHO 2016a). They continue:

> Disability is thus not just a health problem. It is a complex phenomenon, reflecting the interaction between features of a person's body and features of the society in which he or she lives. Overcoming the difficulties faced by people with disabilities requires interventions to remove environmental and social barriers. (WHO 2016a: 1)

As anti-oppressive practitioners we consider how violence and abuse impact on individuals and groups' safety and well-being. We are interested not just in the absence of harm or survival but the capacity for people and animals to thrive. That is why we consider the structural impediments to thriving for people with disabilities (see Anastasiou and Kauffman 2013).

Age-related oppression and privilege can be hard to recognize, with great controversy often surrounding attempts to challenge the control and treatment of the young and old, such as the criminalization of corporal punishment (or "spanking") of children and the introduction of legal provisions to prevent financial abuse of elders by younger relatives or aides. It is well established that age-related vulnerability to abuse peaks when we are very young or very old. Noting global trends in aging and social inequality, the International Federation of Social Workers (IFSW 2012) writes:

> Older adults often experience both social devaluation and poverty upon leaving the labour market; financial market fluctuations contribute to income and social insecurity regardless of employment history, especially in countries with developing and transitioning economies. Groups particularly vulnerable to poverty and social devaluation in old age, due to cultural and institutional biases, which affect people throughout the lifespan, include women, people with disabilities, people with a migration background, and people who do not belong to the majority racial or ethnic group of any given society. Older adults seeking support to maintain independence and quality of life frequently encounter either a lack of social services, especially in rural and remote areas, or services that are poor in quality or unresponsive to linguistic and cultural diversity.

An important point to remember is that the marginalization, impoverishment and devaluing of social groups are all forms of abuse, in and of themselves.

PRINCIPLE 3:
HAVING COURAGE AND FOSTERING CRITICAL CONSCIOUSNESS

AOP workers need to know about social problems and the ways in which these impact on diverse populations. However, to share that knowledge they may also need courage — specifically the courage to raise critical questions about the effects of inequality, especially global inequalities. *Globalization* involves much more than economic interactions — it is "a process of embedding capitalist social relations in everyday life practices throughout the world" (Dominelli 2016: 132). For many, this means living without proper health care, nutritious food, stable housing and access to decent (safe and fairly paid) work (see Phillips and Soeiro 2012), which can affect not only freedom of movement, expression and participation, but actual survival.

Inequalities in Well-Being

AOP workers are concerned about the health and well-being for all — not just those with high or mid-ranked status deemed to be well functioning. We are consumed with questions of justice, fairness and needs rather than the marketing spin of "risk-averse" organizations. We are concerned about those who cannot afford to pay for private assistance, from personal and domestic support to private therapies and adequate housing. Our approach to "user pays" systems is to consider who gets left out. We worry about those who experience great suffering and hardship and find it hard, if not impossible, to get the help they need.

We are willing to acknowledge ongoing inequalities rather than pretend that they do not exist. For instance, we reject the common presumption in Anglo-dominated societies, such as Australia, Britain, Canada and the U.S., that gender equality has arrived and that attention to gender is no longer required or useful. We know that affluent developed countries are neither classless nor egalitarian. We know that globalization has had mixed results across the globe, but that the effects for low-income/waged women and women living in poverty have been mostly negative.

Asking hard questions may not win us accolades or awards, at least in the first instance. As AOP students and workers we must show courage and continue to discuss poverty and inequality, its structural and cultural causes, as well as the personal implications for the impoverished, even when it is unfashionable or unpopular to do so. We do not see poverty as a natural inevitability of human nature, nor poverty eradication efforts as futile. We are concerned with consumption practices, not only as these relate to social equality but also for their impact on habitat for other animals. We do not support the promotion of increased consumption practices of the poor. Taylor (2016) makes the case that with approximately 1.8 billion people comprising the consuming class and 5.2 billion making up the non-consuming class, a radical growth in consumption would have significant, negative environmental implications, not just for the resource production and energy use required but also the environmental waste and degradation that would accompany it. In his view — and ours — the answer is not to allow all to consume at equally dangerous levels, but to transform resource distribution and consumption practices (Taylor 2016).

Human Consumption and Environmental Violations

We know that *poverty* and *waste* are interconnected and both must be targets for reduction (see Gutberlet 2012). We challenge the hunger for exponential economic growth, aware that the core business of multinational corporations and many small businesses alike is to stimulate demand, open up new markets and increase market share of products and services. This includes stimulating demand for disposable products sold in elaborate, wasteful packaging. Hard selling, or the aggressive acts of persuasion used to get people to consume new (revised, updated, improved) products, seems normal, especially now that more and more politicians, community service leaders and non-government executives are drawn from the business class and/or are inducted to neoliberal ways of thinking. With pro-business, pro-profit, competitive cultures infiltrating our formerly public spaces, services and utilities, reducing consumption and the production of waste can seem like a naïve, utopian and amorphous goal, that is, when it goes beyond instituting savings measures for businesses and organizations themselves.

For serious inroads to be made in the reduction of consumption and waste it will require more than self-regulatory actions on the part of particular companies or product lines, as the lowering of consumption is ultimately an anathema to the business principles of those who profit from its growth and proliferation. Health, welfare and education workers, including police, military and other security forces, can participate in a range of activities directed to the two goals of eliminating the poverty of the non-consuming class and the excessive waste from the consuming class. For some, if not many, it will require a shift in thinking about the work that we all, respectively do, and the goals that we are all, ultimately striving towards. The opportunities to be anti-oppressive in your practice orientation are extensive, wherever people are located, in whichever roles they are occupying. While at first glance it may not seem possible to incorporate green, simple-living principles into practice, it is possible on closer inspection, and when alliances are formed across industries and worker classifications.

Critical Reflexivity, Resilience and Emotions

Critical reflexivity refers to the deliberate use of processes and practices to understand more about the self and interrogate one's motivations, actions and impact on others. Critical reflexivity means that we keep questioning our prevailing assumptions about violence and abuse. We take stock of the gaps and contradictions in knowledge, policies, programs and practices relating to this meta (extremely large) topic of violence and abuse. Quantitative and qualitative methods of many varieties may be used in our research, yet, we do not claim — or aspire — to be neutral scientists divorced from our topics. Rather, we are humans embarking on studies where values and processes are enunciated rather than denied or disguised, allowing readers to analyze the material in the full light of theoretical propositions (Mies 1991).

We are cautious of concepts, such as *resilience*, that can be used to blame victims for the abuse and oppression they are subjected to. Conventional definitions of resilience focus on positive adaptation to adversity, particularly the ability to maintain mental health. This is a noteworthy cultural expectation made of people who are facing adversity. As AOP workers we may raise questions about whether such an expectation is fair or healthy. Might the emphasis instead be on how to reduce adversity? In hyper-individualistic societies, there is a tendency to default to personal and biological versions of resilience, which is an easy slide into blaming victims for their predicaments.

We know that work in public health, education and welfare settings, especially in the areas of violence and abuse, requires emotional sensitivity and the willingness to critically reflect not just on one's practices but also operating assumptions, biases and blind spots. We are concerned with processes as much as outcomes, and committed to collaborative, egalitarian and democratic ways of understanding and working with others. Most importantly, working from an AOP perspective means striving to be fair and just, not neutral or objective (Ferguson and Lavalette 2006).

Emotions (traditionally associated with the body) and feelings (traditionally associated with the mind) are not divided from each other or sidelined to thoughts and reason. Nor are they rendered mysterious or considered exclusively individual. Across the spectrum, emotions and feelings are considered important markers of experience, (in)justice and (in)equality. While they so often feel individual and idiosyncratic, they are experienced in social and cultural contexts, not just through individual personalities. Whether someone is experiencing elation, joy and happiness or anger, fear and pain, emotions are emblematic of social and cultural experiences, reflective of contexts not just individual choice or lifestyle. Thoughts, attitudes, behaviours, feelings and emotions often reflect experiences of (unearned) privilege and (unfair) oppression. Self-righteous indignation, sanctimony, smugness and self-aggrandisement are good examples of privilege, just as shame, self-denigration and self-harm can reflect lived experiences of oppression.

Urging us to pay attention to what we and others feel, not just what we think, Airlie Hochschild (1990) gave us the concept of emotional labour, situated within a feminist ethics of care. *Emotional labour* is trying to feel the right feelings for the job at hand, also referred to as emotional management. Hochschild (1990) studied a range of occupational expressions of emotional labour, from flight attendants to debt collectors. Her concern was with the industrial implications of emotional labour and not just how individual care workers manage these often-burdensome expectations. Hochschild (1990) showed us how emotions, not just behaviours, are subject to social rules productive of expectations of how emotional management should be undertaken and by whom. This is particularly relevant to women, for whom caregiving is often taken for granted, or assumed to reflect their inherent nurturing capacities. Violence and abuse relates because it may be used and legitimated in the belief that transgressions from these expectations (such as refusal to perform care) are rightfully punished.

Written on the Body

Feminist, black and queer activists understand the importance of emotions and how oppression can be written on, and into, the body. Racial, sexual and gender oppression all manifest in a range of statistics. For instance, one in four Australian women over the age of 15 have experienced at least one incident of violence from an intimate partner (ANROWS 2015). Notably, women victims/survivors of child abuse and/or intimate partner violence have the highest rates of substance use problems (Call and Nelsen 2007). As Dawe, Frye, Best, Moss and Atkinson (2007: ix) highlight, "women with substance abuse problems are also at high risk of being assaulted. This in turn increases the risk of subsequent substance dependence and heavy use." Call and Nelsen's (2007) study found similar patterns, with the majority of the women reporting that their problems with substance use started after the first incidence of partner violence. Women diagnosed with post-traumatic stress disorder (PTSD) also struggle with substance use problems in greater numbers than women without such a diagnosis (Pollock, Agllias and Stubley 2006). Conditions such as anxiety, depression and PTSD are often (but not always) correlated to and reflective of experiences of material hardship and oppression.

Internalized oppression refers to the process of devalued group members taking on dominant negative stereotypes promulgated about them. Mullaly (2010) refers to this as a process of inferiorization. Allan, Pease and Briskman (2009: 81) note that this often manifests in oppressed people feeling "self-hatred, fear of violence, self-doubt, isolation and powerlessness." In stratified (or hierarchical) societies, one form of internalized oppression occurs for many groups of people because of their devalued class position (Ferguson and Lavalette 2006). Nicely summarized by psychologists Greenleaf and Williams (2009), discrimination poses threats to oppressed individuals' educational and economic potential, their material well-being and psychological functioning. From a psychological perspective, discrimination threatens feelings of self-control, often producing feelings of hopelessness, which can precipitate or worsen depression, anxiety and other mental disorders, and in turn, exacerbate likely exposure to poverty.

Critical Consciousness & Critical Questioning

One way to address internalized oppression is through *critical consciousness*, which is a process of growing critical awareness of the political nature of personal problems and associated experiences of oppression (see Sakamoto and Pitner 2005). Critical consciousness also speaks to a deep awareness of and active opposition to the structural inequalities of political systems and an appreciation of how inequality patterns the personal lives of individuals and collectives. *Activist-scholars* are public intellectuals/scholars/academics, often tied to social movements, who seek to produce knowledge that will advance an issue or cause, often related to social equality and environmental justice.

Feminists have historically been drawn from women's movements that have prioritized women's rights and raising women's consciousness of gender oppression, so as to throw off the shackles of internalized gender oppression. The plural version, *feminisms*, may be used to indicate the wide-ranging, contested body of feminist ideas, research interests and involvement in social movements promoting women's interests, sexual equality and associated causes — across the axes of privilege and oppression. AOP has been influenced greatly by a variety of feminists, of whom many have had close connections, if not membership, to women's activist groups (Adams, Dominelli and Payne 2009). To quote Mies (1991: 62), "the aim of the women's movement is not just the study but the overcoming of women's oppression and exploitation." This means different things to different groups of feminists. For instance, for *eco-feminists* it means combining feminist and environmental concerns and being critical of male privilege and masculinist hierarchies as they play out for humans but also animals and their habitats.

Critical consciousness of the negative impact of economic and moral conservativism is another part of AOP work. *Economic conservatism* refers to a body of "right-wing" ideas and practices that champion the rights of individuals in the free market over the human rights of collectives. It is often referred to as economic rationalism and criticized for being economic fundamentalist. *Moral conservatism*, or "right-wing" approaches to morality that advocate for the ongoing privileging of heterosexuality, traditional gender roles, heterosexual marriage and sexual reproduction, overlaps with but also differs from economic conservatism that prioritizes an individual's right to privately accumulate capital over collective human rights.

Being critically conscious of the negative impacts of welfare austerity is also part of AOP work, whether offering services in welfare, health or education. *Welfare austerity* involves reluctant if not hostile approaches to public welfare provision based on economic and moral conservative ideas about the need to privatize social supports and reduce future claims eligibility (Fraser and Taylor 2016). "Welfare austerity measures" include cost-cutting activities that restrict eligibility and scrutinize the behaviour of recipients. Welfare austerity exacerbates marginalization. *Marginalization* means devaluing someone or something and treating them as unimportant. AOP workers challenge the neoliberalization of public health, welfare and education, as well as the underlying principles and effects of welfare austerity (Ferguson and Lavalette 2006).

PRINCIPLE 4:
ADVOCATING PEACE AND NON-VIOLENCE

Advocacy and social action are important parts of AOP work. *Advocacy* refers to arguments, efforts and actions designed to advance a particular cause or promote the interests of one party over another. Advocacy is often used to challenge unearned privilege stemming from unequal social systems (Ferguson and Lavalette 2006). *Social action* refers to the efforts and actions designed to bring about social change, often on a large scale. This can include any number of protests, including but not limited to blockades, work bans, consumer boycotts, street protests, internet activism and culture jamming (see Chapter 8). Social action and advocacy *with* not just *for* oppressed others is important across communities, institutions (such as schools and families) and in ways that awaken public awareness of systemic barriers that impede the development of oppressed populations (Greenleaf and Williams 2009).

Taking an AOP approach means widening the aperture to explore violence and abuse perpetrated by nation states, including both war and less obvious abuses such as growing social inequality (see Nolan et al. 2014). To paraphrase Indian environmental activist Vandana Shiva (2005), violence occurs through social systems and cultural practices, such as the over-consumption and control of resources by a few, denying the needs of the many, such as the need for clean air and water and decent food and housing. As we will suggest, AOP workers take seriously both the material conditions of life as well as its cultural, social, psychological and interpersonal dimensions.

The Principle of Non-Violence

To be anti-oppressive is to be non-violent, to advocate for non-violence and strive for peace. As the Dalai Lama (UPLIFT 2015) explains, "all forms of violence, especially war, are totally unacceptable as a means to settle disputes between and among nations, groups and persons." Yet, as Martin Luther King Jr. knew so well, the commitment to non-violence can be a very difficult position to maintain, especially in the face of great violence from others. Pacifism can be misread as weakness, passivity and fear. As AOP workers it can be challenging to walk the talk of peace and open dialogue. Speaking across the lines of difference, facing and servicing (treating, teaching, helping) even our most bitter opponents may be required.

At home and abroad, AOP workers care about war and peace, and this is reflected in our practice principles. As Jane Addams, North American social work activist and reformer observed, "peace is not merely an absence of war, but the nurture of human life" (cited in Linn and Scott 1935: 278). She called for the uniting of women in all countries "who are opposed to any kind of war, exploitation and oppression and who work for universal disarmament ... and by the establishment of social, political, and economic justice for all without distinction of sex, race, class, or creeds" (Linn and Scott 1935: 278). As workers committed to fighting oppression we contribute to peace-building activities through our alliances with, or as members of, social movements in pursuit of social justice and equality (see Dominelli 2012b). Some AOP-oriented professionals may be more inclined towards social transformation via macro-political change, rather than just incremental reforms or minor adjustments (Ferguson and Lavalette 2006). Because we understand that social problems are constituted within unfair socio-political contexts, we appreciate the politics of all forms of our work, irrespective of discipline, mode or field of practice.

Critical Questioning for Peace and Non-Violence

Critical consciousness for peace and non-violence begins with *critical questioning,* or questioning that goes beyond taken-for-granted assumptions. Challenging common-sense views enables us to unearth the causes of oppression and privilege, especially those relating to violence and abuse. Critical questions need to start with the self. How have you supported others in their quest for non-violence? What can you contribute to a collective, AOP-oriented understanding of violence and abuse? What strengths, resources and experience do you have to share with others? How might you use these skills, talents and interests for the purposes of peace and non-violence? What blind spots, biases and areas of ignorance might you have? How might you learn about them if they are blind to you? Look for subtle feedback often written on others' faces. Asking others outright for feedback is another option but is best done with those whom we respect and trust to be both critical and kind.

Critical consciousness is central to groups joining together to resist oppression. Resistance can take many forms. It can include acts of defiance but also more subtle acts of subversion, sometimes shown through subversive humour expressed by subordinates to their superiors. It is why so many traditional heterosexual men fear being laughed at by women, or worse still, young girls. Black resistance to white (delusions of) superiority has also used satire as well as more direct political actions including street protests. Class-based resistance to transnational ruling elites occurs in many forms, including the popular uprisings that we have seen in recent decades in and beyond the Middle East. For an interesting discussion of non-violent civil resistance in the Middle East in recent years see Nepstad (2011) and for the role of social media in the Arab Spring Uprisings see Comunello and Anzera (2012).

Adopting an AOP perspective means daring to question some of the most taken-for-granted dimensions of life — those "higher order" questions such as who should own and control the world's resources, how democracy might be operationalized to be meaningful, egalitarian and appreciative of diversity and how we might work towards a society where oppression, disadvantage and stigma no longer poison our clients'/patients'/students' lives. We do so in our own minds, at least, if not with each other and in public forums. Yet, within these broad parameters there is much room for (healthy) dispute and disagreement. We have the courage to question taken-for-granted social practices, including our own. We engage openly with others, making inquiries and opening up dialogues that are not circular or self-perpetuating. Wherever we sit on controversial questions the point is that we do not shy away from them.

PRINCIPLE 5:
WORKING WITH OTHERS IN ALLIANCES

As AOP workers we care deeply about working for social justice across borders. We use the term "borders" broadly, to refer to their many possible manifestations between countries, religions, genders, sexualities, social classes, ages, generations and abilities. As we explain in the final chapter of this book, borders have also formed divisions between humans and (other) animals. AOP workers understand there to be a nexus (or interaction) between power relations and knowledge; for this reason, interdisciplinary knowledge is especially valued.

Forming Alliances Across Borders

As anti-oppressive practitioners we need to create space for new meanings to surface about social problems and potential responses. In practice this can be a creative and inspiring process, however, it may also require pitching new ideas to less than enthusiastic audiences, whether these be funders, managers, board members or the general public. Sometimes this means pushing the boundaries of "received ideas" (Rojek 2012), that is, existing understandings of social problems and their effects, including those that have become dominant within particular circles or interest/activist groups.

We make connections across disciplines and traditional professional boundaries, and in between and across concepts and categories. For instance, we know that domestic abuse and domestic homicide are connected (Smith, Williams and Mullane 2014). Poverty and the burden of disease are also connected. We understand *resilience* as the ability to bounce back from difficulties and recover from hardship, however we are also aware that this is often unfairly expected of oppressed individuals who experience chronic hardship. This can mean that when higher status groups face adversity (such as natural disasters), they are offered more support and have more supports to draw on.

As AOP workers, we do not endorse top-down ways of working, motivated by financial profit and using processes that silence people located at the bottom of social hierarchies (see Sewpaul, Østhus and Mhone 2013). Recognizing and addressing the enforced exclusion experienced by oppressed persons is part of the brief, along with attempts to open up choices and freedoms so often denied to the oppressed (Nzira and Williams 2009). The politics of voice are still important but, as explained by Sewpaul, Østhus and Mhone (2013: 117), "It's not just who gets to speak. It's also who gets listened to and heard."

In this time of neoliberal welfare (Baines 2006; Ferguson and Lavalette 2013; Henman and Marston 2008) we must ask whether we are challenging or reproducing the oppressive social structures operating in our own lives and workplaces. We must ask difficult questions about how we are interacting with clients, workmates, students and community members (see Allan, Pease and Briskman 2009; Mattsson 2014; Sakamoto and Pitner 2005). Are we forming social justice-based alliances that are open to diversity? Do our partnerships with others actively resist being dominating or controlling (see Ife 2012)? Are we unhelpfully conceptualizing people as "passive victims" or instead looking for ways to allow people's experiences of hardship to inform our conceptualization and delivery of services *with* clients, patients and students, not just for them?

PRINCIPLE 6:
INCORPORATING OTHER APPROACHES INTO AOP WORK

AOP perspectives are often used in conjunction with other perspectives, approaches and models. In this discussion we will briefly overview some popular practice perspectives used in the human service professions. For each approach we identify the central concern, main concepts and principles of change, along with its benefits and criticisms. Our aim is to show where AOP perspectives can be used with others but also where there are incompatibilities.

Psychodynamic Theories

The central concern of *psychodynamic theories* is how internal processes (such as needs, drives and emotions) motivate human behaviour, and how childhood casts a long emotional shadow over adults' lives. With reference to the id, ego and superego as levels of consciousness, there is a special focus on the unconscious (thoughts

BRESCIA UNIVERSITY
COLLEGE LIBRARY

that are "hidden" from us) as a key driver of human behaviour. Attachments (later developed by attachment theorists), especially early maternal attachment, are understood as critical to understanding us in adulthood. Theories of human development, personality and abnormal psychology usually also work from these premises.

From an AOP perspective, psychodynamic theories offer us some useful insights about emotions, empathy, positive regard and the therapeutic alliance (see Falkenström, Granström and Holmqvist 2013). They can help us understand some aspects of the inner worlds of individuals, especially individuals who themselves attribute their present social problems to problematic childhood attachments. However, a key limitation of these theories is that they overemphasise the individual, specifically the individual's inner world (or psyche). Change is understood as coming from within the person, but with little regard for social context or structural change. In our view, this is an unfair and unrealistic expectation of individuals, especially when they are subject to violence and abuse.

Cognitive Behaviour Therapy

Cognitive Behaviour Therapy (CBT) is a widely used psychological approach to working with individuals and groups in relation to specific emotional, behavioural and psychological difficulties. CBT principles have been applied in a range of interventions, all of which "share the basic premise that mental disorders and psychological distress are maintained by cognitive factors" (Hofmann et al. 2012: 427). It is related to, and often used in conjunction with, other therapeutic approaches such as mindfulness and Acceptance and Commitment Therapy. The focus of CBT is on increasing the capacity of individuals to regulate their inner experiences. While it has been found effective in helping individuals to achieve discrete, cognitive and behaviourally related goals such as quitting smoking or managing anxiety, it disregards wider patterns of social injustice such as those that produce vulnerability to violence and abuse. Remaining silent on questions relating to power, privilege and oppression, CBT offers little in terms of understanding the causes of violence and abuse nor the collective experience of violation — of which behaviours such as smoking and anxiety may be symptoms. One of the reasons that CBT and related approaches are often attractive to practitioners is because, ultimately, it is easier to affect small changes in the individual, especially those who are motivated to change, than it is to engage in the prevention of violence and abuse.

Narrative Therapy

Narrative therapy or analysis is an approach to practice in which practitioners of social policy, research, community work/development, group work or casework/case management purposefully engage others in and through the use of stories.

Advocates of the use of narratives stress the universality of stories to all cultures and their utility for understanding experiences, especially those of privilege and oppression (seeLopes et al. 2014). The challenge for AOP practitioners, though, is to ensure that the focus on stories does not default to individuals, losing sight of the material and socio-cultural contexts in which individuals live. To be both narrative and AOP in orientation, narratives must be scrutinized for collective — and not just individual — expressions of power, privilege and oppression (see Fraser 2004). Only then can stories about violence and abuse account for the vast differences in susceptibility to and experiences of violence and abuse related to gender, sexuality, class, race/ethnicity, age and ability.

Irrespective of the intervention model or practice approach, AOP workers need to display the personal traits, attributes, skills and abilities conducive to fostering therapeutic working alliances. These include: empathy, respect and sensitivity, intellect, clarity and courage, grit, persistence and tenacity, honesty and consistency, the desire and willingness to learn through a range of mediums, an openness to self-awareness and commitment to humility and a willingness to really enter into other ways of seeing and experiencing the world. Whatever our role or choice of technologies, we do not deny, dismiss or ignore the underlying causes and systems of violence and abuse — even if we feel that we cannot do anything about it.

We need to see how people's experiences — as victims, survivors and/or perpetrators — connect to their contexts. This is a significant contribution that AOP workers can make. We are interested in how experiences of oppression and privilege connect with both risk and vulnerability and exposure to policing and penalty. As we discuss in subsequent chapters, a central goal of AOP work is to prevent the revictimization of abuse victims, including that associated with the stigmatization and blaming of particular groups (such as women who stay with violent men or young people who stay out late drinking).

CONCLUSION

In the last chapter we explored the complexities associated with defining and naming violence and abuse. We noted the importance of language to the conceptualization of violence and abuse, and the ways in which this language signals how interventions are being conceptualized. We return to these ideas later in this book, in Chapter 7, when we explore in more detail the social and material consequences of uncritically adopting dominant constructions of violence, vulnerability, victimhood and danger.

In working through the practice principles outlined in this chapter, we hope that the multiple psychological, cultural, economic and political dimensions of violence and abuse are becoming evident. Emphasizing critical reflexivity, courage and an unshakable interest in analyzing power relations, we have considered the ways in which violence and abuse are caused, or exacerbated, by racism, classism, disablism, heterosexism, ageism and sexism. Oppression, privilege and intersectionality have been emphasized as helping us to understand collective, not just individual, experiences of violence and abuse. We have argued that understanding collective experiences is critical to addressing the causes and prevention of violence and abuse.

Part 2

RECOGNIZING VIOLENCE AND ABUSE

4. CLASS, RACE, RELIGION, VIOLENCE AND ABUSE

- How do class, race, violence and abuse intersect?
- What does inequality have to do with violence?
- Can people described as powerless be violent?
- How are targets of harm constructed?

A central point of this book is that violence and abuse are not just the behaviour of individuals; they are "embedded in social and cultural relationships" (Ray 2011: 21). This is to acknowledge the ways in which contexts, impacts and experiences of violence and abuse are inseparable from social location/positioning. Drawing upon Galtung's "violence triangle," which we introduced in Chapter 2, it is possible to see that what is visible as violence, at a particular time, place and so on is both predicated upon extensive cultural knowledge and truths and embedded in social arrangements and structures — what we might understand as invisible violences. This is not to say that structural and cultural aspects are invisible, but rather that these are rarely visible as violent/violence; they are just "the way things are," the way we live, the normal. As aspects or dimensions of identity, race, culture, ethnicity, social class, dis/ability (discussed in Chapter 6) and gender and sexuality, the focus of the next chapter is relevant to our social location, that is, how we are positioned by and within society. Social structures impact, profoundly, on people's lives — the extent to which they encounter inequality, exclusion, disadvantage and so on — and these structures are justified culturally as the "way things are and should be" and, thus, beyond question.

In this chapter we consider race, culture, ethnicity and social class at a number of levels: as cultural and structural forms of violence; as pivotal to justifications for the use of direct violence (that is, by whom and against whom, when and where); and as crucial for understanding the circumstances in which violence is seen as a problem (that is, whose violence is problematized, when and why).

VIEWING RACE, CULTURE, CLASS AND RELIGION FROM AN AOP PERSPECTIVE

Racial, religious and class-based oppressions often intersect to produce potent negative effects. However, rather than catalogue these effects we draw your attention to the very ways we think about race, class and culture, the assumptions we make and the privileges we enjoy and/or lack, as it is these that provide the fabric for lived personal experiences of violence and abuse.

Race, Culture and Ethnicity

Race has traditionally been understood as representative of biological difference. It is increasingly recognized, however, that race is simply a way of categorizing individuals and groups that is not based on any scientifically valid distinction. Genetic research has shown, for example, that more diversity exists "between individuals *within* a race than between races" (Fozdar, Wilding and Hawkins 2009: 15). This is not new knowledge: in 1950 the United Nations Educational, Scientific and Cultural Organization (UNESCO) definitively refuted the claim that particular groups have "innate mental characteristics," proclaiming that "for all practical social purposes 'race' is not so much a biological phenomenon as a social myth." The idea of race has nonetheless persisted and continues to be drawn upon in popular, professional and public discourses in a way that infers a direct link between physical characteristics ("race") and "other characteristics, such as intelligence, morality, physical prowess or personality traits" (Fozdar et al. 2009: 11). Regardless of the so-called truth of race, the social, economic and political consequences of race for people's lives are very real.

Unlike race, *ethnicity* is commonly associated with culture rather than biology, encompassing "all aspects of daily, family and cultural life that people with common histories share" (Zack 2006). Perhaps the defining characteristic of ethnicity is that of (perceived) difference, whether ascribed by others and/or claimed by the group itself. Ethnicity is produced and reproduced through social interaction, both collective and individual, because "we learn who we are because other people — in and outside of our ethnic boundaries — continually tell us" (Zevallos 2003: 84). Ultimately then, ethnic — or cultural — identity is shaped within a broader context, "through the intersection of the political, economic, social and cultural" (Fozdar et al. 2009: 43). In this sense, we learn to recognize that, despite the loss of credibility of biological notions of race, there is a persistent tendency to equate difference with inferiority. As racial (genetic) inferiority morphs into *cultural inferiority*, cultural difference comes to represent political, social and economic *disability*, perhaps not innate but nonetheless "deeply embedded, unconscious, [and] indelibly imprinted" (Tabili 2003: 128).

An ideology of cultural differentiation, based on the perceived similarities and differences between groups, underlies ideas about race and ethnicity and related assumptions. Widely held but rarely acknowledged, is that ethnicity and culture is something that Others have, "while Westerners remain culture free" (Adelman, Haldane and Wies 2012: 692). These perceptions of difference are critical, particularly their intersections with nationality and status. For instance, within Western countries, reflect on which groups are likely to be constituted as "true" Australians, Canadians, Americans, British and so on. Which groups are likely to be left out? It is not just a case of newcomers (new migrants and refugees) being constructed in this way. Indigenous peoples, whose connections to the countries are deep and longstanding, are also likely to be missed, if not actively excluded. In this sense, being seen as "ethnic" and different is not a compliment or benefit, but carries the risk of devaluation. For white Westerners it means they often know themselves *through* difference; the shape of who they are emerges from the shading out of what they are not.

Notions of race and ethnicity are contentious, evocative and fraught, both constituting cultural violence (the ideology of race and racism) and enabling structural violence (including institutional racism). Racism is complex and emotive: complex because it can be understood in a range of ways; and emotive because talking about it tends to trigger strong reactions and, often, defensiveness. Practices of racism are experienced differently by different groups and at a number of levels — from the structural or macro level, to the everyday and individual (micro) level. Distinguishing between individual racism and institutional racism is important because focusing only on individual acts of racism means overlooking the systematic and structural disadvantages that perpetuate inequality and injustice. When we talk about institutional racism we are acknowledging that society's prevailing views both reflect the interests of dominant groups and are built into its political, economic and social institutions.

Racism is more than prejudice. Racism, as cultural violence, is both ideological and institutionalized (Agozino 2000). As racism shapes individual attitudes and actions it cannot simply be reduced to the intentional rationality of individuals. In this sense, deliberate (conscious) and unwitting (unconscious) racism are, in effect, one and the same, advantaging some people while disadvantaging others. Thinking critically about race illustrates the interconnections of cultural, structural and direct violence.

Privilege

When we talk of privilege in this book we are not referring to the personal favours that intimates, family members and friends share. Nor are we talking about the individual privilege of being invited to a special event or honoured with an award for an achievement. While these single, individual events may be part of a wider repertoire of systemic privileges (consider, for instance, recent debates about the whiteness of Academy Award winners), they are not, on their own, what we mean by privilege. Rather, we are referring to *unearned privileges* granted to people *on the basis of their membership to overvalued groups.*

Privilege intersects all forms of oppression and underwrites our social systems and practices. For the most part, we are born into privileges. For example, vast differences exist in quality of life opportunities across countries, thus the country in which we are born is one very significant determinant of privilege. Similarly, the social status of our birth family, our geographical location and our nationality are also important. However, the privileges that we are born with can also diminish over our life course. Consider, for instance, the ways in which the privileges associated with being heterosexual, young and able-bodied may alter as people age and their circumstances (health, sexuality and so on) change.

Racism colour codes us through a hierarchy that does not favour Black, Asian or Indigenous peoples, but instead favours white Europeans. White privilege is:

> an institutional (rather than personal) set of benefits granted to those of us who, by race, resemble the people who dominate the powerful positions in our institutions ... purely on the basis of our skin color doors are open to us that are not open to other people. (Kendall 2013: 62)

The social construction of whiteness allows white people to assume a position of neutrality, in contemporary and historical relations, offering them many privileges, while at the same time allowing for the denial that they are being received (Puzan 2003). Recognizing the existence of white privilege means acknowledging that what are often presented as race/racial problems are actually "white people's problems with people of color" (Kholsa and McElwee 2016). As a society, because we focus on "people of colour instead of on the dominant culture that marginalizes them," we shift the "burden of improving race relations on the marginalized themselves" (Kholsa and McElwee 2016).

Similar to male and heterosexual privilege (see Chapter 5) and other forms of institutionally and culturally provided privileges based on an overvaluation of particular social identities, white privilege is not something that can be given up as it is not something actively taken or chosen. Rather it infiltrates the ways we interact, do business and think about ourselves in the world (see Kendall 2002).

So rather than thinking of white privilege as the metaphorical ace card privileged people have to play, it is more accurately understood as the advantages associated with being the ones who make up the rules of the game, who instigate and run the game, who change the rules of the game if necessary, all the while declaring no part in the umpiring. As Dyer (1997: 1) so powerfully expresses:

> As long as race is something only applied to non-white peoples, as long as white people are not racially seen and named, they/we function as a human norm. Other people are raced, we are just people.

Social Class

The term "class" has been used in a range of ways and contexts; in short, class means different things to different people. For some, class represents, simply, personal wealth and related status markers associated with education, occupation, authority and material possessions. Understood more broadly, however, social class may be seen as having less to do with money and wealth than it does the less tangible realms of social connections: social standing, family background and lineage and the signifiers of taste, style, behaviour and so forth. Consider, for example, the images associated with "new money" versus "old money." Whether defined narrowly or more broadly, class is, in essence, a system of social division and, as such, it intersects with divisions associated with race, ethnicity and so on, in ways that (re)produce privilege and inequality.

Social class might look different than it did fifty years ago — and the distinction between upper, middle and working classes less clear — but this does not mean that it is any less significant. While wide debates are held about social class in our increasingly complex, unstable and globalized world, it is crucial that class is kept on the agenda as a constant reminder "that not all of our activities are open or free choices" (Bessant and Watts 2002: 320). As explained by Scott (2000: 52), even though class structures are increasingly fragmented:

> it would be wrong to mistake contemporary society's increased individual capacities to manipulate the cultural trappings of identity as meaning that class actually no longer matters ... The fact that we encounter so much political rhetoric about 'classlessness', and the importance of individual choice or the latest fashion in 'achievement', does not mean that class has disappeared. Indeed, we should be asking in whose interests is it to propagate such myths?

There is no dispute that inequality, both nationally and globally, has increased; the gap between the rich/richest and the poor/poorest is ever widening (see Sen and Grown 2013). Differences in socio-economic status underlie class inequality, determining access to goods and services, the ability to speak authoritatively, political influence and so on. Nonetheless, despite the evidence that is all around us, we continue to be expected to attribute personal wealth and success to individual characteristics (passion, hard work, talent and skill) rather than the structural advantages that are built into our societies. Like race and ethnicity, class is a way of dividing people up, of differentiating between types of people. Social division (as cultural violence) is fundamental to social inequality: the "hierarchical distribution of social, political, economic and cultural resources" (Habibis and Walter 2009: 2). As structural violence, inequality is "systematic and enduring"; it is "transmitted across generations, built into institutions and practised in everyday activities" (Habibis and Walter 2009: 3).

Educational Disadvantage and Literacy

Most contemporary societies require literacy, including digital (online) literacy, from their members. The implications of illiteracy are far reaching and present significant obstacles in everyday life, including the capacity to do paid work. Imagine, for example, trying to work out how much medicine to take if you cannot read. Or filling out forms, getting a driver's license, sending an email, querying a bill, accessing banking services, following a recipe, making a shopping list and so on, if you struggle to read and/or write. Street signs, written instructions of any kind and news headlines can all be out of reach for the estimated 800 million illiterate adults around the world (Boughton et al. 2013).

From Canada, Crichlow (2015) discusses how "functional literacy," or the very basic level of literacy required in daily life, continues to be a problem for racialized minorities in white-dominated societies, reflecting educational disadvantage from a young age. Predominantly experienced by people oppressed by class, race (and ethnicity) and gender, poor literacy does not necessarily reflect a lack of interest or ability but rather inadequate educational support and/or encouragement. In her book, *Other People's Children: Cultural Conflict in the Classroom*, Delpit (1995) observes that context is critical when it comes to learning; meaningful activities and tasks are as important as skills training and technical instruction.

On top of the practical challenges posed by not being able to read and write there is the psychological shame to contend with. This is likely to be especially the case for adults oppressed by other devalued identities (see Emslie et al. 2006). As we explore in Chapter 6, "disablism," or the denigration of people with disabilities, provides the wider context in which people struggling to read and/or write can be called dumb, stupid and lazy. It is not hard to internalize negative messages about ourselves, especially if these are repeated often enough. The effects of internalized shame are many and can include clinical depression. In their study of 1,890 South

Korean elders (aged over 65), Kim et al. (2014) found that, after controlling for other variables, participants categorized as illiterate were 2.4 times more likely to be depressed — using the Korean version of the Geriatric Depression Scale — than those classed as literate. Being semi-literate was also associated with an increased risk of depression.

The recognition that education is a basic human right (see Ife 2012; McCowan 2013) is an important starting point for AOP workers. Drawing attention to the ingenuity of people who manage without adequate literacy skills, while important, is not an adequate response to the problem. Rather, positive, respectful and accessible literacy programs should be available to all, including those adults who carry deep-seated anxieties about trusting people to help them with this. This is especially critical for populations known to have had troubled or oppressive relationships with education and welfare authorities.

Education is, however, not the exclusive responsibility of teachers or parents. Community-based programs that offer full support, including basic skills such as holding a pen and pencil or turning on a computer, are needed. Boughton et al. (2013) discuss one such program — "Yes I Can" — a Cuban mass adult literacy model that was piloted in a remote Indigenous community Australia in 2012. Sixteen community members with very low literacy completed the program and, overall, it was deemed a great success. In the words of one of the local Indigenous facilitators:

> this is the best thing that ever could have happened for this little town ... You know, don't stop at one town. Let's keep going. Let's keep it rolling on ... you've got to spread it along, spread the word, take it to other communities, and keep it alive. Keep it alive. (Boughton et al. 2013: 28)

Religious Privilege and Oppression

Religious privilege literally involves the privileging (or advantaging) of some religions over others. In Western countries such as the U.S., Australia and Canada, Christianity underwrites so many systems and structures and is institutionalized in a range of ways, including tax breaks for charities, preferential treatment when applying for building approval for churches (compared to mosques and synogogues), public holidays and other festive seasons and the space to practice religion in schools, prisons and other public places.

Religious privilege enables beneficiaries the freedom from religious oppression such as that generated against Muslims. Since the 9/11 attacks on the World Trade Centre in the U.S., members of the Muslim community have had to live with surveillance, over-policing and, often, open hostility in an environment in which being Muslim has become inherently suspect. In her book, *Islamophobia and the Politics of Empire*, Kumar (2012) argues that while commonly presented as a clash of civilizations — between East and West — Islamophobia in fact represents little more than systemic racism, fueled by the spectacle of terrorism and the (Western) intolerance of religious and cultural differences.

As is the case with other forms of privilege (such as male, white, class and heterosexual), it can be hard for the beneficiaries of religious privilege to see their privilege. This does not mean, however, that it does not exist, nor does it lessen its significance. As Cline (2016) reminds us, to privilege one group over another, on the basis of religion or race or anything else, is to "institutionalize discrimination and bigotry."

Medina (2011), a Muslim feminist scholar living in California, identifies as central to systemic racism the three following concepts:

1. *colourblind racism*, where racism is denied and disguised through claims not to see or notice colour. In this sense, privilege operates — and the profound effects of racism persist — even when there is no deliberate intention of malice (Pearson, Dovido and Gaertner 2009).
2. *otherness*, which is a way of marking others as inherently different to 'us'; of constructing boundaries between people, groups, religions, and nations. Those who are othered are cast as outsiders and often demonised; being othered is a devaluing, oppressive process.
3. *passing* as a member of a racial, ethnic or religious group that is more valued — or has more 'social clout' — than one's own. This is only possible when visual markers of difference, such as religious clothing or other signs often attributed to being homosexual, transgendered, working-class, disabled or elderly, can be concealed. As observed by Nittle (2016), "passing and oppression go hand-in-hand. People would have no need to pass if society valued all groups equally."

Islamophobia refers to the fear and hostility directed towards people who are, or are believed to be, Muslim. In recent years the non-state actor that calls itself Islamic State (also known by is or isis) has received considerable attention, especially in mainstream and social media outlets. For many in the West, isis is seen to pose the greatest threat to their security and way of life. What is less considered, if at all, is that the most devastating effects of the war against isis (and other Islamic militant groups) have been perpetrated against non-Western countries. In countries such as Iraq and Syria, for instance, hundreds of thousands of people have been killed and millions have lost their homes, communities, livelihoods and family members (see bbc News 2016; Khan and Estrada 2015). Yet, with the rise of the far right, such as evident in U.K.'s Brexit and the U.S. Trump presidency, Muslim asylum seekers are not likely constructed as victims but rather as dangerous, threatening perpetrators.

While writing this chapter, aid workers were unable to reach the thousands of people trapped between enemy lines in Aleppo, Syria, leaving them to languish in the most diabolical conditions, produced from years of bombing and the destruction of virtually all infrastructure (Aljazeera Human Rights 2016). Temporary ceasefires to allow aid and aid workers to reach these civilians, most of whom are women and children, have proved unsuccessful. Meanwhile, the focus of public attention in the West is the radicalization of younger Muslims by Islamic extremists, with little regard for the ways in which poverty, discrimination — especially in the labour market — and Islamaphobic abuse (see Khan and Estrada 2015) have contributed to this.

INTERSECTIONS: DIFFERENCE, INEQUALITY AND PRIVILEGE

Systems of privilege and inequality derive from the social statuses of race, ethnicity, social class, gender and sexuality (Barak, Leighton and Cotton 2014). It is the "complex interplay" (Richmond 2002: 24) within and between systems of difference that enables and reproduces the social divisions of hierarchy with profound consequences for people's lives and experiences. Importantly, race, ethnicity, class, religion — and, of course, nationality — are key elements of "boundary making," that is, shaping societal patterns of inclusion and exclusion that contain and constrain people. The creation of symbolic boundaries around "imagined communities" (Anderson 1983) presupposes sameness and belonging while overlooking both interests shared *across* boundaries and the existence of differences (such as those related to social class, gender, sexuality and so on) *within* groups.

Recognizing the complex and intersecting relations of privilege and inequality makes it possible to see how race and racism may be experienced differently by different groups of people. Individual experiences of racist practices, at the everyday or micro level relate specifically to this criss-crossing of class, gender and race. Although we might think of race, ethnicity and class as distinct concepts, classifications and variables, they are "experienced holistically" in the real world; it is the "interplay and intersection" between these that "produces effects that are at once individual and collective" (Habibis and Walter 2009: 244). Acknowledging the complex and varied experiences of living with cultural and structural violence is required not least because "self-experience" or the "way individuals think of themselves" is critical to the maintenance of social inequality (Greig, Lewins and White 2003: 82).

Violence and the Inequalities of Difference

Understanding violence and abuse from an AOP perspective requires us to understand culture in multiple forms, as related not just to ethnicity but also class, gender, sexuality, age and ability. To reiterate, culture is not something that only Other people have. Rather:

> everyone has a culture: a way of thinking, moving, and being that shapes and is shaped by the way an individual sees and experiences the world. There is no such thing as an action, policy, institution, or practice that is culturally neutral. (Adelman et al. 2012: 692)

Aldama (2003) highlights the ways in which cultural and structural violences — the discourses and practices of social division, for example — are intimately connected with the materiality of violence, that is, the lived experience and/or real bodily impacts of violence. Scheper-Hughes' (2013: 75) reference to the "violence of poverty, exclusion and extreme marginality," for example, draws our attention to the inequalities of difference, most markedly those associated with (unearned) social privilege and (undeserved) marginalization. In Australia, for example, Indigenous inequality and exclusion is directly related to, and underpinned by, the conceptualization, both politically and more generally, "of Aboriginal people as 'different'" (Habibis and Walter 2009: 248). "Difference," here, is not neutral but rather is framed as "'the black problem' of primitiveness, non-adaptability and poverty" (Kessaris 2006: 357). Australia's long history of racism is not over and done with, as so many beneficiaries of colonization want you to believe.

From an AOP perspective, we recognize that the impacts of past practices are profound, cumulative and productive of direct violence, both perpetrated *on* and *by* Indigenous peoples. The material effects of social inequality also impact experiences of and responses to abuse and violence in society. Cunneen and White (2011: 117) observe that processes of economic, social and cultural estrangement — of marginalization — are directly associated with "varying degrees of alienation, antisocial behaviour, riots, and violence." For example, the availability and accessibility of community resources varies greatly across the population in accordance with socio-economic status, geographical location (rural as compared to urban areas) and issues of representation and political voice. Because different understandings of equality reflect different ideologies, government interventions, in the form of public policy, can function to either *reinforce* or *redress* social inequalities. Focusing on equality of outcome, for instance, rather than equality of opportunity, is a key social justice measure because this recognizes the "differing needs of differently advantaged groups" (Morley, Macfarlane and Ablett 2014: 5). In other words, because inequalities pre-exist us, fairness cannot be achieved by treating everyone as if they are the same.

In all other respects everyone is *not* treated the same; we know, for example, that disadvantaged and marginalized groups are policed and punished disproportionately. *Criminalization* refers to the "process by which behaviours and individuals are transformed into crime and criminals" (Michalowski 1985: 6). This is to recognize that in targeting particular groups of people and penalizing certain types of behaviour, the "definitions of social harm and crime" embedded in "law and order" policies reflect class, race and other biases (Cunneen and White 2011: 146). We know also that the criminal justice system — including policing, court decision making and criminal sanctions — impacts differently on certain groups in society and that imprisonment, in particular, substantially exacerbates the effects of social inequality. In the following section, we will look more closely at the specific dimensions and manifestations of violence in the lives of Indigenous Australians.

The Violence of Colonization: Indigenous peoples in Australia

Indigenous peoples in Australia, as in many other colonized countries, still experience incredible disadvantage. While "historical in origin," that is, with respect to British settlement/invasion and colonization, these disadvantages are perpetuated through "contemporary structural and social factors" including those relating to "economic opportunity, physical infrastructure, and social conditions," as manifested in "education, employment, income, housing, access to services, social networks, connection with land, racism, and incarceration" (Australian Indigenous HealthInfoNet 2015).

Indigenous health and well-being is significantly poorer, on most measures, compared to non-Indigenous people. For example, Indigenous Australians have not only a life expectancy of around ten years less than non-Indigenous Australians, but also die at younger ages and higher rates. 30 percent of Aboriginal and Torres Strait Islander (AATSI) adults report "high/very high levels of psychological distress" and hospitalizations for "intentional self-harm" have increased by 48 percent over the period from 2004 to 2013 (SCRGSP 2014). In contrast, there has been little change in hospitalizations for non-Indigenous Australians over this same period. Alarmingly, the suicide death rate for Indigenous Australians over the period from 2008 to 2012 was almost twice the rate for non-Indigenous Australians (SCRGSP 2014). The substantially higher rate of Indigenous children on care and protection orders — forty-nine per 1000 children in 2012–2013 as compared to around three to six per 1000 non-Indigenous children (SCRGSP 2014) — further reflects the continuing impacts of colonization and related trauma.

According to the most recent data available, 23 percent of Indigenous adults (defined as those aged 15 years and older) reported having been a victim of physical or threatened violence in 2008, a rate 1.8 times that for non-Indigenous adults

(ABS 2010). Looking at violence more broadly, Indigenous adults are imprisoned at thirteen times the rate for non-Indigenous adults and Indigenous youth (ages 10–17) at a rate that is around twenty-four times higher than non-Indigenous youth. Figures showing that the Indigenous adult imprisonment rate increased by 57 percent over the period 2000 to 2013 (SCRGSP 2014) indicate that this is an ongoing trend. However, accounting for the overrepresentation of Indigenous Australians at pretty much every stage of the criminal justice process is not straightforward. Drabsch (2004) highlights the importance of the following factors:

- The impact of policing practices including police discretion and over-policing;
- The criminalization and policing of particular behaviours, most notably those that occur in public places and seen as disrupting public order (such as disorderly behaviour offences);
- Judicial decision making and, in particular, requirements regarding eligibility for and conditions of bail release (this also applies to parole board requirements regarding conditional/early prison releases);
- Environmental and locational factors including the social and economic effects of living in small rural and remote communities;
- Cultural differences, including those related to ways of communicating and the implications for police interrogation, court appearances and so on;
- Socio-economic factors, including unemployment, poverty, lower educational attainment, poor housing, poor health and so on;
- The effects of marginalization including alcohol and other drug use/abuse and alienation from family and community; and
- The impact/s of specific legislation, including the ongoing effects of colonial policies involving the forced removal of Indigenous children.

Although disadvantaged people are, in general, policed and punished disproportionately, it is clear that the impact for Indigenous Australians is especially dire. Firstly, Indigenous Australians are imprisoned at a rate far greater than non-Indigenous Australians and in relation to what are often relatively minor offences (*over-representation*); and secondly, Indigenous peoples face added difficulty at all levels of the criminal justice system (*differential impacts*). The negative impacts of imprisonment are likely to be intensified due to, for example, separation from family/communities, country or cultural associations, combined with the lack of culturally appropriate policies, services and programs and Indigenous staff. Similarly, eligibility and/or compliance expectations associated with community punishments generally represent particular difficulties for Indigenous offenders.

These might include the imposition of requirements for a fixed residence/address, sustained abstinence from alcohol or other drugs, regular reporting and attendance at appointments and restrictions on associating with certain people — often family members. Conditions such as these are especially problematic in rural areas in which there are long distances to travel, few transport options and more difficulty avoiding restricted family members and friends.

Violence Against Difference: Constructing Targets of Harm

Thinking about violence against difference is to recognize that patterns of violence both mirror and (re)produce existing hierarchies of privilege, dominance and entitlement. As ways of differentiating people and imposing order, race, ethnicity, social class, sex/gender, dis/ability and so on are often used to justify direct violence or used as rationales for who uses violence, against whom, when, where and in what circumstances.

In urging us to think critically about "how we construct targets of harm," Presser (2013: 22) highlights the relationship between the use of direct violence and the ways in which we construct certain others as "not merely different but as bad, destructive, inferior, or subhuman." Ray (2011: 13), for example, refers to the "normative justifications" that are "culturally available" to those who perpetrate violence, whether legitimated or illegal. Granting "ourselves permission to harm," Presser (2013: 24) argues, rests on claims about such things as "our relationship with God, our place in a natural order" and so on, thereby representing this harm as "necessary or inevitable" (25). In essence, then, the positioning of Self/ Other and the associated alignment of difference and inferiority is fundamental to justifications for, and uses of, violence. As observed by Galtung (1990: 298), relations of social differentiation and violence reinforce one another:

> people become debased by being exploited, and they are exploited because they are seen as debased, dehumanised. When [the] Other is not only dehumanised but has been successfully converted into an 'it', deprived of humanhood, the stage is set for any type of direct violence, which is then blamed on the victim.

This is relevant to us thinking about forms of organized and/or collective violence, such as those associated with war and the practices of warfare. For example, Walby (2012: 5) observes that modern wars are "asymmetrical" in that "one side usually has much greater military strength" — including "sophisticated and expensive weapons" — than the other. Therefore war no longer centres upon distinct battles between opposing armies, with "soldiers and civilians" or "combatants and non-combatants" clearly distinguished. As such, contemporary warfare is just as likely to be associated with efforts to dissolve the state (as in intra-state and civil conflicts), as to strengthen it (as in conflict between nations and the World Wars). Modern wars are likely to be "dispersed and decentralised, with low levels of military engagement but over a longer number of years" and to involve the use of "guerrilla tactics, terrorism and genocide" (5). On the one hand, the violences of war are increasingly anonymous and distanced — as in "high-tech" warfare and terrorism — and, on the other, intensely personal as the distinction between military/civilian breaks down, and acts of war move into the realm of the endemic and everyday.

Major or "catastrophic" violence, such as mass killings and genocide, do not appear from nowhere; they emerge through a "continuum of destruction" (Staub 1989). As Flores (2012) explains it, looking back at "horrific instances of violence," such as those associated with Nazi Germany, for example, provides insight:

> [these] all began with the *devaluation* of certain groups, proceeded to *marginalisation* of those same groups (i.e., to covert discrimination and denial of civil, social or political rights, etc.), moved on to overt *discrimination*, and culminated in open *resentment* and *aggression* toward groups identified as suitable targets of hostility and violence. (emphasis in original)

Important here is the almost imperceptible progression through the continuum of violence, such that attitudes become actions and, over time, they form the way things are. So it is that "lower and lower acts of depravity" can be "perpetrated by those who would have never imagined themselves capable of such actions" (Flores 2012). In this sense, we all occupy a place on this continuum; in the words that we speak, the prejudices that we perpetuate and the injustices we fail to challenge.

Violence of the Powerless

No matter how ostensibly powerless people are, they have the capacity to express violence. Ray (2011: 14) argues that culturally available discourses of "justifiable violence" — of violence as "revolutionary or self-defensive" — "authorize" violence by offering perpetrators "a view of themselves as powerless victims" (see Chapter 8). In this sense, it is a mistake to see all violence as merely an expression of status mixed with power. Certainly status, power and violence are interrelated, however, their relationship is not simple but "complex and nuanced" (Ray 2011: 13). They cannot and should not be reduced to an either/or, powerful/powerless binary (or set of oppositions). For example, violence directed at the police by marginalized groups, or by children towards their parents, demonstrates the ways in which violence may be used to express "perceived powerlessness and estrangement" (Ray

2011: 13), rather than social dominance and privilege. Remember, power is not one thing, nor can it be considered a property or possession that some people/groups have and others do not (see Chapter 3). The exercise of power is not inevitably top-down. Rather, it is dynamic, complex and relational, and multilayered and multidirectional as it extends across the micro and macro realms.

Colic-Peisker and Tilbury's (2008) discussion of tensions between Indigenous peoples and resettled African refugees in Australia demonstrates well the complexity of power relations as these are embedded in the intersections of class and race. Indigeneity in Australia symbolizes both "primordial ownership and custodianship of the land ... [and] ... dispossession and social disadvantage." Australia's narrowly defined notion of multiculturalism has also meant that Indigenous peoples have slipped "further down the hierarchy of rights and achievement," resulting in an "almost automatic situation of competition and tension between Indigenous people and migrants" (Colic-Peisker and Tilbury 2008: 47). In this context of "relative deprivation" (48), and especially in urban settings, frustration is "most easily directed towards the newly arrived, highly visible refugee population that, due to its low socio-economic position, shares the same neighbourhoods" (52).

In Colic-Peisker and Tilbury's (2008: 52) account, race — or "shared black-ness" — in the context of the dominating whiteness of Australia contributed to the tension in "unexpected ways." As we have said earlier, the hierarchies of class and race are interrelated and overlap. Colic-Peisker and Tilbury (2008: 52) explain:

> Both the Aborigines and recent African arrivals are at the bottom of the Australian ethnic, as well as class, pecking order as either welfare recipients or workers in low-paid, low-skilled jobs. In this common socio-economic space, they compete for scarce resources, material as well as symbolic, such as public housing, jobs, extraordinary welfare support and "reputation" among the dominant white majority ... Blackness and socio-economic disadvantage [in this context] has not produced a shared sense of iden-tity and solidarity in recognition of similar positioning within the white society, but instead created antipathy, competition and conflict.

PROBLEM VIOLENCE: THE VIOLENCE OF OTHERS

Not all violence is seen as problematic; not all violence is condemned. Discourses of violence enable violence to be represented as the problem of (gendered, classed, raced) Others, rather than indicative of a fundamentally divided and unequal society (see Sen and Grown 2013). The dividing up of violences and designation of some as unacceptable and in the public interest is key here. In observing the various categories and classifications of violence that exist (violence in Indigenous communities, violence against women and children, youth violence, street violence, school bullying, alcohol-related violence and so on), it seems that it is the particular contexts or circumstances within which violence occurs, rather than violence in and of itself, that is of concern. Violence, then, so often manifests as the problems presented by particular groups of people, in particular areas and from whom other groups need to be protected. Problem violence becomes both recognizable as such (we know it when we see it) and contained in way that clearly distinguishes it from non-problem violence (which, of course, might not even be called violence). The conceptualization of violence as atypical, and the associated differentiation of types of behaviours and types of people (violent individuals, violent cultures), diverts attention from the ordinary, unmarked and unremarkable violences of daily life.

Insofar as it is possible to draw any conclusion about the various ways in which violence is thought of and about, it is fair to say that the problematization of violence (what is considered or named as violence), is idiosyncratic and inconsistent; *some* behaviours, actions, individuals and groups are deemed violent in some circumstances and places and not others. Violence is understood and interpreted in different ways in different contexts and the ways in which we respond to violence also vary greatly — from condemnation and punishment to glorification and hero worship. In this respect, who uses violence, against whom, where and in what circumstances *matters*.

Who Should We Fear?: Identity, Risk and Vulnerability

Rarely verbalized let alone seriously considered are questions regarding who is considered dangerous, who is seen as worthy of or in need of protection, what safety means and how this is constructed differently for different people/groups. Ultimately, the range of answers to such questions reveals much about our beliefs and assumptions about identity and difference. For example, ideas about cultural difference and violence overlap so much that these often appear to be one and the same. In the margins of conversations, violence might be talked about as if it is a "cultural attribute" with the related assumption that certain cultural groups are "primitive and prone to violence" and/or that certain cultures are intrinsically violent. In other words, within these contexts that violence is "normalized."

In (previously) multicultural continents such as Australia, United Kingdom and North America, this might play out in the perception that migrants are "not only different from 'us'" but, more critically, that they bring 'their' violence with them (Seidler 2010: 7). Recent events in Trump's America, including the restrictions placed on immigration, illustrate this well (see *Boston Globe* 2017). As Adelman, Erez and Shalhoub-Kevorkian (2003: 110) observe, the "culturalisation of violence" functions to "further distance the majority culture from violence within minority communities." This then justifies both the prevalence of violence and the lack of attention paid to this, for example, in under-policing and so on. The very same argument can be — and is — used to justify the over-policing of certain communities as well as large-scale, targeted interventions and surveillance. In the Australian context, we have seen this in the federal government's 2007 declaration of a "national emergency confronting the welfare of Aboriginal children in the Northern Territory" and the introduction of legislative and other measures to purportedly "stabilise and protect communities in the crisis area" (Brough 2007).

Race, ethnicity, social class, gender and sexuality are significant social divisions connected to the construction of risk and vulnerability and to who is seen as violent. Strong media interest in violence and the narrative of racialized villains and victims, for example, is associated with knee-jerk government reactions that usually "seek to appease public outrage" (Junger et al. 2007: 328). Fear of violence often manifests in fear of particular cultural groups (Seidler 2010: 9), and is reflected in, and amplified by, the media. News headlines and references to "Lebanese gang violence," "ethnic biker gangs" and "militant Muslim youth," for example, frame violence/ crime as a particular type of problem. Fear associated with public violences, is "a key mechanism through which race [and class] privilege is constructed," serving to both "maintain and justify exclusion" (Day 2008: 84–85) and reinforce fixed ideas regarding "who is 'dangerous' and who is 'safe'" (101). In this sense, popular images provide the backdrop for the differentiation of "potential threat" from "potential protector" (Sandberg and Tollefsen 2010: 10).

Constructing an Other — the "them" in relation to "us" — provides the means through which people "make sense of and understand their social world" (Seidler 2010: 8). This is problematic insofar as it flows into and perpetuates fixed ideas about what is so-called normal, natural, right and proper, through making judgements about people "on the basis of how closely they resemble 'us': the 'gold standard'" (Seidler 2010: 8). Our assumptions shape our expectations, which can become our reality when these shape our interactions and movements. The people and places that we choose to avoid are often enshrined in institutional policies and practices including those of racial profiling, targeted policing and so on.

Public Space, Visibility and Community

The emphasis on public violences brings together key concerns regarding social order — and actions seen as disrupting this — and the use of public spaces. Public or street violence is often highly visible, especially in urban settings. As public disorder, violence occurring in and around licensed business venues has tended to be prioritized on the basis that it interferes with the workings of the night-time economy, that is, the profit-making enterprise of private businesses such as pubs and clubs. Notions of (dis)order and antisocial behaviour exemplify how we think about public space and its so-called proper uses, and reflect dominant assumptions to do with the family, privacy and the home. Ross and Polk (2006: 146) observe:

> public spaces have always been used for social activities by low-income, marginal groups. People use the street as a recreation space, a source of entertainment, a venue to meet and sometime a place to live.

For people lacking a space of their own, public places — streets, parks, malls, car- parks — provide them, quite literally, with a place to go and a way to be with others. In other words, these spaces provide them opportunities to connect with others in their communities.

As people who sleep rough well understand, public space and its uses is both linked to broader inequalities and is highly contested, bringing together interests ranging from survival to social to economic. Especially critical is the growing trend towards privatization of public areas as, for example, in the incorporation of public-use facilities such as toilets, baby-change rooms and recreational spaces into shopping precincts/complexes. In such settings, particular people and groups "stand out" and are then more likely to be "seen as nuisances or threats" (Ross and Polk 2006: 147). The ways that we think about public violence — that is, as a particular kind of problem — is therefore linked to what we see as the role of public spaces; as open and designed to fulfil a diversity of purposes, needs and interests, or "as dangerous places that must be under surveillance and control" (Ross and Polk 2006: 149).

Whose Community?

References to "community" evoke ideals of consensus, unity and togetherness. Yet, the lived experience of community is, for many, considerably less positive. Community is a highly contested concept, not least because of the tendency to use it in a way that "effectively defines itself by those whom it excludes" (Faulkner 2004: 9), thereby obscuring complex issues regarding who is and isn't included, whose interests are represented, whose voices are heard and so on (see Adelman et al. 2003).

As observed by Worrall (1997: 58), the "reality of community" is, all too often, "exclusive." This is particularly significant in relation to perceptions of violence and dangerousness — in other words, who we should fear. In this respect, community can mean "segregation, prejudice and the desire for revenge" (Worrall 1997: 58), based on the following assumption:

> there are two clear sides [to violence/abuse]: the respectable law-abiding citizen and the feckless criminal outsider. *This* sense of community reflects an insecure society, suspicious of, and hostile towards, anything and anyone who is different. (emphasis in original)

Safety, then, becomes a matter of us and them: our safety requires, and relies upon, the "exclusion, control, containment, and physical domination" of them — the "feared 'Others'" (Whitlock 2004: 205).

Law-and-order discourses carry considerable power because they invoke community in relation to "risk of victimisation" (Brown 2005: 13), thus capitalizing on the twin "caricatures" of "violating offenders and the violated victims" (Sandor 1994: 156). While we tend to think of victims and offenders as distinct and mutually exclusive groups, the reality is considerably more complex in that people "do not simply exist in one or other of these caricatured roles" (Sandor 1994: 156). Victims can be — and often are — also offenders and vice versa, indeed, "very often the same person can be both simultaneously" (White and Habibis 2005: 320). Furthermore, "victimhood" is a status that is not "given automatically" but rather "results from a social process in which relations of power are central" (White and Habibis 2005: 320). It is important to note, however, that not "everyone who suffers harm or is victimised is labelled as a victim" (White and Perrone 2005: 339).

Ideas about direct violence, specifically "who constitutes a legitimate and deserving victim and what constitutes a legitimate excuse" (Adelman et al. 2003: 113) are relevant, reflecting and invoking gendered, raced, classed assumptions. We explore these issues in greater depth in the following chapter. For now, we can acknowledge that the "denial of victim status" (White and Perrone 2005) to some in society highlights the need to think critically about how "social harms" (such as police harassment, use of force, medical malpractice and so on) are recognized, as well as the tendency to name some activities as "victimless crimes" and some victims as less worthy and/or less harmed than others. Take, for example, the dominant assumption that sexual assaults against sex workers are less serious or have less impact than those who do not perform sex work.

CONCLUSION

As we have shown in this chapter, violence is embedded in social structures and cultural practices. The recognition that "everyone has a culture" (Adelman, Haldane and Wies 2012: 692) is foundational to anti-oppressive work. It means ensuring that we are aware of our own cultural beliefs, values and assumptions and pay attention to the ways in which these shape our perceptions. It also means remaining conscious of the structural violences that are "so ordinary, so deeply engrained in the daily working of our social, political, economic and religious institutions" (Whitlock 2004: 204). This can be especially difficult in the human services field where many of the agencies and institutions who are likely to employ us are, themselves, central to the perpetuation of social inequalities. It is in this context that Whitlock (2004: 206) asks the question:

How is it that in our own desire to obtain justice and create safety and security … so many of us committed to antiviolence work become so willing to accept kinds of structural violence directed by the state against less valued "Others"?

Whitlock's question is powerful and confronting, highlighting the need for a critical view of societal structures. Yet, we must also "turn the critical lens back on ourselves" (Morley, Macfarlane and Ablett 2014: 253), that is, to engage in critical reflection. While we may, in principle, oppose oppression and injustice, we must remain alert to whether "our words as deeds" are "always consistent with this intent" (Morley, Macfarlane and Ablett 2014: 253). While easier said than done, this involves taking a stance of political engagement and awareness rather than adopting a position of silent complicity. To be AOP practitioners, we must remain alert to, and willing to name and question, practices that are unjust and/ or harmful, unintentionally or otherwise.

5. GENDER, SEXUALITY, VIOLENCE AND ABUSE

- **What do we mean when we talk about gendered violence?**
- **How does heteronormativity relate to violence and abuse?**
- **How might we think differently about the idea of violence as a lack or loss of self-control?**

In this chapter we explore further the interlocking privileges and oppressions associated with violence and abuse. Starting with an outline of our conceptualization of sex, gender and sexualities, we examine the complex interconnections between gender and violence, with particular focus on the social and cultural expectations associated with masculinity/ies and femininity/ies.

This discussion furthers the central premise of this book, that is, that violence is not simply an individual problem, rather it is "embedded in social and cultural relationships" (Ray 2011: 21). In the preceding chapter, we considered race, culture, ethnicity and social class as dimensions of identity, or social positioning/s, that critically shape experiences and impacts of, as well as responses to, violence. In this perspective, then, understanding violence requires that we think beyond the acts and motivations of individuals. Referring, again, to Galtung's "violence triangle," we emphasize the extensive cultural knowledge and so-called truths (structural and cultural — or *invisible* — violences) that shape what is seen — what we recognize — as violence at any particular time, place and so on (see Chapter 2). Like race, culture and class, ideas about sex, gender and sexuality represent critical — and powerful — domains of knowledge about nature, the world and the way we are. Telling us what it *means* to be a man or a woman, and in particular what might be considered normal or natural for men and women, shapes both what we see as violence (*visible* violences) and what is seen as amenable to change.

UNDERSTANDING SEX, GENDER AND SEXUALITIES

Taking the time to consider the construction of sex, gender and sexualities is important to ensure that we are not reproducing inequalities, nor unwittingly reinvigorating stereotypical assumptions used to justify the violation of certain groups of people. An important starting point is to have a clear conceptual understanding of sex and gender, and the distinction between these concepts is key to the content that follows. This is necessary given that the terms and concepts "sex" and "gender" are so frequently misused — or used interchangeably — in the public domain. A range of views and perspectives exist, as with any area of knowledge, and many of these are considerably more complex than represented here. The information presented in this section is a starting point. Our goal is to provide you with a foundation for thinking through the issues explored in this chapter.

Perhaps the least complicated way of thinking about the differences between sex, gender and sexuality is to distinguish between:

- having a certain kind of body (*sex*); and
- living as certain kind of social being (*gender*); and
- having certain kinds of erotic desires (*sexuality*).

In our everyday lives we are not likely to experience these as separate and distinct; rather, for most people, sex, gender and sexuality are interconnected — even inseparable — and, for many, just the way we are.

Sex, Gender and Identity

Simply put, sex refers to the categories *male* or *female*, and gender to the ideas, roles and practices that are attributed to (or the social meanings of) male and female bodies, that is, *masculinity* and *femininity*. Yet, in reality, sex and gender do not constitute such neat categories. There is no absolute or necessary relation between gender identity and the classification of bodies as male or female, on the basis of "biological, anatomical and physiological characteristics" (WHO 2010a: 10). Instead, when we consider the range of non-gender-conforming possibilities regarding grooming/appearance, dress, mannerisms, choice of occupations and so on, it seems that gender variance is more likely to represent the norm than the exception. Gender variance is also relevant to understanding the diverse identities included under the umbrella term *transgender*. Notably, the existence of *transsexual* people who experience a profound disconnect between their (assigned) biological sex and their gender identity, represents a significant challenge to the idea that sex and gender naturally go together.

To this list we can add *sexual identity*, that is, a social identity, such as hetero-sexual, gay, lesbian and so on, based on having certain desires or sexual preferences. This is to recognize that, like sex and gender, sexuality and sexual identity are not the same and do not necessarily match; in other words, people who desire (or say that they are attracted to) and/or engage in same-sex relationships may or may not identify as such. Rather, sexual identity is generally understood as encompassing self-identity, sexual attraction, sexual practice and social recognition.

Interestingly though, heterosexuality is rarely talked about as — or in relation to — identity. Rather, heterosexuality is assumed. It becomes the default posi-tion that need not be marked, but is treated as ordinary and non-remarkable — a non-identity. In contrast, non-heterosexuality is usually positioned as a deviation from the norm (of heterosexuality) and, as such, is associated with the idea of a distinctive identity, one that represents difference. Assumptions of universal heterosexuality (that is, *heteronormativity*) are pervasive and overlap with societal gender norms. In this sense, gender deviance is constituted as anything that does not fit within a narrow binary of sex and gender categories. It is commonly seen as proof of homosexuality, as, for example, in the stereotypical association of gay men with femininity (being effeminate) and lesbian women with masculinity (being "butch").

Bodies and Meaning

Certain ideas, roles and practices, then, are associated with certain bodies. In other words, a whole range of assumptions and expectations (gender, including sexual-ity), referred to as masculinity and femininity, flow from the categorization of a body as male or female (sex). This means that our bodies are considerably more than flesh and blood; social meanings are attached to the body and organize men and women's "lives and relations" (WHO 2010a: 10). All too often it is assumed that, gender naturally follows or arises from sex and that male bodies and masculinity and female bodies and femininity automatically go together.

Distinguishing between bodies and the meanings attributed to bodies matters. We need to remain alert to this blurring together of sex and gender. Failing to do so implies — or opens the door to — determinism, or the assumption that particular types of bodies are (in)capable of certain things, and determine our destiny. The assumption that men and women are innately different — physiologically, psy-chologically, emotionally — and, hence, act differently, follows from the idea of male and female bodies as naturally different. If our biology determines who we are — there can be no prospect of social change; for those of us working in human services and motivated by anti-oppressive principles, this is an untenable position.

Whose Gender?

The World Development Report (World Bank 2012: 4) describes gender as the "social, behavioural, and cultural attributes, expectations, and norms associated with being a woman or a man." Gender constitutes, defines and constrains relations in even the most ordinary of settings in everyday life and, most commonly, it does so in ways that are both mundane and unremarkable. This challenges those accounts that rely upon the so-called natural or biological difference between men and women, instead recognizing gender as something that we "do," which tends to be ongoing and largely self-fulfilling, produced in and through our interactions (West and Zimmerman 1987).

Gender is cultural and social, objective and subjective, individually enacted and institutionally embedded. It structures and shapes men's relations with other men (Moore 1994) just as it does women's relations with women *and* men's relations with women. As students and practitioners of AOP, we must be vigilant to the ways in which supposedly neutral practices can, even inadvertently, perpetuate gender stereotypes. For example, the practice of using the term "gender" to refer to women or to designate women's interests and concerns is common across research, policy and service provision contexts. This reflects a narrow understanding of gender as principally relevant to women and women's relations with men, "forgetting or ignoring the different ways in which men and boys are affected by" and invested in "gender power structures and systems" (Kangas, Haider and Fraser 2014: 4).

Rather than view gender as fixed and oppositional (men versus women), we see gender as a complex and powerfully effective domain of social practice (Connell 2000: 18). Reflecting critically on gender, then, means thinking about its impact on the lives of boys and girls, men and women, and the opportunities available to them as well as the ways in which gender shapes relations between women and men and the "resulting differences in power between them" (Kangas, Haider and Fraser 2014: 4).

Inequalities arise from the way in which society is organized (Holmes 2009: 30) and, historically, women have been and continue to be disadvantaged by societal arrangements. This does not mean, however, that gender is only relevant to women's lives. As discussed in Chapter 4, major differences in social power exist between and within groups of men on the basis of race, ethnicity, social class, age and sexuality and so on. Gendered power relations provide the context for the subordination of some men by other men in society, although women are often used "as a commodity to do so" (Hearn and Whitehead 2006: 45). In short, hierarchies of power function *within* as well as *between* sex/gender categories. This is important because efforts to address violence and abuse need to question common assumptions about safety and vulnerability and consider how these are constructed differently for men and women. We will discuss these issues in more depth later in this chapter.

Masculinities and Femininities

Ideas about what it means to be male or female are not universal but vary over time, across and within generations, cultures and societies. Nonetheless, while the *content* of gender norms vary, in terms of the specific expectations of men and women, the very notion of gender *difference* — of gender-specific traits, abilities and affinities — is remarkably consistent. Having argued that gender is a key social/cultural "truth" that cannot easily be explained away through reference to biology and the physical body, we need to recognize the complexity of gender and its interactions with other dimensions of social division.

Masculinity and femininity are generally defined in opposition to each other. Because masculinity usually takes the central focus — as the standard, neutral "everyman" — femininity has traditionally been understood only through reference to masculinity, as its negative or opposite. As so-called natural and mutually exclusive opposites, male and female gender norms tell us that masculinity is synonymous with autonomy and rationality, mastery, active physicality, strength and so on. In contrast, femininity is linked with emotions — with dependence, passivity, weakness and vulnerability. Assumptions that follow about what it *means* to be male or female are symbiotic, based on "widely held dominant and persuasive notions about what men are and, by implication, what women are" (Morgan 1987: 180). Stereotypes fail to capture the diversity among and in between the categories of men and women. It is for this reason that we might more usefully talk about masculin*ities* and feminin*ities*, thereby recognizing the considerable diversity that exists in forms and expressions of gender.

In their study of men's experiences of depression, Emslie and her colleagues (2006) found that, in the process of recovery, some male participants drew upon hegemonic ideals of masculinity such as being strong, in control and responsible for others (Emslie et al. 2006). Other participants, however, took a different approach, instead emphasizing alternative versions of masculinity with a focus on creativity, intelligence and being open to discussing their experiences (Emslie et al. 2006).

From an AOP perspective, there is no single version of masculinity or femininity. Rather these "differ from one culture to another, and from one historical moment to another, even within one culture or organisation" (Connell 2007: 3). This book's focus on structural and cultural violences, then, is underpinned by the following acknowledgement:

> some forms of masculinity and femininity are given social status and legitimacy — praised by others, celebrated in the media, and granted more rights — while others are marginalised, punished and, sometimes, criminalized. (WHO 2010a: 10)

Hegemonic Masculinity

The term "hegemonic masculinity," commonly associated with the social theorist R.W. Connell, refers to the most dominant, or "culturally exalted" (Connell 2000: 84), form of masculinity in a society. As an ideal, hegemonic masculinity is "active, rational and in charge" (Holmes 2009: 90) and includes "having a physically powerful and well-controlled body" and the "rejection of the feminine and the homosexual as utterly opposite to 'real' manliness" (89). That it is also "fundamentally middle class, white and Western" (Holmes 2009: 90) alerts us to the power relations — the tensions and hierarchies — that exist between hegemonic and other subordinated forms of masculinity.

Because gender intersects with class, sexuality and race relations, some men are able to dominate not only women, but also other groups of men. Hegemonic masculinity recognizes that while men in general are advantaged (or privileged) through the subordination of women, some groups of men are advantaged over others (Pease 1999). Some men are able to impose their particular version of masculinity onto others, legitimating and reproducing their own dominance in the process. In this context, subordinated masculinities are those that breach the dominant ideals of manhood, for example, homosexual or gay men who are often symbolically linked with femininity (Connell 2000).

Most of us prefer to attribute our achievements to our own efforts or innate ability (or merit) than we do to unearned systemic advantage. Yet, recognition of unearned advantage — or privilege — is critical for understanding the diversity of lived experiences for men and women. As discussed in Chapter 4, privilege refers to those "unearned rights, benefits, immunity, and favours that are bestowed on individuals and groups" (Davis and Harrison 2013: 28) on the basis of their identity group/s. Those who have (male, white, class) privilege usually have difficulty seeing it, often presuming that the privileges and advantages they enjoy extend to all others (see McIntosh 2015).

Oppression, or undeserved disadvantage, is often accompanied by blame and stigma, underpinned by the idea that we all get what we deserve, good or bad. When achievements and success are seen as the natural consequence of individual talent, ability and hard work, it is assumed that the opposite is also true — that is, that those who lack success are incapable or unmotivated or haven't tried hard enough, and only have themselves to blame. Considered from an AOP perspective, however, personal responsibility and individual achievements are commendable but cannot compensate for the structural conditions of society, advantaging some groups at the expense of others.

GENDER AND VIOLENCE

The discourses of gender, gender difference and violence are so closely intertwined that it is near impossible to think one without the other. In other words, the assumptions that we make about gender come through in — or colour — the ways we think and talk about violence. Interestingly, this is as evident in everyday talk and public/popular discourse as it is in professional and expert knowledge(s) and practices. Perceptions about the relationship between bodies and violence, for example, are central to the "meaning and practice of gender" (Hollander 2001: 88), that is, to our ideas about who is capable of what. In this way, assumptions about sex/gender difference — what men and women are "really" like — shape who and what we recognize as not only violence/violent, but also as vulnerable, in need of protection (from other people's violence) and so on. Sexuality and violence are usually presented together in dominant cultural imagery; what has been referred to as the "cultural coupling" of sex and violence (Eardley 1995: 136).

Gendered beliefs, such as the association of masculinity with power and femininity with passivity (discussed in the previous section), enable and perpetuate gendered violence. Recognizing this enables a shift in focus to that which we commonly take for granted; the imagery of the military for instance, of "our boys defending women and children" (McKie 2006: 7) and, more broadly, the societal positioning of men as protectors. The hierarchy of power relations that exist between men, not just between women and men, speak to our constructions of vulnerability and worthiness.

Why, then, do we refer to some forms of violence as "gendered" but not others? And what are the implications of doing so? Perhaps the most pressing of these is that violence *between* men tends to be overlooked or disregarded and, as such, the relationship of so-called everyday masculinity/ies and violence remains largely unquestioned. This points to a disconnect between understandings of men's use of violence against women in domestic situations and men's use of violence in other (non-domestic) arenas, especially that directed towards other men. In this sense, just as gender tends to be associated with women and women's issues, when the focus is on masculinity, attention is directed towards men's relations with women, and fails to recognize that "men demonstrate masculinity in relation to other men" (Whitehead 2005: 412). In this perspective, gender matters when women are the victims of violence, but is seldom acknowledged or seen as significant when violence is between men. Studies of violence against women, particularly those from a feminist perspective, have come to "occupy a corner that is isolated from analyses of violence in general" (Matthews 2000: 312) and this represents a significant loss in opportunities for collaboration and knowledge sharing.

Gendered Violence

It has been said that the recognition of violence as gendered is the "most important research finding of the past two decades" (Schwartz 2005: 8). Commonly, though, and broadly evident across both mainstream and academic literature, gender is seen as relevant to understanding violence against women and children but not more generally. As highlighted earlier in this chapter, gender is usually equated with women and used to invoke women's interests and concerns. Men's capacity for, or use of, violence against other men is an important gendered problem, yet rarely is this considered "gendered." So domestic violence is understood as gendered violence, as an expression of imbalances in, or abuse of, power, whereas other forms of violence are conceptualized as non-gendered, or not specifically gendered. The implication here is that violence between men is "fair game," an example of an idea that can be understood as "productive" of violence (Shepherd 2009: 214). The association of masculinity with violence is usually so ingrained, so naturalized, that it is neither questioned nor seen as noteworthy. This should be of deep concern to those who care about AOP as understanding gender as only representing certain practices and experiences masks the differential meanings and impacts of violence for diverse bodies and as a result, the adequacy of societal responses(Nayak and Suchland 2006).

The following extract illustrates the complexities inherent in the gender–violence nexus. Highlighted here is the imperative to *see* men's experiences of violence, to recognize and problematize that the greatest harms to men are caused by other men, and that these are deeply connected with, not separate from, women's experiences of violence.

Masculinities and Violence

The cultural enmeshment of violence and gender, manifest in the "everyday bracketing" (Morgan 1987: 180) of masculinity and violence, is a central theme of this chapter. Recognizing that violence is "deeply connected with the taken-for-grantedness of what it is to be a man" (Hearn and Whitehead 2006: 40), however, does not, mean that men are inherently or innately violent. We do not support the claim that men are biologically disposed to or evolutionarily programmed for aggression. Masculinities are multiple and varied; acknowledging that the construction and politics of masculinity/ies are fundamental to the practice and processes of violence (Connell 2000) neither implies a causal relationship between the two, nor that aggression/violence is inherently "male." Rather, it directs our attention towards the ways in which understandings of violence reflect, embed and reinforce gendered discourses, particularly those around men and masculinity.

The links between masculinity/ies and violence are, nonetheless, complex. Masculinities may be associated with the "performance of violence, the potential

Men as Victims of "Gendercide"?

Violence against men in conflict and war is often invisibilized, and is rarely the subject of academic or social debate. The reasons for this range from social constructions of masculinity as aggressive rather than passive, of men as being perpetrators rather than victims to feminist discomfort with men trying to acquire victim status along with women. As Lindler perceptively points out, a man speaking about the ways in which some men suffer violence within patriarchies can easily be construed by women as "the shrewd attempt of a male to weep about victimization in order to hide his factual domination" (Lindler in Jones 2004: 55).

The issue worth addressing in this context is: as with women experiencing violence, is the gendered continuum of violence relevant for men who are victimized by violence? In other words are there, within patriarchies, specific forms of violence against men who are not complicit in women's oppression, who are seen as "non-masculine" or men whose masculinity does not "fit into" or threatens mainstream patriarchal constructions; therefore men who are not "generic men" (Carvell in Jones 2004: 279). In peacetimes, this could include racist attacks against black and Asian men in the U.K. and homophobic attacks against gay men. During times of conflict and war, examples include: denouncing men who refuse to fight in wars as "cowards" (Jones 2004: 102); the shoot-to-kill policy of for example the U.K. police leading to the public shooting of an innocent Brazilian man who "appeared" to the police as an Islamic suicide bomber in 2005; the torture of Iraqi male prisoners in Abu Ghraib prison in 2004 and the killing of Sikh men in Punjab by armed forces in the 1980s. In all such cases Jones and her colleagues argue that these men are attacked, tortured and killed because they are men, hence such attacks are a form of gendercide.

The argument put forward is certainly powerful, and in my view valid. Not all men benefit equally within patriarchies, especially in the context where patriarchies coexist comfortably with other forms of inequalities based on class, race, caste, ethnicity, religious and sexual orientation. The fear that feminists would object to this understanding is, in my view, somewhat misplaced. Most feminists should have few problems with the proposition that some men are indeed vulnerable within patriarchy — as some women can be powerful — as long as feminist theorisations and understandings of female oppression are not negated, or undermined (Carvell in Jones 2004). In reality they would welcome an understanding that is critical of male violence in general, both against women and men.

Source: Gangoli 2006: 537

for violence, the emulation of others violence, the denial of violence, or even opposition to violence" (Hearn 1996: 51). Recognizing the inherent diversity within gendered patterns of violence highlights the importance of thinking about *violences*. Men's violence towards other men, for instance, may reflect a masculinity of status, competition and bravado, whereas men's violence towards women may emphasize a masculinity of domination, control and humiliation (Braithwaite and Daly 1994). Other forms of violence, those predicated on the "feminization" of some men/masculinities, for example, must be understood within the context of hegemonic, subordinated and marginalized masculinities (see Connell 2000).

From an AOP perspective, focusing on masculinity/ies alone is not helpful. Instead, paying attention to the intersectionalities of privilege and oppression, as discussed in Chapters 2 and 3, pushes us to consider the interfaces between gender, class, ability, age, race/ethnicity and sexuality. As noted by the International Research and Training Institute for the Advancement of Women (INSTRAW 2001: 2), "racism, economic disempowerment, political disenfranchisement, geo-political relations, colonial histories, ecological trends and movements of trans-national capital" are all relevant. Thus, approaches that seek to explore the impacts of "men's positioning within these relations" in terms of both their "responsibility *and* vulnerability" (INSTRAW 2001: 2, emphasis mine) enable a dual focus on social justice as well as the specific vulnerabilities of women and children.

"I Just Snapped": Violence as Loss of Control

Responsibility and control are central themes in stories told about both victims and perpetrators of violence, and both can be used to distort and excuse. The association of interpersonal violence with lack of self-control (see Jenkins 2003) illustrates the extent to which we take for granted men's supposed affinity for violence. In the popular imagination, self-control is central to non-violence. For example, it is common to hear violence described in terms of an outburst or explosion, uncontrolled anger or pent-up frustration, as a result of an individual "losing it," "snapping" and so on. This is still evident in the continued reliance on anger management programs in criminal justice, community health and other settings, where (men's) violence is not positioned as a problem in itself, but rather is framed as fundamental and innate yet controllable. In this context, (self-) control means limiting the use of violence to particular, appropriate contexts, settings and victims. Men are fair game, women are off limits, fights must be fair and so on. From this conventional perspective, it is the transgression of limits that distinguishes a man as "violent," his failure to keep in check his otherwise normal and unremarkable capacity for aggression. "Good" men show self-control. They use their powers for good (defending and protecting) not evil (domestic and criminal violence).

VIOLENCE AGAINST WOMEN

Violence against women (VAW) falls within the broader category — or umbrella term — of gendered violence (Shepherd 2007: 248). According to the U.N. Women National Committee Australia (2016), violence against women is "perhaps the most widespread and socially tolerated form of human rights violations," affecting women of "all ages, race, culture and socio-economic situations." The context for VAW is gender inequality; it is perpetrated by governments — the "State and its agents" (United Nations Women 2012a) — family members, intimate partners, friends, acquaintances and strangers, both inside and outside of the home environment. Domestic and intimate partner violence, sexual violence and sexual harassment are most commonly recognized as VAW, however, other forms include: sexual exploitation and trafficking; forced and child marriage; violence committed in the name of "honour"; pre-natal sex selection and female infanticide; and acid throwing. VAW in the form of dowry-related violence and female genital mutilation/cutting is discussed in more detail next.

The term VAW is often assumed to mean, or is used in a way that ties it to domestic violence and abuse — that which takes place in the home and/or within the context of interpersonal relations. The problem with this is that it presents VAW as something that cuts across social boundaries and impacts on all women in similar ways, while obscuring the other violences that women face, specifically those "generated by structures, institutions, and histories" and experienced by women "at the margins" of society (Price 2012: 2). It also perpetuates a false dichotomy between public and private worlds, thereby excluding the experiences of those women for whom "home does not conform to the normative model" (Price 2012: 3), such as in the context of transiency, communal living and couch surfing. Lastly, use of the term VAW has been criticized for implying that gender "can be read unproblematically from sexed bodies" (Shepherd 2007: 246).

Dowry Practices

The dowry system is a tradition associated with marriage that was once practiced widely in many countries including Asia, Europe and some parts of the Americas. Traditionally, in Muslim families, the *dower* was a payment made by the groom to his bride, signifying his honourable intentions and respect for her (Chowdhury 2010). *Dowry*, however, refers to the payment that the groom and his family expect to receive from the parents of the bride. Dowry payments can be in the form of large sums of money, livestock, jewellery, cars, electrical appliances, furniture, crockery, utensils and other household items.

While outlawed in most countries, dowry practices continue to occur, most commonly in India, Pakistan, Bangladesh and Iran, and are closely linked with

Bride Burning

It was after sunset on a Sunday last November when Sushila found her daughter, Laxmi, lying naked on the front step of the house she shared with her husband and two children on the outskirts of Bangalore.

Laxmi had burns to more than 80 percent of her body and in the darkness Sushila could hear more than she could see.

"I heard her crying, she was in agony, but I didn't know how bad it was," says Sushila. "There was no one to help her, no one wanted to come to her. I was the only person she could call for help and I live 12 kilometres away."

Laxmi was eventually taken to the Victoria Hospital in central Bangalore, which has a 50-bed burns ward, one of the most advanced in the country.

She survived three days, enough time to describe to police how she came to be doused in kerosene by her mother-in-law and set alight by her husband.

Bride-burning, as this type of crime is most commonly referred to, accounts for the death of at least one woman every hour in India, more than 8000 women a year.

"We also call it dowry death," says Donna Fernandes, the founder of Vimochana, a women's rights organisation established in Bangalore in 1975 with the aim of preventing violent against women.

"The husband's family believes they have not received enough money for their son at the time of the wedding, perhaps because they are of a higher caste or some such reason, and that's when the harassment starts."

Often, says Fernandes, the husband's family begin pressuring the wife's family right after the wedding.

"They start asking for cash, or gold, or consumer goods like washing machines or televisions. Whatever it is they believe is owed to them or was promised to them, luxury goods that they can get the bride's family to pay for."

In many cases the husband's family decide after the marriage has taken place that the original dowry was not sufficient.

"They know the bride's family is vulnerable, because of subjugated role of women in our society, and what begins is a process of extortion. Demands for money turn into threats of violence, and when the family can't pay any more, the bride is killed."

Source: Koutsoukis 2015

local laws and customs. In Pakistan, for example, while divorce is not illegal, it is associated with great stigma and, largely because wives are "entitled to the return of dowry upon divorce," is rarely granted (Ali, Arnadottir and Kulane 2013: 88). Women who choose to leave a marriage, no matter the circumstances, are likely to be stigmatized and socially isolated. The dowry system is also associated with a range of other damaging practices. Families might restrict girls' access to education, for example, in an effort to maximize the funds/assets available for dowry expenses. Further, because younger girls generally attract lower dowries, child marriages are more likely to occur (Babu and Babu 2011: 36).

Incidences of violence within dowry marriages are a particular concern. Reports from rural India indicate that dowry practices are associated with abuse and violence after the marriage ceremony is over, as a way of demanding further dowry payments (Bloch and Rao 2002). Chowdhury (2010) argues that dowry-related violence is consistent with the lower status of women in India in the context of deeply embedded gender norms, beliefs about gender roles, social order and so on, implying that, for women, even an abusive marriage is preferable to being alone (see also Huda 2006).

India has the highest number of dowry-related deaths in the world; according to India's National Crime Records Bureau, 8,455 "dowry deaths" were reported in 2014 (Government of India 2014) while estimates sit at around 106,500 cases per year of "cruelty" perpetuated by husbands and their relatives (Bhadoriya 2016). According to Bhadoriya (2016), the majority of dowry-related deaths occur when "the young woman, unable to bear the harassment and torture, commits suicide," most often by hanging, poisoning or fire.

Female Genital Mutilation

Female genital mutilation (FGM), also referred to as female circumcision, has been practised for thousands of years in many regions including, but not limited to, parts of Africa, Indonesia and Malaysia. The term FGM refers collectively to procedures involving "partial or total removal of the external female genitalia, or other injury to the female genital organs for non-medical reasons" (WHO 2016b). In line with global mobility and patterns of migration, practices of FGM are increasingly being performed by health professionals and in "less traditional" countries (Engle 2004) including Australia, North America, Europe and the United Kingdom. According to the World Health Organization (2016), over 200 million girls and women, in thirty countries across Africa, the Middle East and Asia, have endured some form of FGM. Mostly carried out on young girls between infancy and age 15, FGM offers no health benefits and has serious health consequence including "severe bleeding and problems urinating, and later cysts, infections, as well as complications in childbirth and increased risk of newborn deaths" (WHO 2016b).

FGM is generally described as a cultural norm or practice and, as such, is intertwined with cultural identity, beliefs and tradition. It nonetheless reflects "deep-rooted" gender inequality and "constitutes an extreme form of discrimination against women" (WHO 2008: 1). The grounds for FGM vary widely between groups and regions but commonly relate to "cultural ideals of femininity and modesty" (WHO 2016b) and marriageability. In some areas, for example, FGM "ensures a girl's virginity", making "men more willing to marry her and pay more money for her" (FORWARD 2012: 5). This means that while FGM is widely condemned, it is extremely difficult to address and requires substantial community engagement and education in addition to legislative measures. The following excerpt, from the WHO report, encapsulates the complexities of the issue:

> In every society in which it is practised, female genital mutilation is a manifestation of gender inequality that is deeply entrenched in social, economic and political structures. Like the now abandoned foot-binding in China and the practice of dowry and child marriage, female genital mutilation represents society's control over women. Such practices have the effect of perpetuating normative gender roles that are unequal and harm women. Analysis of international health data shows a close link between women's ability to exercise control over their lives and their belief that female genital mutilation should be ended. (OHCHR et al. 2008: 5)
>
> Where female genital mutilation is widely practised, it is supported by both men and women, usually without question, and anyone departing from the norm may face condemnation, harassment, and ostracism. As such, female genital mutilation is a social convention governed by rewards and punishments which are a powerful force for continuing the practice. In view of this conventional nature of female genital mutilation, it is difficult for families to abandon the practice without support from the wider community. In fact, it is often practised even when it is known to inflict harm upon girls because the perceived social benefits of the practice are deemed higher than its disadvantages. (OHCHR et al. 2008: 5)

It cannot go without mention that another form of genital mutilation is widely practiced in developed, Westernised countries, namely cosmetic or elective genital surgeries. Labiaplasty, for example, is performed primarily for aesthetic reasons (Sharp, Mattiske and Vale 2016) and aims to modify the size and/or shape of the labia. Interestingly while FGM is concerned with controlling women's sexuality, procedures such as labiaplasty are associated with enhancing this. Social and cultural norms are critical, influencing perceptions of what a "normal" vagina looks like and what is sexy and desirable. Braun (2009) argued that the cosmetic surgery industry preys on women's insecurities about their body image, which is also reinforced by the role of media, in the form of magazines, movies, advertising and pornography. The extent to which FGM and cosmetic surgery are comparable though, is up for debate:

> Some people argue that cosmetic surgery such as breast enlargements/ reductions, facelifts or "designer vaginas" (an operation to change the way the vagina looks) are equally harmful cultural practices similar to FGM, as they both affect health, both physically and psychologically. However, the most important difference is that in cosmetic surgery women give their consent for the operations; usually without a deeply embedded pressure from their community. In terms of FGM the decision is made for the child or woman, who is usually neither informed nor old enough to decide for herself. Also the extreme societal pressure makes it difficult to determine if a girl is freely deciding to undergo the procedure without pressure from others. (FORWARD 2012: 11)

GENDERED HIERARCHIES OF DIFFERENCE: HETERONORMATIVE VIOLENCE

Heteronormativity, or the promotion of heterosexuality as "normal" and "natural," underpins much violence at both the structural level and in the form of direct acts of violence. In many parts of the world, the human rights and full citizenship of lesbian, gay, bisexual, transsexual and transgender, intersex and queer (collectively LGBTIQ) people are systematically denied (Padilla, Vásquez del Aguila and Parker 2007: 217), often via the criminalization and associated punishment of homosexual acts. Homosexual activity is still treated as a criminal offence in at least seventy-nine countries worldwide, including Egypt, Iran, Afghanistan and Singapore. Penalties are harsh, ranging from forced psychiatric treatment (such as in Dominica) and prison sentences, to life imprisonment (in countries including Uganda, Gambia, Tanzania, Barbados and Bangladesh) and hard labour (Angola, Jamaica) to death (Sudan, Mauritania, parts of Nigeria, Iran, Saudi Arabia, Yemen). Structural violence, which includes the "systematic and institutionalized abuses and social cleansing practices perpetrated by governments or their functionaries" (216), facilitates direct violence. Reporting by the International Gay and Lesbian Human Rights Commission, for example, indicates:

> torture is a widespread means for regulating sexuality and enforcing norms of gender and sexuality, and that the effects of sodomy laws in many parts of the world justifies detention of people based on their sexual orientation, denial of public services, and the abuse of LGBT persons by police, doctors, and health practitioners. (Padilla, Vásquez del Aguila and Parker 2007: 217)

Homophobia and Transphobia

While global responses to gender variance differ, whether expressed as sexuality (such as homosexuality or bisexuality) and/or identity/identification (such as transgender), heteronormativity continues to shape the lives of LGBTIQ people, including those living in queer-friendly urban spaces. Heterosexual privilege refers to the many benefits extended to people who are identified as heterosexual. In contrast, *homophobia* speaks to the rejection and contempt for people who are seen not to conform to the cultural conventions of gender, particularly in relation to (hetero)sexuality. *Transphobia* refers, broadly, to "hostile responses to perceived violations of gender norms and/or to challenges to the gender binary" (Bettcher 2014: 249). It might be expressed in a range of ways, including the belief that transgender men/women are not "real" men/women and the refusal to use their correct name or acknowledge a transgender person's nominated gender.

Many transgender people who work in and/or use the services of organizations also experience institutional discrimination (see Gates and Sniatecki 2016). As explained by Talusan (2015), transgender people are especially vulnerable:

> unlike other marginalized groups, trans people find it much harder to hide our status or seek support from people close to us. On the whole, being gay is less visible and easier to conceal from bigots than being trans ... Trans people are much more visible and prone to isolation.

Passing, which we discussed in Chapter 4, describes the purposeful or knowing concealment of "undisclosed discrediting information" (Goffman 2009 [1963]: 42). Passing is only possible where there are visual markers of difference that can be concealed through, for example, clothing or cosmetics, physical and voice training and so on. While passing may be interpreted as duplicitous and dishonest, it can be a strategy to avoid the negative and potentially far-reaching impacts of association with devalued groups. Mitra and Doctor's (2016) qualitative study reveals the complexities of attempts to pass by gay, corporate professionals in India. Here, the individuals used strategies such as partitioning their lives and distancing themselves from others in order to *pass* as heterosexual and avoid homophobia in the workplace. Some also looked for ways to push back against heteronormativity and protest homophobia but in doing so risked "standing out" (Mitra and Doctor 2016).

Evidence consistently demonstrates the negative impacts of heteronormativity and related homophobia on LGBTIQ health (see Dysart-Gale 2010). The broader contexts of marginalization, stigmatization and discrimination against LGBTIQ people and communities are also relevant to their experiences of violence and abuse. For instance, U.K. researchers Donovan and Hester (2010) note that the dominant narrative, or, as they term it, the "public story" of domestic violence is that it is a heterosexual phenomenon and an experience of violence that is primarily physical. These stereotypical assumptions have ignored both the significance of non-physical violence, including emotional, verbal and psychological forms of abuse, and the diverse experiences of LGBTIQ people. The availability and appropriateness of services for non-heterosexual victims of domestic violence is an important concern. An Australian survey, for example, found that victims of same-sex partner abuse perceived mainstream domestic violence services as "unsympathetic if not unsafe" (Leonard et al. 2008: 48). Interestingly, though, in a recent study into practitioners' attitudes to working with transgendered clients, Australian researchers Riggs, Fraser, Taylor, Signal and Donovan (2017) found a high level of support for instituting trans-friendly practices, yet still noted the need for ongoing education and sensitivity training.

Given the long history of homophobia, conscious remedial efforts are required to prevent the isolation and exclusion of members of LGBTIQ communities from mainstream society. In Chapter 8 we take these ideas up in more detail, but for now the central points to remember are that heteronormativity, homophobia and transphobia are all forms of abuse that can be hard to see, especially for people who enjoy heterosexual privilege. Services and practitioners who assume heterosexuality to be the norm perpetuate heteronormativity and contribute to the stigmatization of LGBTIQ people, which in turn can lead to them downplaying or hiding their identities so as to pass as "straight." Without deliberate efforts to involve LGBTIQ communities, policies, programs and services will not reflect the diversity of gender expression, identities and sexualities.

Gay Panic

Direct violences perpetrated against LGBTIQ people, in particular gay men, have been institutionally supported in a range of ways. Stephen Tomsen has examined Australian social and legal responses to fatal violent attacks in which "the sexual identity and marginal social status of an apparent homosexual victim had a significant relation to the motives of offenders" (Tomsen 2003: 92). He observed that a substantial proportion of these resulted from "personal disputes and resulting violent conflicts," usually in private settings and between two men, in which the (heterosexual) perpetrator "alleged that he was subjected to a sexual advance or sexual attack by the deceased" (92–93). In examining the criminal justice response to these offences, it was not only evident that they were taken less seriously than might otherwise be expected, but also, ironically, that there were tensions associated with who (the perpetrator or the deceased) should be afforded "legitimate victim status." Specifically, Tomsen (2003) noted the increasing, and increasingly successful, use of "sexual advance allegations" in such cases, in which defendants claimed that the use of violence resulted from their "shocked" and "outraged" reaction to another man's sexual advance.

The so-called "homosexual panic defence," to which Tomsen (2003: 93) refers, has "no formal existence in Australian law." However, it draws on existing provisions regarding provocation and self-defence in relation to a perceived "threat to male honour and sexual identity" (98). Tomsen concludes that the "success of offender claims about the horror of being subjected to homosexual desire is premised on the certainty of the homo/hetero divide" (107), reflecting the association between masculine identity and the "integrity" or "sanctity" of the (heterosexual) male body.[1]

Community, Victims and Perpetrators

The notion of "community" is a common reference point in public debate. Yet, as suggested in the previous chapter, it warrants closer analysis because it so often perpetuates divisions by "effectively defin[ing] itself, by those whom it excludes" (Faulkner 2004: 9). Patterns of inclusion and exclusion in society are underpinned by the ways that we think about, or construct, community. Is community based on the "risk of victimisation" rather than "bonds of commonality, trust, sharing, equality, and recognition of difference" (Brown 2005: 13)? Relevant here is the "all-agent or all-victim dichotomy" (Mahoney 1994: 64), which is the predominant Western idea that "you are an agent if you are not a victim, and you are not a victim if you are in any way an agent."

It is important that AOP students and workers understand the complexities associated with the ways in which so-called victims and perpetrators are constructed in relation to violence and abuse. Commonly we see these reduced to roles, if not caricatures, with little room for neither ambiguity nor recognition of victimhood as a status that is not automatic, but rather "results from a social process in which relations of power are central" (White and Habibis 2005: 320). For example, victims of violence in public spaces may be denied victim status on the basis that they have contributed to their own victimization by being drunk or choosing to go to a particular "rough" location (see Tomsen, Homel and Thommeny 1991). The drawing of boundaries between victims and perpetrators as if these are mutually exclusive categories is also problematic, denying the possibility that, over the course of a lifetime, people can — and do — occupy both positions, as victims *and* perpetrators of violence and abuse.

This is also relevant to representations of violence against women in which clear boundaries are drawn between victim and perpetrator based upon an either/or binary of innocence and guilt. Innocence and guilt, however, are neither self-evident nor value neutral concepts but, rather, are societally and culturally relative to time, space and place. Engaging with these issues more thoughtfully means asking difficult questions. How might notions of the "worthy victim" in this context be reliant upon particular assumptions about gender roles (regarding appropriate femininity for example)? What does this mean for the women seen to be "difficult," such as women who use drugs, perform sex work, are involved in crime and/or use violence? The focus on (some) women as worthy victims can also get in the way of thinking more critically about "women's power, issues of domination, agency and choice" (FitzRoy 2001: 13). When women perpetrate (criminal) violence, society is quick to account for this as "mad" and/or "bad." Women are often pathologized and understood as either not fully competent (that is, coerced by a male partner and/or their responsibility diminished by trauma), or as unequivocally bad, gender deviant and deserving of harsh punishment. In her research with women who use violence, FitzRoy (2001: 26) explores these issues in depth and concludes that it is possible — and necessary — "to acknowledge women's oppression in the broad social fabric of their everyday lives, but still name women's agency and make women accountable for the violent crimes they choose to commit."

Conceptualized as distinct categories, the terms "perpetrator" and "victim" fail to represent the scope and complexity of experiences of violence and abuse. For instance, over the course of their lives, men are more likely than women to experience violence and, like women, this is most likely to be at the hands of other men. Unlike women, however, male-to-male violence is most likely to occur in a public place, yet public safety campaigns continue to focus predominantly on women in this context. The popular view of women as vulnerable and men as powerful significantly impacts upon perceived fear of crime and public confidence, reinforcing the accepted wisdom that men, and not women, should feel confident and safe in the public sphere. Paradoxically, although the private realm of the home and family is commonly associated with safety, women are, in fact, most unsafe when they are in the privacy of their own homes. Nonetheless, the potential for victimization is a constant presence for women who venture into the public world.

Acknowledging the intersectionalities of identities and power relations is essential, as explained by FitzRoy (2001: 26–27):

> Women (like men) are socialized within a hierarchical social order where they learn to categorize "different" members of society into oppositional dichotomies. In other words, women also learn to think about and respond to different people in our community as superior or inferior ... [and while] these forms of abuse are [not] always overt or violent in action ... women participate in, benefit from and perpetuate power relationships, which maintain the dominant capitalist and patriarchal order. Therefore, it is not a difficult step to acknowledge that some women also learn to abuse power in the public arena of their workplace or the street or more often in the private realm of the family. In reality, for many women the family is the primary place where they can feel a sense of power and have the

opportunity to enact power against others — a child or an elderly or disabled relation — who are defined as inferior to them. In addition, women also live within a social context whereby "violence" is legitimized as an appropriate individualized response to difficult or problematic situations.

CONCLUSION

This chapter focused on the interconnections between gender and violence within the context of globally and locally structured power relations. The issues explored here have significant implications for understanding and intervening in abuse and violence. Widely held, culturally dominant beliefs about men and masculinity and women and femininity, most notably in relation to the association of masculinity with power and femininity with passivity, reinforce a view of gender relations that positions man as aggressor and woman as, invariably, his victim (Naffine 1997). Men's violence against other men is usually positioned as, in itself, unremarkable and to a large extent inevitable; consequently, the idea that men, masculinity and violence naturally go together remains largely unquestioned. Secondly — and more broadly — hierarchies of difference constitute the structural and cultural contexts for all violence in society.

As we argue throughout this book, an appreciation for — and commitment to engaging with — intersectionality(ies) is required for understanding violence and abuse from an AOP perspective. The existence of interpersonal violence in same-sex relationships further highlights the need to re-visit common assumptions about sex, gender and vulnerability. Most notably, the idea that the exercise of (gendered) power is only relevant to understanding male–female relations contributes to the lack of recognition — and services — for LGBTIQ victims of violence. That this can result in the exclusion of LGBTIQ people from the protections offered to other victims of violence is a critical concern.

In this chapter we have examined the profound and interconnected relationships between sex, gender and violence. The issues discussed here are complex and nuanced; they are far from settled and warrant further thought, critical reflection and debate. AOP practice demands that we be both ever mindful of the ways in which we talk about violence and abuse, and also willing to challenge public/popular (mis)perceptions by acknowledging people's diverse experiences of and engagements with violence.

Note

1. More recently, and from the U.S., Tomei (2016) takes up these questions in her doctoral thesis entitled, "The Gay Panic Defense: Legal Defense Strategy or Reinforcement of Homophobia in Court?"

6. ABILITY, AGE, VIOLENCE AND ABUSE

- **How do oppression and age- and ability-related privilege intersect violence and abuse?**
- **What makes something a hate crime?**
- **How can we understand child abuse and elder abuse from an AOP perspective?**

As we have shown in the previous five chapters, violence and abuse take many forms and can produce noxious and long-lasting effects. In this chapter we focus on violence and abuse related to age and (dis)ability. Our aim is to stimulate thinking, make connections between personal and political experiences, raise questions and point to some insights about AOP practice. We begin by noting the potential impact of age-related privileges and oppression, which we take as forms of abuse. As we will suggest, child and elder abuse need to be seen within the broader sociocultural and political contexts in which they take place. Only then can we, as AOP workers, address the causes, not just the symptoms of vulnerability to abuse.

Throughout the chapter we connect people's susceptibility to being abused and violated with disablist and ageist attitudes, policies and practices. This includes abuse perpetrated against the old (people over 70 years of age), against the young (under 18 years of age) and against people with disabilities of all ages. Collectively, these are groups of people often denied rights, exploited and marginalized — and who are at risk of internalizing their devalued status. With reference to intersecting oppressions, we discuss able-bodied and age-related privileges with particular reference to poverty as it constitutes a major threat to the health and well-being of the disabled and the very young. We raise questions about hate crimes and whether time and energy should be dedicated to rehabilitating those who commit them.

In the second part of the chapter we examine child and elder abuse that occurs within families and domestic homes. We pay particular attention to the violence and abuse that prevents people from living safely in their homes and communities. We note that abuse can happen in public as well as behind the closed doors of homes and care. As AOP workers we are interested in the politics of care and care work, in family and supported care homes, from the perspectives of both the cared for and the carers. This informs how we understand age, ability and, most importantly, the attribution of worth and value.

PRIVILEGE AND OPPRESSION ON THE BASIS OF ABILITY AND AGE

Privilege and oppression occur on the basis of group membership in line with socially constructed classifications (see Chapters 1, 2 and 3). Ability and age are two important classifications used to distinguish people, separate them and accord them a value in social hierarchies — at the top of which sit the able-bodied adult, free from impairment, disease, injury and chronic conditions. As we discuss below, age hierarchies intersect those of function and ability. Both systems make stereotypical assumptions about humans' capacity, value and worth — assumptions that can be oppressive for those in the devalued categories, and unfairly promote those in over-valued categories (see Pease 2010).

Able-Bodied Privilege and Disability

From their *Privilege Uncensored* website (n.d.), Carleton University women's and gender students describe *able-bodied privilege*:

> assum[ing] that everyone can see, walk, hear and talk, for example, constructing environments around these "non-negotiable" attributes. However, it is obvious that not everyone can see, walk, hear or talk, and as a result, those with specific weaknesses are set at a disadvantage … the notion of disability as "abnormal" [assumes] … that disabled individuals must be returned back into the normal state of ability, reinforced as a problem within society that must be "cured." <https://privilegeuncensored.wordpress.com/what-is-able-bodied-privilege-3/>

Able-bodied privilege may go unnoticed until it is lost. Soldiers, for instance, are often disabled in the course of their military service. Despite the rhetoric, returned soldiers who sustain chronic or permanent disabilities are likely to find their social status dramatically decline along with their place in society. The loss of able-bodied, adult privilege can be severe and hard to bear. Soldiers who return amputated, disfigured, and/or with post-traumatic stress are likely to experience multiple losses — of identity, authority, command over resources, social status, cultural respect and, perhaps most critically, the regard for them as fit, strong and able-bodied. Kinder (2015) takes up these issues, while calling for disability studies to include the experiences of veterans more systematically, in *Paying with Their Bodies: American War and the Problem of the Disabled Veteran.* The point of AOP practice is to neither deride people for their (former) privileges nor ignore the suffering of those who have become accustomed to privilege; rather, it is to engage openly, respectfully and from a position of empathy, not pity.

Able-bodied privilege is often expressed through a tragic view of disability, which assumes a clear distinction between ability and disability. In this view, disabilities are abnormal and undesirable, and it is wrongly assumed that all people with disabilities long to be "normal" again, and will undergo whichever medical intervention it takes to achieve this. These assumptions are so ingrained that having a disability is thought to spell the end to all hopes, dreams and possibilities for happiness. From this view, disability is a tragedy to be avoided at all costs, rather than one of many possible differences to be negotiated (French and Swain 2004). From the U.K., French and Swain (2004: 34) write:

> such are the negative presumptions held about impairment and disability, that the abortion of impaired foetuses [sic] is barely challenged ... and compulsory sterilisation of people with learning difficulties was widely practised in many parts of the world, at least until the 1970s.

So taken for granted are these assumptions that we fail to notice the ways in which societal beliefs, systems design and physical environments can be disabling. The "disabled person's problems are perceived to result from individual impairment rather than the failure of society to meet that person's needs in terms of appropriate human help, accessibility and inclusion" (French and Swain 2004: 34).

As a set of criteria for access to programs, services and benefits, there is wide variation in what is seen as constituting *disability.* Hall and colleagues (2014: 195) note that around the world the criteria used to define disability varies from time spent being disabled to extent of disabilities. For instance, to qualify as disabled in Australia, substantial impairment of functioning must occur for six months or more, while in U.K. requires twelve months or more and Sweden does not impose time requirements (Hall et al. 2014). In India, "one-eyed persons" (that is, people who literally have the use of only one eye) were not considered disabled until 2011, and references to mental illness, mental retardation and mental disability are constantly changing (Office of the Registrar General and Census Commissioner, India New Delhi, 2013). This may not seem important until you reflect on the ways in which access to services, programs and benefits is directly related to disability status.

People with disabilities are estimated to be the largest minority group in the world (Palombi 2012). For instance, in Canada, 3.8 million adults reported a disability in 2012, representing 13.7 percent of the (adult) population, with the majority of these reporting problems related to pain, mobility and/or flexibility (Statistics Canada 2015). Categories of disability are extensive, though, including but not limited to physical, sensory, mobility-oriented, cognitive and intellectual disabilities as well as emotional disorders and mental illnesses. The causes of disabilities are equally diverse, from congenital (pre-birth) and genetic factors, to infection, illness and injury, including non-accidental injuries as a result of violence and abuse.

In simple terms, a disability is something that gets in the way of, or prevents people from having the same opportunities and quality of life as others. While this "something" can be related to something inside the person (such as a disease), it also reflects societal barriers to the participation of people with different abilities. Taking this into account, the causes of disabilities are not just carried within the person; rather it important to shift the focus away from disabled individuals and towards *disabling* environments.

Disablism

The term *disablism* was introduced by a disability action group, Scope, in 2004, to describe the ways in which people with disabilities are discriminated against, excluded, devalued, exploited and intimidated (Shakespeare 2004). Disablism speaks to the wider culture of placing people on a hierarchy of ability and rating their worth and value on the basis of achievement within standardized environments. It highlights the ways in which differently abled people are prevented from participating in everyday activities. Minor accommodations can, in many cases, significantly impact on access and participation; for instance, the provision of alternate communication options for people with anxiety and agoraphobia, feedback loops for people with a hearing impairment, mobility access for buildings, allowance for service dogs who are assisting people with visual impairments and other conditions including post-traumatic stress, epilepsy, autism and diabetes.

Goodley (2013) explains the emergence of critical disability studies, which is an interdisciplinary effort to examine the ways in which disability becomes entangled with other forms of oppression, including those relating to gender, class, ethnicity and age. Studies prefixed by the term "critical" usually refer to critical theory, or the examination of power relations, across domains, including global capitalism. From the U.K., Deal (2007) argues that while blatant forms of prejudice towards disabled people are decreasing, more so-called subtle forms of prejudice remain, obstructing the attempts of disabled people to become equal, respected and valued members of society. Deal points to the concept of *aversive disablism* to draw attention to the many assumptions of able-bodied superiority that are cast — unwittingly and unintentionally — upon disabled people. Palombi (2012) refers to these as *micro-aggressions* and notes that even egalitarian able-bodied people may engage in domination over disabled people. This may include, for instance, talking about the need to "soldier on" and push through pain, discomfort and illness in order to achieve goals and prove high functionality.

For people managing chronic conditions including acute episodes, this talk of "toughing it out" and clichés of "no excuses," "just do it" and so on, is likely to be the source of significant pressure. The prohibition on whining about health, especially in highly productive workplaces, can, for instance, result in people concealing their illnesses and conditions. Apart from the public health risks of cross-infection, accident and injury, the personal costs for individuals can include missed health appointments, failure to access necessary treatment and exacerbation of symptoms and existing workplace dangers (see Palombi 2012). Work-intensified practices associated with neoliberalism and the corporatization of public utilities, health, welfare and education systems have exacerbated these problems as workers and managers are pushed to prioritize cost efficiencies over quality and service provision (see Chapters 3 and 8).

Irrespective of whether or not they are professional and able-bodied, not wanting to jeopardize employment is a pressure many workers experience, and for good reason. As illustrated by Strandh et al. (2014) in their longitudinal study, unemployment carries enormous costs. Unemployment and underemployment are strongly correlated to poverty, social exclusion and poor mental health outcomes (see Crowe and Butterworth 2016), and long-term unemployment can have especially devastating impacts for those groups who have been historically excluded or prematurely expelled from the labour force. With the demise of manufacturing jobs in traditionally masculine areas such as car making, young, able-bodied, working-class men may find it hard to get work, especially if they are not well placed to take on serving roles such as those in hospitality, tourism and personal care. Disabled young men from poorer backgrounds may be even further behind and are likely to lack the support needed to train for, seek and maintain employment. Older and younger working-class women may also find it difficult to get work, especially if they live in suburbs with high unemployment. Depending on their disability, disabled women might find it even more difficult than peers who have not yet experienced the obstacles of disability, to be taken seriously as an employee.

Ableist discourses would have us believe that anyone who tries hard enough can become a highly functional, socially esteemed free agent living the dream of unfettered autonomy. The truth is that even the most accomplished, wealthy and celebrated person on Earth relies on others, sometimes armies of support, including brokers, lawyers, accountants, managers, personal assistants, housekeepers, nannies, cooks, gardeners, drivers, masseurs, therapists and so on (see Mullaly 2010). Simply paying for a service does not erase mutuality of benefit; dependence on the networks of infrastructure allows high-flying individuals to shine. Dropping this cultural pretense requires recognizing that we are, in fact, all connected in networks of activity, interdependent and intradependent in ways that change over time (French and Swain 2004; Palombi 2012). Acknowledging our collective embeddedness is important to AOP work and pivotal to developing and sustaining therapeutic alliances (see Chapter 7; Palombi 2012).

Age-Related Privileges and Oppression

Much is made of the chronological age of humans, with confident assertions about what can be expected when we are young, middle-aged and very old. Although age-related assertions might seem credible and authoritative, they are context and time specific. Butler first used the concept of ageism in 1969 to refer to the stereotyping, discrimination and prejudice experienced by elderly people (Butler 1989). In 1978, Ansello described ageism as a subtle stereotype that associates aging with decline and can become a self-fulfilling prophecy. Today, ageism can be seen to apply to any age-related discrimination, from the very old to the very young.

Adulthood — young to middle-aged — has long been considered the peak of human functioning. Turn on the television, log onto the internet or read through the newspapers and the vast majority of people shown in positions of power are 20 and 50 years old, though in some areas such as electronic gaming, fifty is considered old. The usual targets of ageism are, therefore, the very young and the very old, both of whom are assumed to be dependent and, often, pre- or beyond cognition and moral reasoning (see Dalrymple and Burke 2006).

Anglo-dominated cultures such as Australia, New Zealand, Canada and the U.K. have a reputation for not cherishing their elders, at least when compared to other more collectively oriented cultures (such as Indigenous Australians, Maori, Japanese). People over 70 years old are often assumed to be chronically ill, dependent and needy, with little to offer society. Stereotyped as having little to no capacity for learning, they are often are locked out of employment in growth industries involving automation and computer coding (Lemish and Muhlbauer 2012). Older people are then depicted as non-contributing members of society and, ultimately, a burden on their family, relatives and friends (see Butler 2009; Kosberg and Garcia 2013), as well as institutions including health/hospitals and social security.

DIFFERENTIAL AGING

Most communities, including those in (ex)Commonwealth countries such as Australia, New Zealand, Canada, India and Britain, are experiencing a dramatic aging of populations. Yet, how we age varies significantly, and is influenced by our social status and place in social hierarchies, as well as access to resources and cultural capital. Older adults can find it hard securing paid work, especially if they have been out of the workforce for a while. For instance, over the period 2013–2104, the Australian Human Rights Commission (2015) found that a quarter of Australians aged 50 and over experienced some form of work-related age discrimination. With the loss of economic productivity and assumed authority that often accompanies this, ageism has a habit of trivializing, if not ignoring older people's interests, hopes and plans.

Ageing and Social (In)Equality

The widening gap in social equality means that longevity and so-called successful or productive ageing can be elusive (Romo et al. 2013), and that retirement practices are changing as the value of many aged pensions is decreasing and/or only extended to older and older populations. Dhillon and Ladusingh (2013) note that in India, longevity has resulted in women, but not men, staying in the workforce longer. Also from India, Vera-Sanso (2012) notes the significant contributions that older women make to the informal economy; their work distributing agricultural products, for example, provide funds to support their husbands, subsidize younger relatives and reduce levels of family poverty overall.

Ageism is cast onto sexed, gendered, classed and racialized bodies. Premature aging is often reflective of multiple forms of oppression across the years. Oppression produces stress. From large-scale empirical studies we know that people in low socio-economic circumstances are more adversely affected by stress than those in more affluent settings, not just mentally but also physically, manifesting in diminished cardiac functioning and greater receptivity to stroke (see Lazzarino et al. 2013).

Ageism occurs when people are underestimated and devalued because of prejudices and stereotypes associated with their age (Butler 2009; Pease 2010). Ageism can be conveyed through humour, with oppressed persons regularly the butt of jokes (Mullaly 2010). While many jokes are made about growing old, the supposed naivety and dependency of the very young is also a frequent source of amusement. The young may be seen to "know nothing" while, according to other clichés, "it's all downhill from forty." Jokes about disability are even more prolific; although not always voiced in polite company, such jokes consist of degrading references to people who lose control over various functions, whether muscles and movement, emotions, sanity or cognition, and/or bladders and bowels. Donald Trump, during his U.S. presidency campaign, provided a good example of this when he mocked a reporter with a physical disability (CNN.com 2015), an incident that was caught on camera and broadcast across the world.

Although often accompanied by the claim "I was only joking," jokes such as these would not exist without the power of ageism and disablism to reinforce the already corrosive conditions in which the old, young and disabled exist. Ageist assumptions, expressed in a range of ways, including humour, set the scene for the very old and young people to be excluded from decision-making processes, including those central to their own lives. The inclination to disrespect and dismiss seriously undermines people's well-being and opens the door to other forms of abuse.

Ageism is toxic to social equality but not always easy to see. Ageist stereotypes can include presuming elders have only memories, not current and future interests, hopes and plans. This can result in older people wondering whether they are even entitled to still have hopes and plans. Then there are the sexual stereotypes of old men as dirty (sexually and otherwise) and older women as asexual and invisible (see Lemish and Muhlbauer 2012). Effectively, such stereotypes operate as a slur that hovers overhead, warning sexually active older people to police their own behaviour if they want to avoid drawing unwanted attention (such as disgust). For aging disabled people across the sexual spectrum, these sexual stereotypes can be even more toxic, denying people the right to consensual sexual relationships and casting their relationships as inferior, if not transgressive.

It is not surprising, then, that ageism may be internalized and can have significant consequences. For instance, Nelson (2016) showed how affective (or feeling-based) responses to ageism influence older people's cognition, rates of healing from illness and recovery from accidents. Hausdorff, Levy and Wei (1999) found that people's style of walking — their gait — changed depending on whether they were exposed to positive or negative stereotypes of aging. Makris and colleagues (2015) found that when people internalized the negative effects of ageism, they were less inclined to seek help for restrictive and chronic back pain, which in turn limited their mobility and quality of life.

Children and Ageism

Children can also be subject to ageism, that is, being automatically ignored, underestimated and undervalued because of their age. Ageism against children is not new. In many countries, childhood (under 18 years old) has historically been associated with a lack of agency, rights and responsibilities. This has occurred even when children, and working-class and/or racialized children in particular, have been put out to work; they become miniature adults but with none of the associated rights and entitlements.

The struggle for children and young people to be afforded legal and civil rights, as individuals in their own right and not their parents' property, has occurred over centuries. Children across the world have been both cherished and dominated at the same time (Thompson 1997). While in the West children are stereotyped as indulged and overprotected, the reality is that the fun and innocence of childhood is not evenly distributed. Some children are denied childhoods as they are conventionally portrayed. Across the world, many children do paid work for more than mere pocket money, yet stereotypes of children often deny their contributions. In some countries, children are the primary breadwinners for families (see White 2002 in relation to child workers in Bangladesh). Though rarely recognized, children can be the engines of families, performing physical and emotional labour that far exceeds assumptions of what children of that age are capable of.

Advocates of child welfare and rights know that class, caste and skin colour influence the life chances provided to children (see Eriksson, Bruno and Näsman 2013; Chapter 8). Privileged children do much better on so many developmental scales, and for those who fall behind, the support and remedial actions on offer can be impressive. Wealth matters as it opens so many doors and purchases so many services. From an AOP perspective, monetary wealth does not simply flow to those who work hard, but rather is exchanged, mostly amongst those who already have wealth. As Swedish researchers found after studying the trajectories of children adopted into very wealthy families, it is neither talent nor initiative but wealth that generates (more) wealth in adulthood (Black, Devereux, Lundborg and Majlesi 2015).

Poverty as Child Abuse

Class, gender and age oppression can intersect with serious consequences in both developed and developing countries (see Boston and Chapple 2014; White 2002). Children make up whole segments of societies who are living with chronic environmental abuse and deprivation. All who live in chronic poverty face severe and sustained challenges to flourishing — personally, educationally, physically and sexually. Exposure to other environmental hazards, such as lead poisoning, is also a critical concern (WHO 2010b). For the children who manage to survive into adulthood, the effects of poverty and pollution routinely follow them through their life.

As AOP workers we know that pollution and poverty are forms of child abuse. We also know that child servitude and slavery continue to be major social problems associated with poverty, exposing many children to the risks of better-resourced adult predators (see Schwartz 2013; van Doore 2016). The International Labour Organization's (ILO) (1999) *Worst Forms of Child Labour Convention* comprises the following:

a. All forms of slavery or practices similar to slavery, such as the sale and trafficking of children, debt bondage and serfdom and forced or compulsory labour, including forced or compulsory recruitment of children for use in armed conflict;

b. The use, procuring or offering of a child for prostitution, for the production of pornography or for pornographic performances;

c. The use, procuring or offering of a child for illicit activities, in particular for the production and trafficking of drugs as defined in the relevant international treaties;

d. Work which, by its nature or the circumstances in which it is carried out, is likely to harm the health, safety or morals of children.

The risks of children being enslaved were often higher than adults because they were easier to kidnap, more malleable to train and less demanding to keep than adults, and because of their susceptibility to being sold by impoverished parents to discharge debts (Schwartz 2013). Most child slaves are oppressed on multiple levels. The risks of becoming a child slave show exactly how racism, sexism and ageism can intersect.

HATE CRIMES

Human history is riddled with extreme, hate-fuelled violence (Tyson and Hall 2016). Galtung's (1990) violence triangle reminds us that structural and cultural violences provide the context for — and enable — direct violences, a conceptualization that is especially valuable for thinking about hate crimes. Broadly defined, a *hate crime* is a crime motivated by prejudicial hate, that is, hatred driven by prejudices such as racial prejudice, homophobia and misogyny, all of which can intersect the hatred associated with ageism and disablism. Hate crimes can be perpetrated by either individuals or groups who direct their rage towards others deemed inferior.

Oppression and Hate Crimes

Perry (2001: 1) reminds us that, "racial, gender ethnic and religious violence persist as mechanisms of oppression." In essence, a hate crime is an "assault against all members of stigmatized and marginalized communities" and, as such, is "much more than the act of mean-spirited bigots" (Perry 2001: 1). Tyson and Hall (2016) consider the meanings attributed to hatred, including whether hatred might ever be seen as normal, or conversely, a mental illness.

Beck (1999) explored the question of why perpetrators of hate, in war but also domestic violence, often believe that they are doing good. He argued that those responsible commonly possess distorted beliefs about the legitimacy of their (violent) actions — whether they be kidnap, rape, murder, war and so on — which in turn shape their thinking and emotions to justify their violence. One of the many challenges of anti-violence work is to make sense of violence that is used in the name of justice, often by oppressed persons who, because their faith in criminal justice systems is low, put their faith in "street justice." Forms of vigilantism such as this feed off and into military discourses about justice, often endorsing widespread violence and abuse, including the use of incendiary weapons and chemical warfare (see Berndtson et al. 2014).

Questions remain regarding hate crimes. Couldn't all forms of violence and abuse be seen, at some level, as expressions of hate? Don't rapists hate their victims? Might parents who repeatedly and deliberately violate their children be seen as engaging in acts of hatred? How could a white football supporter verbally abusing and throwing a banana at a black player not be read as racial hatred? What about priests who molest the children in their care? Might they be seen to hate children or, at least, hate children's rights to autonomy, safety and protection from harm? Many more examples could be cited.

Child Soldiers

Hate crimes are common in war but are not necessarily what we have in mind when we think about hatred; that is, hatred is often attributed to individuals and groups rather than nation states and international alliances. Ostensibly, hate crimes seem straightforwardly wrong and deserving of heavy punishment, however, on closer inspection there are more complicated issues at play. Child soldiers, for instance, engender important and difficult questions about hate crimes and culpability. In spite of the United Nations Convention on the Rights of the Child, and the principle of the best interests of the child, there are hundreds of thousands of child soldiers (aged under 18 years) fighting in armed conflicts (Grossman 2007). While known to perform heinous violence, the age of child soldiers — and the fact that they often have been forced into military operations — surely mitigates, if not negates, culpability. Rather than prosecuting child soldiers, Grossman (2007) advocates treating them as victims rather than perpetrators, including international law trials for grave human rights violations. Controlling for specific individual circumstances, our position is to consider them as both victims and perpetrators; attention to their experiences as both is necessary to ensure that history is not repeated.

For two years Boothby, Crawford and Halperin (2006) studied the rehabilitation of former child soldiers from Mozambique; children who were accepted back into their families and communities and taught how to become caring, responsible adults. They found that effective interventions included teaching self-regulation and promoting behaviours that enhanced feelings of security, addressing trauma and grief, providing training opportunities supportive of future livelihoods and strengthening coping skills, especially those related to processing trauma and grief, as well as culturally specific rituals of forgiveness and healing practices. Together these interventions helped former child soldiers to reintegrate back into their families and communities (Boothby, Crawford and Halperin 2006).

One of the attractions of calling a particular form of violence a hate crime might be to underline its seriousness. Hate, after all, is a strong word. Might it, however, be counter-productive, serving to deflect attention from broader societal and collective prejudices (Hall 2013)? Our view is that it will depend upon the context in which hate crimes are discussed and whether critical questions are posed. From an AOP perspective, it is both ethically and pragmatically necessary to rehabilitate people who commit hate crimes. Since there are so many hate crimes perpetrated in war (and beyond), we have to attempt to rehabilitate offenders, particularly if they are young, or hate crimes will proliferate. This reflects our measured optimism for the possibilities of transformative change, which extends to individuals whose actions may be driven not only by hate but also by their distorted beliefs about their own rights, privileges and ways of seeing the world. Debates about how this might best be achieved cut in and across social justice movements, with implications for policy and decision making regarding victim compensation, prison alternatives and restorative justice practices.

Disability Hate Crimes

A British study by Emerson and Roulstone (2014) found that disabled adults were significantly more likely than able-bodied adults to have been exposed to violent crime. They noted that disabled adults with mental health problems were the most likely to be subjected to disabled hate crimes, and that poverty strongly moderated risk, with impoverished disabled adults much more susceptible to being assaulted than those from more wealthy respondents. In writing on disability hate crimes, Sherry (2016) posed — and answered — the question "does anyone really hate disabled people?" with a resounding "yes." In order to demonstrate the extent of this, Sherry (2016) incorporated the vile, hurtful words that disabled people from around the world had reported to him, arguing that "hate speech" is central to hate crime, indeed, hate speech can be an important piece of evidence that the act is not simply a random crime, but is directed at an individual because of a particular identity.

The recent Sagamihara massacre by an estranged care worker of disabled people in a Japanese residential home illustrates the deep hatred felt by some towards people with disabilities. The murderer in this case, Satoshi Uematsu, was later reported to have told the police, "It is better that disabled people disappear" (Findlay 2016). In line with Beck's (1999) idea of "doing good," Uematsu justified his crime on the basis that he was doing the world a favor by eliminating disabled people. In a report in the *Independent* newspaper, however, Hennessy (2016) clearly identified the massacre in Japan as a "hate crime that disabled people like me live in fear of." Noting the oppression of disabled people across the world, Hennessy (2016) pointed to the warning Uematsu had given Japanese authorities through the letter he wrote to them in which he offered, to "methodically 'wipe out' Japan's disabled community. His letter repeats the claim that 'all disabled people should cease to exist.' 'I envision a world where a person with multiple disabilities can be euthanised' he [Uematsu] wrote."

A week later, Findlay (2016), in a piece for the *Sydney Morning Herald*, asked why the "mass murder of 19 disabled people in Japan barely" rated a mention. Writing as a disabled person, Findlay noted that she and her friends had all been told, at some point in their lives, that they should kill themselves. She argued that disabled people have long endured the indignity of being portrayed as worthless and that their risk of experiencing violence was much higher than able-bodied populations, both in Australia and internationally; disabled people's fear of crimes of hatred being committed against them, she concluded, are neither inflated nor unfounded.

From an AOP perspective, the concept of hate crime, like so many others, is both useful in illuminating experiences and also problematic on multiple levels. Our approach is to use the concept cautiously, with awareness of its potential to unduly individualize and close attention to the links between love, hate, privilege and oppression. Terms such as *disablist hate crime* are nonetheless useful in connecting individual hate crimes with the wider context of disablism, reflecting a social rather than medical model of health (see Hall et al. 2014). Whichever terms we use, we must not lose sight of the negative effects of violence, abuse and hate on whole communities. In Canada, for instance, Perry and Alvi's (2012) analysis of the community impacts of hate crimes highlighted the intense distress experienced by both the immediate victims and those around them. Being in the presence of, or connected to, a victim of abuse resulted in symptoms of vicarious trauma including shock, anger, fear, vulnerability, inferiority and a sense of futility. Trauma such as this can precipitate depression, a disabling condition for growing numbers of people across the world and especially risky for those who were physically punished during childhood.

AGE- AND ABILITY-RELATED VIOLENCE AND ABUSE

In recent decades, *elder abuse* has been recognized as one of many possible forms of domestic or familial violence. At the interpersonal level, elder abuse involves physical, sexual, psychological/emotional and financial abuse and neglect perpetrated by family members and others including paid carers. Elder abuse also encompasses cultural forms of disrespect and systemic abuse, however, including that perpetrated by government authorities (Ploeg, Lohfeld and Walsh 2013).

Similar to reactions to other forms of domestic violence, elderly victims may experience shock, disbelief and denial, as well as shame and self-blame.[1]

The effects of interpersonally committed (or direct) *child abuse* are well documented across regions, nationalities and other groupings. The legacy of these abuses can be devastating (Arias 2004), affecting health and well-being over many years (Krieger 2003). As is the case for so many survivors of abuse and violence, opportunities in education, training and work can be impaired or sacrificed. In other words, the losses associated with child abuse are multiple and cumulative, extending beyond victims'/survivors' immediate needs and relationships, well into the future.

Much has been written about child abuse. Because the existing body of literature is extensive and widely available, our aim here is to highlight aspects of abuse and violence that are significant but commonly overlooked.

The Early Years: Chronic Abuse and Deprivation

It is widely agreed that the early infancy years provide a critical foundation for healthy development. Diversity of opinion exists, however, in relation to the exact relationship between child health, well-being and development and factors including brain chemistry, neighbourhoods and families (Shonkoff and Phillips 2000). What we can say is that there is a link between adult diseases and conditions and early life deprivations and maltreatment, which paediatricians Shonkoff et al. (2012) refer to as "toxic stress." They write:

> altered brain architecture in response to toxic stress in early childhood could explain, at least in part, the strong association between early adverse experiences and subsequent problems in the development of linguistic, cognitive, and social-emotional skills, all of which are inextricably intertwined in the wiring of the developing brain. (Shonkoff et al. 2012: e236)

Classifying something as child abuse is a deeply significant and political act. Flaherty et al. (2014) detail the challenges faced by medical practitioners in trying to decipher whether children's fractures are due to abuse, accident or other health conditions such as vitamin D deficiency, rickets, copper deficiency and osteogeneis imperfecta (very brittle bones). The consequences of getting the diagnosis wrong are serious. The implication of failing to identify a child's injuries as abuse is that no action is taken to prevent further injury; conversely, wrongly identifying abuse is likely to cause great distress and disruption to children and their families, including the possibility of child removal (Flaherty et al. 2014).

South African researchers Meinck, Cluver, Boyes and Ndhlovu (2015) examined risk and protective factors for young people (aged between 13 and 19 years) who have been emotionally and physically abused. In talking about their experiences of violence and abuse, the young participants referred to a wide range of practices that might not conventionally be thought of as abuse, these including food insecurity and/or unequal access to food, AIDs-related stigma, and inconsistent discipline by the adults around them (Meinck et al. 2015).

Canada's Ontario Child Health Study is a province-wide health survey of children aged 4 to 16 years. It was first conducted in 1983, then again in 1987 and in 2000–2001. In their analysis of this study's data from the 2000–2001 period, MacMillan et al. (2013) found that the children of parental adversity were at increased risk of physical and sexual abuse; and that the risk was especially high for children living in urban areas, living in poverty and/or whose parents were young at the time of their birth. The figures also showed a higher proportion of childhood physical abuse reported by males (33.7 percent of males surveyed) than females (28.2 percent of females surveyed). The physical abuse experienced by males, however, was less severe than that reported by females, and males were significantly less likely to report child sexual abuse — specifically 8.3 percent of males as compared to 22.1 percent of females (MacMillan et al. 2013). This is important information that helps us understand violence and abuse. Yet, caution needs to be shown, as statistics do not tell the whole story. For example, the risk of uncritical reliance on statistics is that we concentrate on the groups more likely to be victimized and don't pay enough attention to others, including in the planning and delivery of services, support and related social policy. It can take years for people who have experienced abuse to come forward, perhaps waiting until they feel safe enough, piece together their experiences and use the language of violence and abuse to describe it to others. This affects statistics and studies of violence of all kinds.

Many researchers have studied the cumulative impact of multiple violence and abuse experiences, including early life stressors. The long-term implications are many and include the greater risk of adult obesity (see Bentley and Widom 2009). Decades ago, AOP-inspired researcher Boushel (1994) analyzed the ways in which structural, cultural, personal and interpersonal factors combine to create a child's protective environment, emphasizing the importance of ongoing safety nets for children and their parents/carers to prevent future abuse. In other research, Shalev et al. (2013) found a direct link between cumulative childhood stress, particularly exposure to violence, and telomere erosion, a condition of premature cellular aging with serious lifelong health implications, including increased susceptibility to disease and early mortality.

Depression or Oppression?

Depression can be disabling and rising numbers of people across the world are reported to be suffering from it. More than twenty years ago, Acheson (1993), a medical doctor, asked a question that is especially compelling for AOP workers: "Depression or oppression?" While Acheson was referring to a specific case — the depression experienced by a female victim of domestic violence — there are many other instances in which oppression and depression collide. Depression and suicidal ideation are particular risks for children who have been emotionally maltreated (Khan et al. 2015). High levels of depression, anxiety and distress are also reported by adults exposed to childhood sexual and physical abuse (Lindert et al. 2014). In a meta-analysis of the long-term health consequences of childhood abuse and neglect, Norman et al. (2012) found clear evidence that all forms of child maltreatment pose serious health risks and, over the long term, significantly contribute to the burden of disease across the world. This is a consistent finding from researchers, irrespective of theoretical and political orientation. Interestingly, while it has long been known that survivors of child sexual abuse experience higher rates of mental illness, drug dependence and so on, it is increasingly apparent that these impacts are associated with *all* forms of child abuse and neglect.

The Corporal Punishment of Children

At first glance it would seem that physical abuse is self-evidently child abuse. However, the voices of those who advocate physical punishment for children indicate that the line between abuse and discipline remains unclear, at least for some (see Gershoff 2002). In our view, the corporal punishment of children reflects ageism in action. In his book, *Beating the Devil Out of Them*, Straus (2001) argues that parents who spank and slap in the name of corporal punishment are physically abusing their children and that these supposedly "minor" acts are the precursor to violence that occurs in the wider world. Smacking advocates argue that without corporal punishment, children will not learn to listen, comply and obey the adults in charge (Gershoff 2002). This belief is not substantiated in research. In her meta-analysis of whether corporal punishment works for parents in the U.S., Gershoff (2002) found that while corporal punishment did produce higher levels of immediate compliance, it also generated in children higher levels of aggression, less internal morality and compromised their overall mental health — all factors that contribute to anti-social behaviour.

The corporal punishment of children is legally prohibited in thirty-two countries, but still legal in other countries including Canada and Australia. Researchers such as Doucette, Harris and Jaffe (2014) in Canada are strong advocates for making the physical punishment of children illegal, while also recognizing the need for communities to be supported in establishing alternative forms of discipline.

In Australia, Bernadette Saunders (2013) takes the same position, and has long advocated for Australians to stop ignoring the evidence of harm that physical punishment causes children.

We recognize that people, including professionals such as psychologists, are divided as to whether the corporal punishment of children can ever be considered ethical or reasonable. Nevertheless, we hold the position that the physical domination of children through smacking and spanking is wrong, not least because it models the use of violence as an appropriate way to resolve issues and treat others, particularly those with less power. For us, it is important to notice how seemingly innocuous terms, such as "smacking" and "spanking" are used in a way that empties relationships of their power and obscures the ethics of domination. Notwithstanding the risk of serious assaults being enacted against children, the possible consequences of physical punishment include long-term harm to physical, emotional and mental health that prevents children from reaching their potential. There is also an argument that it can impact on children's capacity for moral reasoning in culturally specific contexts (Saunders 2013). Most critically, the physical punishment of children is not only harmful but ultimately counterproductive in terms of an AOP aspiration of non-violent future citizens.

Thinking Differently about Age and Ability

How we conceive of aging — individually and as a society — effects how we experience getting older. Given the negative stereotypes about aging in popular circulation it is likely that we all carry some kinds of fears about aging, at the base of which lie deep insecurities that reflect these disempowering messages about what to expect of old age. As critically reflexive practitioners, it is worth exploring our own feelings about aging: do we fear aging, and if so, what fears do we carry and how have these come about? Nelson (2005), for example, asks whether ageist disrespect is related to younger people's fear of their future selves. Interestingly, a group of Serbian researchers observed children's mostly positive perceptions of old age and concluded that ageist attitudes are more likely to be adopted later in life (Davidovic et al. 2007).

From an AOP perspective, it is important to think about age as a rough marker rather than a self-evident fact of capability. Chronological age provides a general indication of developmental milestones and reasonable expectations in this regard; for instance, the age range at which we might expect children to walk, talk, problem-solve and be capable of independence. It might be predicted that, at certain stages of development — such as infancy — individuals will not be in a position to fully participate in decisions, even those about their own lives. However, much variation exists among groups and individuals with regard to physical, intellectual, emotional and moral development. Age may or may not be relevant to fair and reasonable expectations, rights and responsibilities.

Child rights movements — mostly but not exclusively comprised of adults — have pushed for the recognition of issues including child abuse, child workers' industrial conditions and the oppression of young people in residential facilities (see Chapter 8). Taking their lead, we recognize that, for the many children and young people who live and work independently from birth families or who parent siblings and/or their own children, conventional portraits of adolescence as a time of growth, parental support, education/training and (consensual) sexual exploration are far from accurate. Recognizing the wide diversity of experiences, including developmental experiences, is crucial. We must avoid lazy over-generalizations, based solely on age, regarding what people can and cannot or should and should not do. In practical terms this means seeing age and developmental milestones as elastic and culturally relative, and viewing the individual within these terms of reference. Avoiding ageism requires an open mind regarding what people in certain age brackets might be thinking, feeling and experiencing. Similarly, we must think about contributions to society in broader and more inclusive ways. People contribute to society in a range of ways; this might be through paid work but, equally, might involve contribution in the realm of the emotional, artistic, community and/or social.

The experiences of oppression for working-class and/or Black disabled children are multiple and multi-layered; communicated in people's attitudes, in social policies that deny them the chance to participate in community activities, in town planning that prevents them from free movement and in societal arrangements that deny them the opportunity to do paid work and share in the economic benefits (Mullaly 2010). Oppression can snatch away innocence, as well as trust, respect, hope and well-being, from the most robust of victims. Shame, isolation, deprivation of resources and loss of opportunity remain common experiences for young disabled people, especially those with multiple disabilities (intellectual, learning, behavioural or mobility based).

Embedded in ableist discourses, as discussed earlier in this chapter, is the expectation that people defy their disadvantages to not just survive, but also succeed like few before them. In other words, disadvantaged people must (over-) compensate for their assumed deficits. For the disabled, the very young and the very old, these messages, and the associated (self-) expectations, can make life considerably harder. As AOP workers, we should not hold oppressed persons, especially multiply oppressed persons, to a higher standard of behaviour than we do people with privilege. While we are keen to see all people flourish, this should not require the superhuman efforts of those who are already devalued.

THE POLITICS OF CARE

The concept of care infers emotional warmth, engagement and careful attunement. Twenty-five years ago, Ashworth, Longmate and Morrison (1992), for instance, explored the meaning and significance of patient participation in the context of nursing, which they described as a caring profession. Characteristics assigned to participatory nursing care practices included emotional attunement, an acceptance of diverse identities and attempts to mutually build knowledge between patient and practitioner (Ashworth et al. 1992). Caring is often assumed as self-evidently "good"; that caring for others means that we are not dominating them and that power relations are not in play. Certainly in naïve views of care, altruism and goodness prevail. Dig deeper into care, though, and more complex dynamics become evident — patterns of privilege and oppression including those associated with who cares for whom.

Giving and Receiving Care

While more men are involved in direct forms of care than in previous generations, women still provide the bulk of care in both formal and informal settings (Baines and Cunningham 2015). Maternal images of care abound in the popular imagination: ideas about who has a so-called natural affinity for caring, the association of caring with love and self-sacrifice rather than money and so on. Given the cultural expectation that women perform the role of primary carers, both in relation to children and otherwise, it is not surprising that feminists have a longstanding interest in care provision, in both informal and formal systems of care.

The needs of caregivers are not often heard or taken seriously. Because caring work is, in general, undervalued, carers — whether unpaid or paid — are vulnerable, unsupported and may have few options. The abuse, deliberate or unintentional, of carers by the people they care for — and/or their extended family — is a significant concern. Nonetheless, many disabled people, like some elderly and very young people, have little to no control over who cares for them, and how. Because much of this caring work happens in private, without independent witnesses, it is possible for abuse by caregivers to continue over protracted periods of time. As a case in point, it is only relatively recently that religious institutions have been exposed for their refusal to support victims/survivors of abuse and collusion with perpetrators.

As we have indicated throughout this book, chronic poverty is both a form of abuse and closely intertwined with disability:

> Poverty creates disability and disability creates poverty. People with disabilities are often among the poorest of the poor. The World Bank estimates that disabled people make up 15-20% of the poor in developing

countries. (The Danish Bilharziasis Laboratory for the World Bank, People's Republic of Bangladesh 2004: 2)

As observed by Dominelli (2016: 236), "poverty is not just about inadequate incomes but also the right to experience fulfilled lives within one's community, share in a common sense of identity and belonging with other people, and control one's life oneself."

Care, Gender and Moral Development

Feminist notions of care giving and reciprocity are linked with questions about public ethics and morality. Carol Gilligan (1977) explored the limitations to Kohlberg's (1971) theory of stages of moral development, which involved a sample of seventy-two Chicago boys aged between 10 and 16 years. Noticeably, no girls were included, a practice that was common in many Western countries during and post-WWII. Gilligan (1977) studied how girls and women's morality developed and found it was different to the ways Kohlberg described. One of her main arguments was that developmental theory needed to integrate a "feminine voice" (Gilligan 1977). Gilligan was writing during a time when it was common to present women as a unified group with universal needs and interests. The homogenization of women, or the process of making women's differences disappear through the assumption of commonality, has subsequently been widely critiqued (see Fraser 2008). Yet, the spirit of Gilligan's (1977) message remains: girls and women have so often been ignored and excluded in studies about moral development. This is not a small omission and serves as a reminder of the need to be cautious regarding the claims and generalizations of so-called science.

The politics of caregiving flows through health, welfare and education service provision. Care workers can be exploited and abused by their employing organizations, including those claiming to use best practices. Baines and Cunningham (2015) examined the impact of neoliberalism, specifically the effects of welfare austerity and the outsourcing of care services, on workers' employment conditions and quality of care services in Canada, the U.K. and Australia. They discuss the financial crises facing so many care organizations as a result of budget cuts and new public management-based market reform, noting that what was formerly known to be the non-profit sector has been radically reformed to prize more aggressive, commercial operations (Baines and Cunningham 2015). They note that for the primarily female workforce, who are at the front line of the care professions, welfare austerity has meant both cuts in the services they can provide to others as well as substantial cuts to their pay and employment conditions.

In so many health, welfare and education activities, older women — those aged over 50 years — make up the majority of officially recognized volunteers who give their time, energy and expertise without remuneration (Bussell and Forbes 2002; O'Neill and Gidengil 2013). These are the women who help out at schools, in the canteen and in the classroom; who sit on boards and head up community campaigns. They are the ones most likely to make and help distribute food, including through food banks and programs such as Meals on Wheels, and through visiting people at risk of isolation (see Gonzales, Matz-Costa and Morrow-Howell 2015). If there are trees to be planted and stray pets or injured wildlife to be rescued, it is most often older women who step forward. Likewise they provide substantial amounts of care for their grandchildren and other relatives (see O'Neill and Gidengil 2013). Most importantly, many older women work without pay, even though their own economic situations are precarious, to help those — animals and humans — who are most disadvantaged (see Bussell and Forbes 2002).

Poverty and Women's Caring Work
Able-bodied and disabled women alike may provide care to others. We already know that being disabled increases the risks of poverty. The same can be said for women providing unpaid care. Women's unpaid care work has long been associated with poverty in old age (regarding the U.K., see Victor 2013; regarding India, see Vera-Sanso 2012). Expected to care "for love not money," the income-generating sacrifices that many older women make mean that little money gets set aside for their own future. For some older women, the double shift, that is the expectation that they be responsible for both paid work and domestic labour, continues into their seventies. The ageist assumptions that often negatively pattern the lives of older lesbians are also noteworthy — for example, the historical, heterosexist tendency to erase lesbians' sexuality and disregard and/or devalue their intimate relationships. On this basis, Langley (2001) emphasises the necessity of services that recognize and value the experiences of older lesbians and gay men, their intimate partnerships and preferred family forms.

Three decades ago, in *Counting for Nothing: What Men Value and What Women Are Worth*, Marilyn Waring (1988) showed how accounting has come to dominate the way policies are made, with the practice of counting privileged over qualitative assessments of worth and meaning. Most importantly, Waring (1988) illustrates from her work in developed and developing countries that when something is not formally counted it is usually taken for granted and not valued. Good examples include clean, accessible drinking water, a pollution-free environment and work that is not measured in formal systems of economics, especially so-called women's work.

When work is not measured, counted and valued, it can disappear not just from formal ledgers, but also from collective thinking, with informal workers redefined as unproductive non-producers. While national censuses often try to capture some of this informal care, the vast majority of government reports leave it aside.

This is important for the millions of women across the world, but also men and transgendered people, whose care efforts are also rendered invisible and whose own care and safety needs may be denied in the process. It is equally important that we, as AOP students and workers, recognize the wide variety of work — paid or unpaid — that is done and the ways in which this contributes to health and well-being. While ensuring that we advocate for broader organizational and policy recognition, acknowledging this informally, if not formally, goes some way towards making visible the otherwise un(der)valued caregiving we see around us.

Case Study: Rhonda and Ken

The case study below highlights some of the issues relating to providing, receiving and valuing care in a context of neoliberalism and welfare austerity. Many other examples could be cited and this case is by no means rare or extreme:

> Rhonda loved her job. She worked for a company that provided supported accommodation for older people who have difficulty looking after themselves. While the pay was low, Rhonda derived great satisfaction from the interactions she had with the people she worked with. One of her favourites was Ken.
>
> No one from Ken's family came to visit him and on his birthday, his only present was from Rhonda. Meanwhile, the company that Rhonda worked for had been taken over by a large corporation that prided itself on its modern techniques of staff management and its high returns for shareholders. The work people like Rhonda did with residents like Ken was considered wasteful of time and Rhonda's emotional investment with Ken was not within the boundaries of professional care. Intervention from Rhonda's manager meant that she was not allowed these family-type relationships with service users. Rhonda was saddened by this — her years of experience in the sector meant she knew that the extra steps she took with Ken gave him happiness, which in return gave her job satisfaction.
>
> Rhonda decided to leave the company and took up a job in retail that paid her better and where she was allowed to be friendly with customers. Ken's condition deteriorated markedly and he passed away a short time later. The aged care company didn't mind — they had a waiting list for accommodation and were able to fill Ken's place within a week.

In this case study, we see Rhonda personalizing the services provided to Ken by getting to know him as a person and helping him to celebrate his birthday. This was subsequently reinterpreted as boundary-crossing behaviour, as the (assumed) unnecessary excess of care. Rather than obeying management, Rhonda resisted their framing of this situation and resigned, moving into an area where her willingness to care was welcomed. She was fortunate to have this opportunity to do so.

The case study illustrates the ways in which caring can be radical, even deviant, especially in the context of care provision with oppressed populations. Baines, Cunningham and Fraser's (2011) study of care providers in Canada, Australia and the U.K. further demonstrates this point: many of the predominantly female voluntary social services workers in their study actively pushed back against managerialist pressures by refusing to drop the caring from their work with people with disabilities.

The undervaluing of care in formal service provision and lack of recognition given to informal care work has many negative consequences. The risk of exploitation is especially critical in the context of social policies that assume that those who aren't formally employed are staying at home and doing nothing. The implications for recipients of informal care include the denial of benefits and rights and possible exposure to violence and abuse by caregivers.

The promotion of social justice requires that AOP workers recognize not only the full gamut of violence and abuse, but also the value of care and associated physical and emotional labour, as well as the ethics of care and reciprocity integral to caring relationships. This includes respecting and valuing the volunteers in our services, the families and informal supporters of our clients, patients and students. It means appreciating that these networks of support — unpaid and often unseen — provide at least as much care as the network of formal organizations and professionals.

CONCLUSION

Ageism and disablism represent two axes of privilege and oppression that are of critical concern to anti-oppressive practitioners committed to the advancement of social equality. By unfairly privileging some and oppressing others, ageism and ableism provide fertile ground for abuse and violence. Whole segments of society can be written off, at least temporarily, for being too old, too young and/or too "feeble." In itself this is a form of abuse, both on a large scale and systemically. Crucial for AOP workers, though, is the ways in which this renders the very young the very old and those with disabilities vulnerable to abuse and violence, not just directly, but also indirectly through structures and culture.

Note

1. For an excellent overview of elder abuse across countries, see Kosberg and Garcia (2013).

Part 3

UNDERSTANDING RESPONSES TO VIOLENCE AND ABUSE

7. LEGISLATIVE AND POLICY RESPONSES

- How are the vulnerable constituted in laws and policies?
- What does it mean to operate in the best interests of the child?
- How might we think about the prevention, perpetrator and victim programs?
- Why do we need to think globally as well as locally?

This chapter provides an overview of the range of legislative and policy responses to violence and abuse while raising critical questions for deeper thought and discussion. As discussed in this chapter, the legal and policy context for abuse and violence is broad, encompassing global, national and local arenas of governance and ranging from international conventions and commitments to legislative provisions and organisational policy.

GLOBAL GOVERNANCE AND LEGAL PROVISIONS

United Nations conventions and declarations and other international regulations provide the global context for legislative and policy responses to abuse and violence. Collectively, these recognize (some) forms of abuse and violence as human rights violations and emphasize government accountability with regard to the entitlement of all people to the "full enjoyment of their human rights" (Howe 2008: 202). The Universal Declaration of Human Rights (1948) applies to all people and states that "no individual may be discriminated against or hindered from enjoying his or her human rights." International conventions and commitments with a direct focus on gender equality and freedom from violence include the United Nations' Convention on the Elimination of All Forms of Discrimination against Women (CEDAW) (1979), the Declaration on the Elimination of Violence against Women (1993) and the Beijing Declaration and Platform for Action (1995). Countries that have endorsed (or ratified) international conventions, including Canada, Australia and the U.K. (but not the U.S.), have made a commitment to uphold the principles and incorporate these into national legal frameworks.

The United Nations' Convention of the Rights of the Child (Australian Human Rights Commission 1989) recognizes that all children require "special safeguards and care" on the basis of their "physical or mental immaturity." Serving as a key reference for many government and non-government organizations, it "provides a common, ethical, and legal framework" and is notable for its conceptualization of children as the "holders of rights" rather than "passive recipients" (Bylander and Kydd 2008: 2326). As such, the Convention provides the basis for child protection legislation, an obligation made explicit in the requirement that participating countries:

> take all appropriate legislative, administrative, social and educational measures to protect the child from all forms of physical or mental violence, injury or abuse, neglect or negligent treatment, maltreatment or exploitation including sexual abuse while in the care of parents(s) legal guardian(s), or any other person who has the care of the child. (Article 19)

U.N. conventions are, however, extremely difficult to implement. As is the case for many socially progressive laws and policies, obstacles are plentiful and encompass complex and high-stakes issues such as disputes and tensions over sovereignty claims (that is, what is "good" for a particular country) and international responsibility (what is "good" for the world overall) (Weiss 2016). The same kinds of problems beset policies aimed at the protection of animals and habitats.

International agreements also exist in relation to the certain aspects of the protection of animals and their habitats. These include the United Nations Convention on International Trade in Endangered Species of Wild Fauna and Flora, the Convention on Migratory Species and the Convention on Biological Diversity. Nonetheless, there is currently no overarching, global or intergovernmental agreement concerning animal welfare more broadly. Since 2000, organizations including the World Society for the Protection of Animals and the International Fund for Animal Welfare have been petitioning the United Nations to put "animal welfare on the global political agenda" by adopting a Universal Declaration on Animal Welfare (IFAW 2016).

Legislative Responses

Legal provisions that relate either explicitly or indirectly to abuse and violence are multiple and serve a diverse range of purposes and interests. *Constitutional law*, for instance, encompasses the protection of human rights and related frameworks for reporting, investigating and responding to these. It is likely to include legislation outlining the country's responsibilities in relation to international/U.N. conventions as well as specific acts regarding various forms of discrimination. For example, in Australia, the Human Rights Commission administers the Australian Human Rights Commission Act 1986 and also has statutory responsibilities in relation to the Age Discrimination Act 2004, Disability Discrimination Act 1992, Racial Discrimination Act 1975 and Sex Discrimination Act 1984.

Criminal law may include both federal (or country-wide) and state/territory/ provincial laws in relation to acts of violence designated as a crime. As indicated in earlier chapters, violences deemed criminal vary greatly over time and context. Considerable variation also exists in relation to the ways in which legal definitions are interpreted and applied. As such, criminal law is only ever likely to capture a small proportion of violence, a recognition that is critical to interpreting crime data and statistics. Criminal law also tends to focus on physical forms of violence and this is reflected in the emphasis placed on evidence, witnesses and so on in court proceedings. Non-physical violence is, however, legally recognized as a crime in some countries. The U.K. government, for example, has recently introduced a new offence, the "offence of coercive or controlling behaviour in intimate or familial relationships" (under section 76 of the Serious Crime Act (2015)), which explicitly recognizes the cumulative impact of controlling behaviours that "stop short of serious physical violence but amount to extreme psychological and emotional abuse" (Home Office 2015). The inclusion of emotional abuse and other coercive behaviours in legal definitions of domestic violence represents a significant shift in policy making, however, the practical implications of policing, let alone prosecuting this are likely to be substantial.

Civil law concerns the rights and responsibilities that people have towards each other. Unlike criminal law, it is not enforced by the police but rather is initiated directly by individuals through the court system; a person might sue another person for damages in relation to, for example, negligence, defamation and so on. Intervention orders — or restraining/protection orders — also generally fall under civil law although criminal penalties may apply if the order is breached.

Family law is generally made and administered at the federal level via the family court and deals with issues that may arise following the breakdown of a relationship, including the care of children. While family courts, generally, will not have a direct role in relation to domestic and family violence, this must be considered by the court in deciding upon the residential arrangements and ongoing care of children. In this sense, family law plays a major role in either maintaining silences about or clearly acknowledging abuse experienced within family relationships.

LAW, VIOLENCE AND PROTECTING THE VULNERABLE

We tend to think of the law as our chief defence against abuse and violence; as working in our interest to keep us safe, protect us from disorder and so on. It is important though that we think critically about the "we," the "us," and the "them." In other words, the boundaries we draw between us/them shape the violences we see (and do not see), and the voices that we hear. Recognizing that the experience of violence is inevitably subjective is not to deny the objective reality of violence, but rather underlines the importance of context and standpoint.

As we explored in the opening chapters, being anti-oppressive implies a commitment to thinking, feeling, reflecting and exploring social problems in different ways, resisting the temptation to get caught up in busily "doing" in accordance with current conventions. This applies equally to appreciating the use of laws and social policies to address the problems of violence and abuse. For all the legal advances being made around the world with respect to criminal violence and abuse, it would be naïve to think that laws only protect the vulnerable. Rather, laws themselves can be violent:

> the relationship between law and violence is a long and tightly interwoven one. Violence has played fundamental and symbolic functions in the development of contemporary law. Violence has been employed to establish new laws and social orders as well as preserve existing laws and social orders. (Curry 2008: 1134)

That violence is done in the name of the law makes this neither reasonable nor ethically justifiable. Indeed, the grounds for abuse and violence should never be beyond question, as the only option or necessary for a "greater good." Essentialist ideas about difference on the basis of race, ethnicity, culture, sexuality and so on must also be resisted; it's a small step from believing that certain people are fundamentally different to accepting violence against those people as just. Numerous examples of legally endorsed violence exist; clearly the issues are incredibly complex and defy simple solutions, nonetheless a commitment to AOP requires that we critically reflect on the ways in which violences are both used and justified.

The introduction of any legislation (purportedly) concerned with the protection of vulnerable groups has instant appeal; what possible objection could there be to stepping in, taking responsibility and doing what is (morally) right and proper? Protectionist legislation allows the rights of target groups to be overridden "for their own good," on the basis that that group itself is incapable of exercising these in a responsible manner; in short, that the government knows best. Australia is not the only country with a history of this, however, the continuing story of Aboriginal and Torres Strait Islanders (AATSI) — presented next — provides an especially vivid case study. Following this we look at some other areas of law that have an orientation towards protecting the vulnerable, including children and disabled persons, yet enable direct and indirect forms of violence.

Whose National Emergency?

As a colonized country, Australia, like Canada and New Zealand, has its origins in the "dispossession and removal of Aboriginal people from their lands, their violent elimination, and the denial of their political rights" (Stokes 1997: 158). This is not only historical. The impacts of historical events negatively accumulate and ripple through the generations of Indigenous peoples, and current policies are often leveraged through colonial attitudes and practices. The Northern Territory National Emergency Response Act 2007 (NTER) is a good example of this.

The Northern Territory (NT) is the third largest but least populated of Australia's eight states and territories. AATSI people comprise 30 percent of the total NT population, this being the highest proportion of any state or territory (ABS 2013b), many living with multiple disadvantages, in poorly serviced, underfunded remote communities. In 2006 the NT government responded to allegations of serious sexual abuse of children in Aboriginal communities by establishing an inquiry, the NT Board of Inquiry into the Protection of Aboriginal Children from Sexual Abuse. Following the release of the Little Children are Sacred Report in 2007, the response of Australia's federal government response came quickly:

> In response to the national emergency confronting the welfare of Aboriginal children in the Northern Territory, the Australian Government today announced immediate, broad ranging measures to stabilise and protect communities in the crisis area. (Brough 2007)

The overriding of a state or territory government by the federal government is not a common occurrence and, here, was justified on the basis of "clear evidence that the Northern Territory government was not able to protect these children adequately" (Brough 2007: 10).

The Northern Territory National Emergency Response Act was presented as the solution to sexual violence experienced by Indigenous women and children in remote Indigenous Australian communities. The Intervention, as it came to be known, incorporated a broad range of intrusive measures, the more notable of which included a strong policing and military presence (the Emergency Taskforce

Operational Group), the banning of all alcohol and pornography, compulsory income management, the physical examination of all AATSI children, the abolition of the NT Aboriginal Land Rights Act, compulsory acquisition (by government) of land/township leases and controlled tenancy arrangements, the imposition of external controls on Indigenous organizations and appointment of government business managers with absolute powers. Significantly, the intervention was declared exempt from the Racial Discrimination Act 1975, enabling the federal government to specifically target AATSI people; they did this by arguing that "special" or "race-specific" measures were warranted and for the "benefit of Aboriginal people."

The NT Intervention was initiated as a necessary response to the so-called national emergency of violence in Aboriginal remote communities. The NT National Emergency Response Act, however, included no specific measures to address child abuse, indeed "child abuse" is not mentioned in the legislation. Funding accompanying the implementation of the Act was directed towards the costs associated with enforcement, administration, monitoring and management. Notably, measures such as income management were geographically targeted — that is, compulsory for all those individuals receiving welfare payments regardless of their circumstances and whether or not they had care of children. There was no funding or other provision for child- or family-focused programs and services, however, or schools, teachers, classrooms and so on.

Rather than it being seen as good policy badly implemented, critics point out that the control and regulation of Indigenous peoples was always the intention of the NTER. The Little Children are Sacred Report was the ostensible trigger for the government action. It is a lengthy and detailed document (320 pages) and included ninety-seven recommendations. It has been argued that the report was used "as a shield to force the imposition of an existing federal government agenda" (Brown and Brown 2007: 622). While it might be expected that there be strong connections between the actions recommended and the subsequent legislation, this was not the case here:

> There's not a single action that the Commonwealth has taken so far that … corresponds with a single recommendation. There is no relationship between these emergency powers and what's in [the] report. (Siewert, Parliamentary Debates, cited in Senate Hansard 2007: 42)

Protecting the vulnerable, framed here as saving the children, enables the imposition of controls that, otherwise, would be seen by most as unacceptably intrusive. In this sense, protectionist rhetoric can function as a "moral imperative that hides unstated, untested, but very evident ideological motivations far removed from concerns of child welfare" (Altman 2007: 2). This is further evident as we track the progress of the NT National Emergency Response Act. Following a change of (federal) government, a review board (the NT Emergency Response Review Board) was established to undertake an independent review of the Act. In the report, released in October 2008, the Board made a number of strong criticisms, noting that the "design and implementation of the NTER were not based on a consideration of current evidence about what works in Indigenous communities" (Commonwealth of Australia 2008: 34) and had failed to "engage constructively with the Aboriginal people it was intended to help" (9). It recommended that the "blanket application of compulsory income management in the NT cease." Most damning, however, was that they found no evidence that the intervention had produced any improvement in child safety. The NTER was further criticized by the United Nations Special Rapporteur on the situation of human rights and fundamental freedoms of Indigenous peoples, who noted that, in its current form, it is "incompatible with Australia's human rights obligations" (Anaya 2010: 2). The government nonetheless maintained its position, as follows:

> The Government believes that income management should continue because it is doing a good job. It is helping children, making families more financially secure and improving community safety by diverting money away from alcohol and gambling. (Commonwealth of Australia 2009: 11)

The Northern Territory National Emergency Response Act expired in 2012 but was extended until 2022 under the new name of the Stronger Futures in the Northern Territory Act. The actions described here, undertaken in the name of the "sacredness" of children, illustrate the ways in which government intervention can represent a sledgehammer approach to issues that are multilayered and complex and, as such perpetuate violence both structurally (in the assumptions made about people and problems) and directly through the coercive actions of policing and enforcement.

In the Best Interests of the Child

Interventions undertaken in the best interests of children have a long history. Those involving the forced removal of children from their families are perhaps the most obviously violent, both in the sense that abuse and violence might constitute the grounds for this and the act of removal is, in itself, likely to be experienced as violence. As observed by Carson and Kerr (2014: 253), *child protection* is a "contested concept," both with respect to what children need protecting from and what constitutes protection. Child protection policies enable the imposition of society's dominant values and assumptions about "childrearing and family life" (257). This is to say that ideas about child abuse and poor parenting are, largely, historically, socially and culturally specific. Child protection legislation, policy and practices can be seen as both implicitly and directly coercive, legitimizing the intrusiveness of monitoring, surveillance and intervention that impacts most heavily on the disadvantaged in society.

Over the course of the twentieth century in Australia, at least 500,000 children were placed in care outside of their family home. In accordance with the policies of the time, children were placed in care — an orphanage, home or institution — for many reasons:

> including being orphaned; being born to a single mother; family disloca-
> tion from domestic violence, divorce or separation; family poverty and
> parents' inability to cope with their children often as a result of some form
> of crisis or hardship. (Commonwealth of Australia 2004: xv)

Many of the care environments experienced by these forgotten children were "emotionally and physically punitive"; children were "subjected to criminal assaults and had no emotional relationships with any adults or personal interaction with significant people in their lives" (Commonwealth of Australia 2004: 17). Child protection practices, specifically the forced removal of children from their families within the context of assimilation policies, have been targeted at specific groups. Up until the 1960s, for example, the children of Indigenous peoples in Australia (the Stolen Generation), Canada (the Sixties Scoop) and the U.S. have been removed and placed in institutional care or adopted by white families in accordance with an "assimilationist colonial model that assumed Aboriginal people were culturally inferior and unable to adequately provide for the needs of the children" (Sinclair 2007: 67). Child removal has also been justified on other political and economic grounds such as China's one-child policy, which has resulted in the forced adoption of at least 80,000 Chinese babies, mostly to North American families, since the early 1990s.

Child Migration

Records indicate that practices of child removal date back to the 1600s with the transportation of British children — with or without parental consent — to the colonies. Euphemistically referred to as child migration, it is estimated that between six thousand and ten thousand child migrants came to Australia throughout the twentieth century. This is substantially less than the (approximately) 100,000 children who were sent to Canada over the period 1869–1935 (Commonwealth of Australia 2001). Within the context of British imperialism, sending children to commonwealth countries including Australia, Canada, New Zealand and Southern

Rhodesia (now Zimbabwe), was central to colonization, providing farm labour and populating the "colonies with good British stock" (Coldrey 1999), as vividly captured in this quotation from the Archbishop of Perth in 1938:

> At a time when empty cradles are contributing woefully to empty spaces, it is necessary to look for external sources of supply. And if we do not supply from our own stock we are leaving ourselves all the more exposed to the menace of the teeming millions of our neighbouring Asiatic races. (Child Migrants Trust 2017)

The stated motivation for taking children to other countries — and Australia in particular — over the mid- to late 1900s included removing them from the danger associated with World War II and the threat of invasion (1940s), strengthening immigration (late 1940s–50s) and providing deprived children, sometimes orphans, with a better life (1950s). Church-based and philanthropic organizations played a substantial role in implementing policy, including the provision of institutional care in Australia. For many children, the experience of institutional care was brutal: "abuse and assault, both physical and sexual, was a daily occurrence and … hardship, hard work and indifferent care was the norm" (Commonwealth of Australia 2001: 7). A Senate Inquiry into Child Migration, released in 2001, concluded that although the policy of child migration "reflected the values of the time and was well-intentioned," it is now recognized as "seriously flawed" with "obvious serious and long-lasting deleterious impacts on the lives of many former child migrants" (Commonwealth of Australia 2001: 41).

Protecting the Disabled

The term "forced sterilization" refers to the practice of sterilization after a person has "expressly refus[ed] the procedure, without her [or his] knowledge or is not given an opportunity to provide consent" (Human Rights Watch 2011). This may consist of surgical intervention such as a hysterectomy or vasectomy, or hormone treatment such as the implantation of contraceptive devices. The forced sterilization of people with a disability occurs, with or without legislative backing, across the world. It is often justified on the basis that ending menstruation and taking away fertility will provide "greater quality of life and dignity for disabled individuals" and that "pregnancy, childbirth and childrearing are beyond their intellectual grasp" (Bufkin 2015).

The U.N. special rapporteur on torture identified forced or "non-therapeutic" sterilization as constituting "torture or cruel or inhuman treatment." As explained by Sifris (2010), this expands customary understandings of torture to recognize those forms that are uniquely gender specific. Forced sterilization also contravenes the

U.N. Convention on the Rights of Persons with Disabilities and U.N. Convention on the Rights of the Child and, according to the United Nations Special Rapporteur on violence against women, "violates a woman's physical integrity and security and constitutes violence against women." Unlike most other Western countries — and despite criticism from the United Nations — Australia has no laws to prohibit the forced sterilization of women with disabilities (Frohmader 2013); instead it is left to the courts to decide whether it is in the "best interest" of an individual to undergo such a procedure.

SOCIAL POLICY

Social policy is centrally concerned with the social life and welfare of citizens and, as such, is closely linked with social change. While definitions vary, social policy can be understood as encompassing the range of "systematic public interventions relating to social needs and problems" (Fawcett et al. 2010: 7), most commonly in the form of government action and, critically, inaction. Social policy is generally distinguished from public policy on the basis that it relates to welfare and quality-of-life issues rather than higher-level national interests such as monetary and taxation policies, immigration, employment and industrial relations. In reality, though, the distinction between these is far from clear and, arguably, not particularly useful in terms of people's everyday lives and the issues they face.

Human services organizations and workers play a central role in social policy: "human services are produced by social policy and are key players in the production of social policy" (Fawcett et al. 2010: 20). Social policy provides the context within which organizations exist and, to a large extent, determines how they operate. Human service agencies also influence policy in a range of ways, both overt and covert, most notably in shaping representations of the nature and scale of problems through data gathering and classification, outcome recording and so on. Crucial to an AOP perspective is the recognition that workers in the human services can and do "change policy as they implement it" (Carson and Kerr 2014: 83), for example, through the use of discretion. While this implies the potential for bias and inequity in service provision, it also highlights the ways in which workers can take action to minimise the impact of oppressive policies on vulnerable people. The "role of local resistance in shaping policy bottom-up" (Ayres and Marsh 2013: 655) is critical to AOP; in other words, passion — for social justice, for AOP principles — really does matter. We must all "bear responsibility for structural justice" because each one of us, through our actions and inactions, contributes "to the processes that produce unjust outcomes" (Young 2011: 103).

Policy Making

Social policy is the outcome of "political processes in which interpretations of problems and their solutions are made and resisted" (Morley, Macfarlane and Ablett 2014: 65). The ways in which problems are interpreted invariably reflect particular assumptions about human nature and society. In this sense, what ultimately becomes policy represents, at best, a "compromise resulting from contest and debates between groups" (Dalton et al. 1996: 15). The purpose and process of social policy can be understood differently depending on one's perspective. Policy making may, for example, be seen as a sequential or linear process through which rational solutions are applied to objective problems. Such perspectives tend to assume the existence of a "socially and politically stable system" (Carson and Kerr 2014: 77) in which there is wide agreement on issues of concern, as well as broader consensus regarding important questions, such as the nature of society and the role of government.

Taking an AOP perspective, we must dig beneath these assumptions in order to understand the ways in which the needs and rights of the oppressed continue to be overlooked. We know that, in practice, rationality is rare in policy making, that "information is often incomplete. People disagree over objectives. Parameters shift" and social problems are not "clear, separate and stable" (Bridgman and Davis 2004: 40). Social policy exists within a social and political context and issues of power are inherent. There will always be a range of interests and agendas regarding, both, the issues that constitute social problems and the appropriate solutions. The significance of pragmatic concerns such as budgets, time frames, organizational structure and decision-making processes and so on, should not be underestimated, nor the growing bias towards "policy impacts that are tangible and certain" (Carson and Kerr 2014: 77).

The establishment of inquiries, committees and advisory groups is increasingly recognized as an important means for ensuring wider participation and representation in policy, in response to "demands for greater participation in public decisions" (Fawcett et al. 2010:. 33). Critics point out, however, that this "contracting out of policy advice" (Hazlehurst 2001: 13) enables governments to maintain control while seeming to encourage participation. The membership of such committees, for example, may be carefully orchestrated, with the selective appointment of particular experts and interest groups ensuring that the advice provided is that which the government "symbolically wanted" (Prasser 1994, cited in Hazlehurst 2001: 15). Even committees or inquiries that might be considered truly impartial may still be limited in their ability to create change due to narrow/limited terms of reference, unreasonable deadlines, lack of resources and so on. Should the findings, despite all of this, turn out to be politically unpalatable, strategies to effectively neutralize their influence can include criticizing and/or discrediting the people involved, recommending further investigations and/or failing to release the report/findings. In Australia, use of the former strategy was illustrated vividly in the federal government's reaction to the 2015 Australian Human Rights Commission (AHRC) report, as summarised here by Human Rights Watch (2016):

> An AHRC report into conditions in Australian mainland immigration detention centres and facilities on Christmas Island in February found that mandatory and prolonged detention had profoundly negative impacts on the mental and emotional health and development of children. More than 300 children committed or threatened self-harm in a 15-month period in Australian immigration detention, and 30 reported sexual assault.
>
> Following the report's release, senior government officials made personal and unsubstantiated attacks on the credibility and integrity of the president of the AHRC, Professor Gillian Triggs, including calling for her resignation. The chairman of the International Coordinating Committee, the U.N. body responsible for accrediting national human rights institutions, described these attacks as intimidating and undermining the independence of the AHRC.
>
> In March, the U.N. special rapporteur on torture, Juan Mendez, concluded that by failing to provide adequate detention conditions, end the practice of detaining children, and put a stop to escalating violence in processing centres, Australia was in violation of the Convention against Torture. Former Prime Minister Tony Abbott responded by stating that Australia was "sick of being lectured" by the U.N.
>
> In September, the U.N. special rapporteur on the human rights of migrants postponed a visit to Australia due to the "lack of full cooperation from the government regarding protection concerns and access to detention centres."

In Chapter 2 we introduced the idea of problematization and the need to think more critically about the ways in which certain phenomena become or are constructed as contemporary social problems. As AOP students and workers, we need to keep questioning why certain violences, and not others, are problematized — why public and social policies target some forms and not others. Recognizing that different policy approaches reflect different perspectives on and/or explanations for violence enables us to see policy as, to a large extent, ideological: value-laden, firmly grounded in gendered, raced and classed assumptions, always and inevitably political. The adoption of particular definitions, terminology and categories significantly shapes the structure and content of social policy. Policy responses to problem violence are based upon certain understandings of violence, both in relation to the nature of violence and the circumstances in which this is seen as constituting a problem that is worthy of state intervention.

Policy Approaches: Violence as a Public Health Issue

Violence is commonly framed as a public health issue on the basis that it "causes a large number of injuries, disabilities, and deaths" (Powell et al. 2008: 1806) and is preventable. At first glance, public health models have much to offer AOP, especially considering their focus on evidence, collaboration, and the prevention of harm, disease and injury. A key criticism of neoliberal public health models, though, is their tendency to shift responsibility for social problems from the state to individuals and communities, thereby "privileging the collective well-being of society over the interests of individuals and groups, and in practice neglecting the collective and institutional factors shaping health" (Flood 2015: 6). It has also been noted that preventive approaches tend to prioritize the amelioration of "adverse effects" over a comprehensive or in-depth understanding of an issue (Powell et al. 2008: 1807). Dominant public health approaches, then, are likely to consider abuse and violence more narrowly as "contributor[s] to poor health" and "morbidity and mortality," rather than as matters of "social injustice" (Flood 2015: 6). The pursuit of social justice via broader social changes to the ways in which we think about people is, however, fundamental to AOP.

According to Broom (2008: 130), preventive approaches to health are commonly associated with a "distinctive neo-liberal political economy," incorporating a focus on the individual and emphasis on evidence and quantifiable risk. Ill health and disease are largely understood as the sum of individual behaviours resulting from poor lifestyle choices. Importantly, positioning "lifestyle" as a key determinant of health focuses attention on individual responsibility and self-regulation rather than the longer term and more intractable realm of the social — the ways in which societal arrangements create and perpetuate inequalities. Social factors are understood through this prism of individual behaviours; accordingly, the capacity to respond to the environment by making the right (healthy) choices and so on is a primary aim of public health programs (Bacchi 2009). From this perspective, awareness-raising is pursued as a mean of informing individual choice. The implication of framing health as the sum-total of individual decisions and actions, however, is that "unhealthy" individuals are seen as having put themselves at risk, so are personally responsible for their ill health (see Robertson 2007). Good health is thereby framed as the "duty or obligation" of individuals (Scott 2003: 289) and linked to the greater good of protecting the "vitality and integrity of the population" (279).

The concept of "risk" is central to dominant public health approaches to violence and abuse, with their emphasis on the economic costs of violence and associated burden on the nation's economy. Risk, here, is narrowly defined, though, with an emphasis on individual deficits and as a means of distinguishing between healthy (responsible, motivated, self-regulating) and unhealthy or at-risk (irresponsible, wilful, imprudent) individuals (see Kemshall 2003). In this context, violence is reduced to certain "attitudes, values and beliefs" (Lohan 2007: 498) and violence prevention a matter of managing risk factors and risk(y) individuals/groups. The focus of policy then is the stimulation of individual behaviour change and the identification of risky groups so that their riskiness can be managed (Williams et al. 2009; Bacchi 2009). In AOP we are not just concerned with changes at the individual level, or narrower still, the individual behavioural level. Nonetheless, through this lens, violence becomes a problem of and for certain individuals and groups rather than integral to the structures of society that ensure the privileges of some are built upon the disadvantages of many.

As highlighted in the discussion of child migration earlier in this chapter, the recognition of violence against children as a significant public health issue is relatively recent. The contemporary focus on familial and institutional sexual abuse, child prostitution, child pornography and exploitative child labour, for example, has not always been an issue of public concern. Currently, however, attention is primarily directed towards the ways in which "children are at a particular risk of being victimized by violence" (Bylander and Kydd 2008: 2323). Important though this is, focusing on children as passive victims obscures the broader contexts of violence: of "child exposure to armed conflict, preventable poverty, environmental trauma, exploitation, homelessness, and other deprivation" (2323). In other words, acknowledging structural violence is fundamental to understanding children's "experiences of and reactions to violence," including those in which children have a more active role. As both a society and a global community, we continue to exhibit:

> greater tolerance for economic violence (e.g., child poverty, homelessness, and absence of affordable healthcare or daycare), community violence (e.g., unsafe physical and mass media environments), and developmental violence (i.e., failure to provide each child the necessary nutrition, love, care, education, culture, and play to realize their developmental capacity). (Bylander and Kydd 2008: 2319)

Evidence Based?
Preventive approaches are said to be evidence based, that is, derived from scientific (positivist) approaches and characterized by "narrow standards of evidence," but represented as knowledge that is authoritative and value free (Flood 2015:

6). The assumption that it is possible to scientifically know, predict and quantify human and social behaviour lies at the core of preventive/public health models, as exemplified in the dominance of actuarial approaches via the identification, targeting and management of risk. Actuarial techniques use mathematics and statistics to assess risk by placing "people into categories and estimat[ing] the riskiness of these groups rather than looking at individuals as unique cases" (Bull 2010: 56). *Risk factors* are those factors that increase the likelihood of a negative event — such as disease, an injury, death, crime, violence and so on — occurring and include things like individual traits, family and peer networks, employment and so on. From this perspective, policy problems are understood as objectively real, existing outside of any social and cultural context and manageable through the application of evidential knowledge. Such approaches may be contrary to the spirit and principles of AOP should the knowledge upon which they are based be assumed as impartial and apolitical.

Recognizing that social problems emerge through "shifts in understandings" (Fawcett et al. 2010: 26) is critical to countering apolitical, individually oriented perspectives. This directs our attention towards "definitional practices" and the ways in which "certain phenomena and/or issues in society come to be defined and understood as problematic by some portion of the citizenry" (25). For instance, to say that domestic violence was discovered as a social problem in the 1970s does not mean that violence did not happen prior to this. Rather, it is to recognize that it was not until then that it was named and politicized as a systemic, not merely individual, issue of public, and not just private, concern (see Powell and Murray 2008).

Thinking critically about what is seen to count as evidence is important for an AOP perspective. An emphasis on "counting, efficiency and effectiveness" (Bacchi 2008: 171) as the basis of valid evidence, for example, equates to a reliance on certain bodies of knowledge and impacts, in turn, on the commissioning and funding of research, the questions asked and so on. *Evidence-based policy*, as it is commonly understood, does not represent all available evidence. Instead, particular forms are credited as authoritative, actively chosen, drawn from certain disciplines and seen as "fit for purpose," that is, consistent with a neoliberal emphasis on individual — not structural — factors.

AOP practice respects and facilitates diverse forms of evidence and sources of knowledge. We do not, as most public health and preventive models do, treat gender as a variable nor reduce it to "specific biological characteristics" (Doyal 2000: 934). Oversimplifying gender in this way, as discussed in Chapter 5, is problematic in a number of respects, most notably because there is no one "reality of 'maleness' and 'femaleness,'" (Doyal 2000: 954), nor is it possible to understand sex/gender as factors that operate in isolation. An AOP perspective recognizes that there are no easy answers or simple solutions. No matter how tempting quick fixes might seem, we recognize the significance of social structures, social inequality and, in particular, the power relations inherent within diverse masculinities and femininities.

Violence Prevention

Violence prevention, often referred to as primary prevention, refers to efforts directed at stopping violence before it occurs in order to reduce its prevalence (see United Nations Women 2012b). Violence prevention often focuses on young people in the belief that early education can change attitudes and behaviours productive of violence. Population-wide campaigns aim to raise awareness across age brackets of domestic violence through, for example, television advertisements linking it to sexist beliefs and attitudes. A recent Australian campaign, "Stop it before it starts," is a good example, targeting "so-called influencers, such as mums, dads, teachers and coaches, who unwittingly excuse disrespectful behaviour by young people" (Norman 2016). While it is widely agreed that "violence-supportive and sexist attitudes" (Flood 2015: 5) are a significant determinant of men's violence against women, the reality, or applying this to practice, as discussed next, is considerably more complex than this.

Approaches to violence prevention commonly emphasize direct violences and overlook structural and cultural forms of violence. For instance, prevention programs have conventionally been conceptualized within a disease framework such that the behaviour — in this case, violence — is constructed as "amenable to diagnosis, prescription and cure" (Miller and Rose 2008: 211). Violence prevention policies — as seen in Australia, the U.K., Canada and the U.S. — have tended to represent violence as akin to a disease that must be prevented and "managed as a threat to public health" (Bumiller 2008: 79). This plays out in a range of ways. The need to protect children from the damaging effects of exposure to violence, for example, invokes ideas about generational "contagion." Symptoms of disease become early indicators of violence, requiring early intervention and attention to risk factors and protective factors. As a policy problem, domestic violence is framed as preventable — in much the same way as other problems such as drunk driving and smoking — through the application of expert knowledge and intervention to influence individual choices.

AOP students and workers should be alert to the problems associated with equating social problems with disease. Such approaches not only pathologize — and thereby, depoliticize — but also misrepresent the complexities of human experience. In "turning the marks of violence into symptoms of a disease" (Bumiller 2008: 79), violence prevention policies commonly address "all women as potential victims" (80) while targeting only certain groups or types of boys/men as posing a risk of violence. Violent men are positioned as either rational individuals who "choose" violence (who can choose *not* to use violence), or inherently bad (violent men as distinct from "normal" men). From here, policies are likely to incorporate both awareness and behaviour change strategies for perpetrators (and often victims) and criminal justice pathways to monitor, manage and/or punish those violent perpetrators marked as bad. Violence perpetrated by more privileged groups, such as white, middle-class, heterosexual male professionals, for example, is more likely to be presented as "out of character" and the perpetrator as "low risk." Racialized working-class men, however, are more likely to be categorized as violent men who require punishment and/or treatment to change their attitudes and behaviour. As AOP workers, we must be careful to avoid falling into this trap.

Other problems ensue from the expectation that we are ever-strategic, that we deliver value for money and so on. For instance, under neoliberal governance violence prevention is often talked about in the context of "investments in public health," with the pitch that education provides the "best start in life" and is the "solution to disadvantage" (Bacchi 2009: 206). Representing violence as a problem related to ignorance or lack of education opens the door to educational solutions that equip us to become "experts" of ourselves by promoting an "educated and knowledgeable relation of self-care" with respect to our bodies, minds and conduct (Miller and Rose 2008: 215). Not only does this shift attention away from the "deep structural asymmetries of power" (Bacchi 2009: 207) that shape society, but it also, by suggesting a linear and straightforward process, it misrepresents the complex nature of behaviour change.

The link between attitudes and behaviour is complex and contextual. Attitudes do not necessarily determine behaviour as "people might say one thing and do another," nor is human behaviour always "reasoned or planned" (Pease and Flood 2008: 552). Available research shows that attitudes are, in fact, "very poor predictors of actual behaviour" (Ajzen and Fishbein 2005, cited in Pease and Flood 2008: 552), thus, attitudinal change will not necessarily result in behavioural change. In practice, these approaches often default to an emphasis on improving communication and interpersonal relationships, unhelpfully reinforcing the idea of violence as individually chosen and used without socio-structural context.

As observed by VicHealth (2014: 230) in their report on the findings from Australia's 2013 National Community Attitudes Towards Violence Against Women survey:

> While attitudes play an influential part in the problem of violence against women, they are among a myriad of factors. Moreover, attitudes are a product of cultural and structural influences, as is whether they are ultimately manifest in behaviour. This suggests while strategies targeted to individuals to strengthen their attitudes are valuable, an effective prevention approach will need to also address the community, organisational

and societal-level determinants of attitudes, and of violence against women itself.

Prevention, whether this seeks to address survivors and/or perpetrators, is "a joke when it isn't backed up by serious and systematic responses to violence" (Greenberg and Messner 2014: 246).

Policy Responses

Policy responses are widely understood as falling within the category of secondary prevention, strategies aiming to minimize the immediate harm of violence once it has occurred and prevent re-victimization, and tertiary prevention including longer term treatment and rehabilitative services for victims and perpetrators. Examples of both are considered here. It is important to state at the outset, though, that the policy responses discussed reflect a narrow vision of violence as perpetrated by men against women. While this reflects current policy directions and practice, readers are encouraged to maintain a critical perspective, keeping in the mind the range of issues discussed throughout the book, especially Chapter 5.

Victims of Violence

Policy responses encompass the crisis, short- and long-term needs of victims, as well as the early identification of violence. Systems to facilitate early identification and intervention can include those associated with mandatory notification of child abuse, as well as screening assessments administered within the health system through antenatal, maternal and child health services. Ensuring that a broad range of services are available for victims is fundamental. These include health care/ medical treatment, including that in relation to sexual and reproductive health, financial and/or housing support, ongoing counselling/therapeutic intervention and access to the police and criminal justice system. Income support provisions and other forms of material aid are practical measures that are pivotal to anti-oppressive practice. The importance of an integrated, multi-agency approach is also widely agreed upon and should address both immediate safety needs and planning for the short- to medium-term future with due regard for the victims' own priorities, including their relationship/partner choices. Ensuring that different agencies communicate and work together is now recognized as critical to women and children's ongoing safety, as is the importance of services that are both inclusive and culturally responsive to diverse needs.

Multi-agency responses include those situated within the justice setting with a strong victim focus and emphasis on perpetrator accountability and mandatory intervention. More recently there has been a shift in emphasis towards removing perpetrators of violence from the family home rather than expecting women and children to leave/escape. Many of these initiatives are relatively new and their effectiveness is not yet clear. Inter-agency collaborations may bring together police, refuge workers, women's support workers, correctional staff, perpetrator program staff and representatives from health, child protection, legal services and other community organizations. Programs such as this, variously referred to as violence intervention programs, specialist family violence courts, DV integrated responses and abuse prevention programs, are now relatively common in Australia, Canada, the U.S., the U.K. and New Zealand.

Failure-to-protect policies are intended to better ensure the safety and protection of children, however, in practice may actually increase danger for children and their mothers. While failure to protect is not always made explicit in policy documents, the focus on holding mothers, rather than male perpetrators, responsible for violence in the home is common practice. Most often it is marginalized and already oppressed women that are targeted on the basis that they are unable or unwilling to protect their children, notwithstanding the factors — such as poverty, racism, intimate partner violence and inadequate housing — that are well beyond their control. Throughout this book, we cite a range of writers from Canada, the U.S., the U.K. and Australia, all of whom highlight the ways in which the concept of failure to protect differentially impacts on people by virtue of their gender, race and class positions. The issues explored in Chapters 5 and 6 in this book also illustrate just how ineffective failure-to-protect policies can be at keeping women and children safe.

There is a pressing need for new policy initiatives and practice approaches that are grounded in social justice and genuinely fulfill the mandate of protecting children. The challenges are many and varied, especially given the recent ascendancy of radical conservatism both within and beyond the U.S. and U.K. Yet, this context only heightens the imperative to talk and think about policy alternatives. A first step is to open up discussions about the nature and meaning of protection and to ask questions about the appropriate responsibility and responses to safety failures. It is especially critical that responsibility for those who are most vulnerable does not fall onto those with the least status and resources.

Other policy responses aimed broadly at actual or potential victims of violence include those with a focus on risk reduction. *Risk reduction* in this context refers to both making public spaces safer through better lighting and so on, and strategies that are claimed to make individuals less likely to experience violence or be victimized. Programs might cover self-defence techniques as well as advice for staying safe, including avoiding poorly lit places and public transport at night, watching your drink, situational awareness and so on — in other words, not making oneself vulnerable to attack. Many colleges and universities, for example, hold annual information sessions such as this for female students who will be residing on campus. Approaches such as these emphasize individual responsibility to keep safe and address all women as potential victims while positioning all men as, at least potentially, dangerous. They also obscure the reality that girls and women are most unsafe in their own homes and/or with people that they know. Ironically, while it is boys and men who are most at risk of violence in public places, rarely are such safety programs directed at them.

Perpetrators of Violence

As we have suggested policy responses regarding violence are often disjointed. Generic mentions of violence in policy and related documentation commonly refer to men's violence against women and children (family violence and/or domestic violence). Violence, between men for example, is otherwise seen as a criminal justice issue or, more rarely, is referred to in the context of combat/war and defence. In practice this means that policy responses to violence are generally not grouped together or the responsibility of any one minister or area of government.

Policies are not just written documents, rather policies shape both programs in action and service integration across all fields of health, welfare and education. In their 2007 review of violence-related policies, Junger and colleagues (2007: 327) observed "surprisingly similar" trends across seven countries: Australia, Canada, Germany, the Netherlands, Spain, the U.K. and the U.S. These included the lack of a "coordinated policy approach" and a strong media interest in violence associated with "management by crisis with the result that policies are not based on evidence, but instead seek to appease public outrage" (Junger et al. 2007: 328).

When it comes to policy making and the programs that this enables, it matters who uses violence, against whom, where and in what circumstances. The tendency to separate public and private violences, for example, as in the distinction drawn between violence against women and children and other forms of violence, including criminal violence, implies that there is no connection between the two. Policy responses are also highly contextual, as evident in the complex rules and interpretations regarding what constitutes the acceptable use of violence in sport. Similarly, in a military context, the rules of engagement outline the terms for appropriate use of force in combat situations. From an AOP perspective, this raises difficult questions regarding which violences are — and are not — deemed problematic, as well as who is deemed worthy of or in need of protection and in what circumstances.

The correctional system is one of the few contexts in which interventions that specifically address violence — as compared (or in addition) to domestic or family violence — are run. As discussed above, policies relating to (non-domestic) violent crime often frame and respond to violence as the actions of abnormal or deviant individuals who are "bad," "mad" or otherwise different to the rest of us. An emphasis on professional experts — specialist and intensive in nature — usually follows with a treatment orientation requiring the expertise of highly skilled clinicians with backgrounds in behavioural science and/or medicine. Such interventions are invariably based on mainstream psychological principles, with a strong actuarial focus and an emphasis on either/both pathology and/or cognition, emotion management, impulse control and decision making. Consistent with a neoliberal emphasis on the individual, responses to criminally designated violence usually assume a lack of capacity or an unwillingness to self-manage. In other words, violence is explained through reference to deviance and is positioned as a problem related to certain "types of people" rather than societally and structurally embedded.

Perpetrators of Violence Against Women

Policy responses regarding the perpetration of violence against women most commonly include intervention programs, protection orders and criminal/court proceedings. The purpose of civil protection orders, discussed earlier, is to protect women victims of violence from further acts or threats of violence. As such, the onus is on victims to provide evidence of prior and/or imminent abuse. Many jurisdictions, including Australia, the U.K. and the U.S., now have family/domestic violence legislation with specific provisions for police intervention, including the capacity for police to act on behalf of victims of violence in applying for protection orders — a small but significant indication of progress.

Intervention programs are used extensively throughout the world and aim to address the behaviour, attitudes and beliefs of perpetrators. Most commonly they are group based. Yet, they also "vary widely in their approach, design, content, and mode and manner of delivery" (Mackay et al. 2015: 5). For instance, perpetrator interventions in Australia include both voluntary and court-mandated programs, whereas those in the U.K. and U.S. are mostly court mandated. While there is a growing commitment to programs that are specifically relevant to men who are Indigenous and of culturally and linguistically diverse backgrounds, the majority are generic — that is, developed for an Anglo/white audience.

Currently there exists a lack of sound, high-quality evidence regarding the effectiveness of perpetrator interventions. As noted by Day (2015), overall, despite some promising but early indications, the "evidence relating to the effectiveness of perpetrator behaviour change programs remains weak" (see also Tappis et al. 2016; Eckhardt et al. 2013). In the Australian context, a recent evaluation of a small number of Australian programs found "modest but positive" results, but concluded that evaluation evidence is, on the whole, limited and that there is a pressing need for further research (Mackay et al. 2015: 6). From an AOP perspective, we recognize the difficulties associated with measuring — and even defining — effectiveness in this context. Important questions to be asked include how best to capture success, whether to use measurements and/or qualitative methods, and if so, which ones. It is also critical to acknowledge the inherent limitations of interventions that focus on interpersonal, direct forms of violence and assume a relatively straightforward link between attitudinal and behavioural change. Reports of positive changes also need to be viewed critically, most importantly with regard to whose views are sought in making such assessments. It is also worth considering the extent to which observed changes are attributable to professional interventions as compared to other circumstances and events (and how it might be possible to discern one from the other).

Despite the relative lack of definitive evidence regarding their effectiveness, perpetrator programs exist across both the government and non-government sectors. Increasingly, community organizations compete for funding to deliver these services. Programs may be voluntary or court-mandated. However, "voluntary" in this context may be both a misnomer and euphemism given the significance of other motivating circumstances (such as the threat of a relationship ending). As discussed earlier, there is a growing movement towards integrating responses to family/domestic violence, with police, community correctional services and other government and non-government agencies expected to collaborate to ensure women's and children's safety. These might be pre-sentence, that is, in the form of a court diversionary program, or an aspect of the sentence itself, as a condition of a suspended sentence bond for example. Access to domestic violence perpetrator intervention programs in custodial settings is often limited and the courts generally have no influence over program availability and access in the prison environment. While symbolically significant as an acknowledgement of criminality and censure, imprisoning domestic violence perpetrators, is, at best, a temporary solution, providing victims with little more than a short-term reprieve. At worst, it can traumatize and harden the incarcerated and exacerbate the problems of violence, especially for under-resourced and marginalized communities.

CONCLUSION

This chapter has explored a range of examples of policy approaches to abuse and violence. The importance of paying attention to the ways in which policies construct abuse and violence has been a strong focus. Social problems, as argued by Bacchi (2000: 48) are "created or given shape" in the very policy proposals that are offered as responses. Ensuring a critical focus on policy with respect to issues that make it onto the political agenda, are seen as amenable to change and so on, is fundamental to an anti-oppressive approach. As individuals committed to AOP principles, and to social justice more generally, we have an obligation to ask difficult questions concerning societal understandings of violences as a problem for some, and in some circumstances, but not others.

8. SOCIAL MOVEMENTS AND COMMUNITY RESPONSES

- How have social movements responded to systemic forms of violence and abuse?

- How can critical consciousness develop and what is accidental activism?

- Why connect with community groups and social movements campaigning against abuse and violence?

In the previous chapter, legal and criminal justice responses to violence and abuse took centre stage as we discussed law reform and criminal proceedings as important elements of the overall suite of responses needed to address violence and abuse from an AOP perspective. In this chapter we examine community responses to violence and abuse, and social movements that have coalesced around particular violence and abuse causes and campaigns. By using illustrative snapshots, our purpose is to then link the personal with the political and show how AOP workers across health, welfare and education might lend their support.

We begin by defining what we mean by "community" and "social movements" as we explain some of the many methods community groups and social movements use to draw public attention to issues. Illustrative examples are provided to inspire, but also ground our discussion of how AOP workers and students might get involved and/or support others in the pursuit of social equality, peace and non-violence. With each example we make suggestions for how AOP workers can connect with social movements and community campaigns that address and try to prevent violence and abuse. A discussion of critical consciousness and accidental activism is included and makes for an interesting exploration of how people can get involved in advocacy campaigns, sometimes unexpectedly. This is relevant to the health, welfare and education practitioners and managers who are already involved in such campaigns, but it also applies to many of our clients, patients and students who are active, or could be active, in anti-violence and abuse campaigns that include but go beyond direct violence.

COLLECTIVE STRUGGLES FOR SOCIAL JUSTICE AND NON-VIOLENCE

Throughout this book we have stressed the importance of language, especially the need to clarify operating terms and maintain awareness of the problems all concepts and terms carry from their multiple applications. Before we provide an overview of some past and present international anti-violence campaigns, we draw your attention to the concepts of communities and social movements, and provide an exploration of key elements of movements for change: expressing and regulating emotions; alliance building across divisions; using media and creative outlets to forge connections and share information through alternative networks of support; and deliberating on methods, funding and overall strategies for actions.

Conceptualizing Communities and Social Movements

Around the world, social movements or mass collectivities have advanced causes that could not have been advanced if members had been working alone (Byrne 2013). These movements have been built through communities who come together, at least for a time, to pursue issues and advance campaigns, which we define not in the military sense but as an organized pursuit of an espoused (or stated) goal, albeit through a wide range of methods, tactics and strategies.

Since they entail networks of community activity, social movements are more accurately seen as fluid and overlapping spheres of action rather than distinct and discrete organizations (Meyer and Whittier 1994). Similarly, communities need to be understood in multiple ways, taking multiple shapes, forms and processes. They can be based on (any mix) of the following: geographic communities (such as neighborhoods and regions), communities of identity (such as LGBTIQ, women and men against violence), communities of circumstance (such as those affected by particular disasters) and communities of interest (such as Indigenous rights or the farmers' lobby), most of which exist alongside, if not built by, virtual online communities (Fraser 2005).

Tarrow and Tollefson (1994: 3–4) define *social movements* as, "collective challenges by people with common purposes and solidarity in sustained interaction with elites, opponents and authorities." From this perspective, social movements can be seen to involve collective expressions of resistance (including those politely, artistically and/or musically expressed) and resistance that recognizes pain, suffering and inequality, and strives to address both the causes and effects of it. Across campaigns and fields of practice, we/they know that, "to ignore the oppressive environmental conditions that contribute to client problems is metaphorically akin to ignoring a contaminated water supply even after scores of citizens have become deathly ill" (Greenleaf and Williams 2009: 6).

However, Tarrow and Tollefson's (1994) definition fails to account for *right-wing social movements*. Founded on hierarchy, social stratification and inequality, these right-wing movements fight to keep or increase the privilege of particular groups over others who are systematically devalued. It is why Rydgren (2005) describes them as "movements of exclusion." They are a force with which to be reckoned, often garnering mass support and infiltrating formal political parties and electoral systems, as demonstrated recently through campaigns by Brexit (Britain's exit from the European Union), the Tea Party, the gun lobby and those supporting the Trump presidency.

Across national borders and political party lines, right-wing social movements share the tendency to blame the oppressed for being exploited. This *victim blaming* (see Ryan 1976) is not just the precinct of hotheaded members of right-wing movements but also reproduced through the neoliberalization (privatization and marketization) of health, welfare and educational products and services (see Fraser and Taylor 2016). "Targeting the hard to reach" has often meant more punitive responses, including strict surveillance (such as through urine testing) (see Duvnjak and Fraser 2014). The "new normal" is to offer brief crisis interventions for the very serious cases deemed most risky. Otherwise, narrowly focused services tend to be provided on a single-issue basis to individuals profiled to be more likely to help maximize success testimonials and, in turn, profits.

To maximize success and efficiencies, inviting in those on the edges of oppression is the temptation, as is the weeding out of people who have complex, chronic issues, from families that have experienced generations of such issues. Meanwhile, the poor, destitute and serially abused are often blamed and discredited as lacking in functioning, not having the capacity to solve problems, failing to be sufficiently resilient to rebound from difficulties, being unable to amass cultural capital and/or initiate wealth-creating innovations and so on. These beliefs can then be attributed to oppressed groups' assumed failures and failings, and used by even some who are well meaning, to encourage victims to self-blame.

Divisive methods are used by members of right-wing movements and those who support them, often with seemingly innocent questions and comments made to fake interest and openness in discussion. For members of these exclusionary social movements, the oppressed can be blamed for each and every part of their problems (see Mendes 1997, 2000). Oppressed, impoverished and exploited people are blamed for a range of issues, from those that are *regional*, where there are serious perils in the physical environment such as drought, floods, civil war ("Why would they live there if conditions are so terrible?"), to the attribution of poverty and isolation, to specific races/ethnicities ("Violence is in their blood"; "They don't know anything but poverty") and problems caused by religions ("Why do people insist on practicing such a violent religion?"), sexuality ("What do you expect is going to happen when people choose to live such flagrantly homosexual lifestyles?") and gender ("Fortunately the ladies here know their place. They aren't strident, childless ambitious types.").

Right-wing social movements are often unashamedly racist, sexist, Islamaphobic and/or homophobic, and routinely encourage mob violence to be carried out against women and visible minorities (see Rydgren 2005). Hate and hostility to others are primary motivations. However, these violent and abusive groups are also built from social networks formed in communities and have goals pursued through collective, purposeful actions. It explains our need to distinguish these movements from progressive, social justice movements that promote respect for diversity, social equality for all, peace and non-violence.

AOP workers take an interest in right-wing social movements, including those described as radical and extreme, because they are possible homes, ideologically speaking, for our clients, neighbors, families, friends and in some instance, among AOP workers who may be blind to some forms of bigotry (or the refusal to allow for differences from the norm). We remain mindful of right-wing arguments that gather steam and are used to collude with or incite violence against others (see Chapter 6 regarding hate crimes). As AOP workers, however, our ultimate focus is on *socially just and progressive* collective activities, because they help build communities across diversity and divisions, and can result in powerful alliances being forged (see Calhoun, Wilson and Whitmore 2014).

Emotions, Alliance Building and Non-Violence

No community is free from politics, internal and external, without difficulties. Even so, it can be a creative and deeply democratic process when people band together to get attention and pressure authorities to respond to their claims (Staggenborg 2015). While there are times when participants form loose, cordial collaborations that are more instrumental (or task focused) than affective (or emotional) in nature, there are many other times when social movements produce tight, emotional, intellectual and, for some, spiritual or religious bonds.

Writing about social movements and the transformation of emotions through mass activities, Collins (2009: 28) explains that Durkheim's notion of *collective effervescence* can occur, which has three parts: (1) The bodily awareness of co-presence through the physical assembly of people; (2) focusing attention on a shared goal; and (3) producing a collective awareness that "fus[es] cognitive and moral unity." When these ingredients are present, Collins (2009: 28) asserts that the following four sets of emotions are likely to unfold:

1. feelings of group solidarity;
2. emotional energy... [as participants] "become pumped up with enthusiasm and confidence";
3. emotional connectedness to group emblems (such as logos, banners, t-shirts and so on) used to promote issues, causes and campaigns and keep movement members engaged; and
4. feelings of morality from the collective pursuit of the "highest good" and identification of opposition, often as "unworthy, evil or inhuman."

In such morally and emotionally charged environments, as so many justice campaigns tend to be, it is not always easy to stay even-tempered, openly communicative and focused on long-term goals. Despair can evoke rage, which can then be unhelpfully turned inwards, and sap energy for participating in collective change activities (Hopkins 2013). Community groups and social movements committed to non-violence face the delicate challenge of using emotions to motivate membership and members into action, without overwhelming members to the point of paralysis or, conversely, revenge through retaliatory violence. These are issues the organizers of the recent international Women's Marches Against Trump needed to manage.

Non-violence can be a difficult stance to maintain, particularly in the face of extreme, sustained and life-threatening violence. Newly instituted radical, and what might be considered fascist, regimes — such as the Trump administration — also make the stance of non-violence difficult to maintain. Finding safe ways to allow members to feel and express intense emotions about the violence and abuse they are campaigning against is necessary and is especially important for protecting the ethics and efficacy of campaign messages and representations (see Harris and Morrison 2012). For group organizers in intense conflict situations, this can feel like walking a tightrope, balancing critical analyses of power relations and measured optimism about the possibilities for change. It may be tempting to resort to violence, but we must resist this because it is exactly this — vengeance, hate and the violation of others — that we stand against. Justifications of violence being provoked needs to be carefully inspected, including when used by activists, to ensure it is not an excuse for retaliation (see Wahlström 2011).

Peace building relies on the recognition of the interconnectedness of all parts of life, or all parts of the whole, from relationships with oneself and others, to all other interactions with other cultures and species (Harris and Morrison 2012). Whatever our role or field of practice, AOP students and workers appreciate that peace building calls for us to assess situations and respond thoughtfully, not just reacting to our most immediate thoughts and feelings (see Dickinson and Schaeffer 2015; Hopkins 2013). We know there may be times we need to temper our emotions and bite our tongues, that is, stop ourselves from speaking out, or if we do speak out, stop ourselves from always tackling the problem in the same way, with the same self-righteous indignation. At other times we may need to compel ourselves to speak out, in spite of the social disapproval to do so. Along the way we appreciate the need to recognize and value small victories, while also finding ways to enjoy the company — or collective co-presence — that advocacy and campaigning can bring (see Dickinson and Schaeffer 2015; Rostosky et al. 2015).

We take the view that to support peace is to support gun control, a position supported by empirical evidence:

> Americans might value reflection on Australia's recent experience in reducing deaths from firearms. The U.S. has 13.7 times Australia's population, 104 times its total firearm-caused deaths (32,163 in 2011 vs. 236 in 2010), and 370 times Australia's firearm homicide rate (11,101 in 2011 vs. 30 in 2010). Importantly, in the 16 years since the law reforms, there have been no mass shootings. (Chapman 2013: 5–6)

We do not accept the argument that arming more people helps protect them from future harm, or ensure their safety if future threats arise. On the contrary, violence begets violence. We do not accept, for instance, that more guns would have helped the victims of the Florida gay nightclub shooting. Add alcohol and party drugs to the mix of armed crowds taking matters into their own hands, and the results may have been even more catastrophic, opening up the possibility of people killing each other by accident or mistake. Admittedly, the challenges facing gun control advocates in the U.S. are more extensive than Australia and other countries such as Canada, Britain, New Zealand, Bangladesh and India, where gun ownership is not seen to be an emblem of freedom and national pride to the same extent that it is in the U.S.

Collaborative Practices across Differences, not Heroic Individualism

Earlier in this book we stressed the need for AOP workers to articulate the theoretical underpinnings, not just pragmatic imperatives of their work. A key goal is *praxis*, that is, the integration of theory and practice (see Glasser 2014). Describing the convergence of research and activism in the global justice movement, Bevington and Dixon (2005) urge researchers to move beyond theoretical schisms (or divisions) to prioritize the production of movement-relevant theory. Doing so means turning scholarly attention to what social movements have done and are doing, rather than being preoccupied with abstract theoretical questions.

As AOP workers we are interested in engaging others in socially progressive change. If not already members, AOP workers are likely to come into contact with members of community groups and social movements through the course of their work, such as teachers, social workers, police, doctors, nurses, physiotherapists and a host of other professionals. We appreciate the need to collaborate with others, across different identities in community groups and social movements (Calhoun, Wilson and Whitmore 2014; Mendes 1997, 2000, 2012). Active efforts to attract underrepresented sections of communities might be needed. To quote Mendes (2012: 5), "particular care should be taken to encourage and validate groups traditionally excluded such as gays and lesbians, people with disabilities, and racial or ethnic minorities."

We recognize the need for ongoing learning, no matter how experienced we are. We guard against inducements to create inner and outer circles in social movements, even minor versions of celebrities and outliers. We know that for priorities and strategies of community groups and social movements to have meaning and engender commitment, they need to reflect the broad interests of the membership-based, not just the leadership group (Mendes 1997, 2000, 2012; Meyer and Whittier 1994). While we may like and respect (or conversely dislike and/or disrespect) particular individuals in social movements, we try to disrupt any tendency to revere particular members over others, such as researchers over frontline activists, or leaders over members (see Reiter and Oslender 2015), and drop any fantasies of the heroic individual "expert" saving the day.

For the many people who live in urban, suburban and regional areas, global communications produce quick sound bites and short stories, which jostle for audience attention. Many of these stories carry the theme of *competitive individualism,* or the naturalness and rightfulness of people competing with each other for status, resources, others' affections and respect. Often these stories or narratives are of triumphant individualism, where particularly downtrodden individuals rise up from their treacherous circumstances to defeat the odds of them failing and to succeed in some way that the dominant, privileged and esteemed recognize as important (see Chapter 6). For instance, a refugee may win a gold medal at the Olympics, or a young man physically disabled from a car accident studies information technology at university and goes on to make a fortune developing a smart phone app, or the 90-year-old woman who just graduated with a PhD (see Hooper 2016). Underlying these stories of triumph is the celebrated can-do attitude with the individual winning accolades, prizes or grant money. As uplifting as these stories can be, they have a tendency of overinflating the power of individuals while disaggregating them from their support systems and denying their interconnectedness.

AOP workers are analytical of power relations. So, we know that conflicts and divisions are a possibility in community groups and social movements. As with any collection of people, social movements and community groups can be sites of thoughtless and indulgent behaviours, such as dominating temper tantrums, sulking, refusal to allow others to express dissent, all-or-nothing ultimatums, passive aggression and so on. Structurally, there can be the challenge of sustaining adequate operational resources, including time and expertise (Ife 2012; Mendes 2012). Opponents may try to pick off key members of campaigns with grant offers, personal inducements and/or the promise of minor reforms, in turn producing discord within the group or wider movement. Many other possible divisions can occur, making social movements not just possible sources of inspiration and empowerment, but also sites of control, conformity and domination (see Conway 2003). If this happens, the aim is to look for ways to bridge divisions, heal conflicts and any other efforts to prevent segments of groups and movements permanently shutting down from each other.

In all of our work, AOP workers must avoid the trap of placing efficiency over fairness. We cannot stress enough how challenging a task this is. Compared to the slick wins of brilliant individuals who forge ahead with plans unburdened by the responsibilities of consultation, collective and democratic group practices can appear cumbersome and frustrating. This can produce a cultural impatience for alternative ideas and egalitarian practices and an undemocratic, hierarchical appetite for celebrity experts. As we have already indicated earlier, respectful, open dialogue across differences poses several challenges, especially if there are vast differences in members' income, status, education, access to technology and ability to physically participate in movements. Skill, patience and self-discipline is required from AOP workers if they/we are to truly show respect for difference by, for instance, sharing airspace, being open to discussing new ways of framing old problems and allowing members to express dissent (see Dickinson and Schaeffer 2015; Ife 2012). These attitudes, aspirations and practices are crucial for social justice and anti-oppressive practice across fields and disciplines. It is helped but also complicated by our use of media communication.

Managing Media and Branding

Media, including mainstream and social media, are important platforms for communication for social movements, particularly non-profit groups (see Guo and Saxton 2013). However, care must be taken to negotiate the sea of media texts that flood our lives to decipher their utility for progressive social change. We cannot rely simply on what mainstream media offers. Mainstream, commercial media crafts news, solicits attention from audiences and then sells that attention as advertising space to commercial sponsors. For all the variety that appears in mainstream media, much of it reinforces rather than challenges collective ways of seeing, believing and valuing. Alternative positions, views and experiences may remain buried, with little known about the dramatically different, perhaps even much better, ways that others live, especially if these differences occur outside of the West. A good example is the relative lack of attention given to radical examples that work, such as in Costa Rica, which was demilitarized in 1948 after civil war, redirecting military funds to health and welfare for Costa Ricans, who experience less social inequality than North Americans (see Rosero-Bixby and Dow 2016).

Having a strong web presence is important to many campaigns against discrimination, harassment, marginalization, abuse and violence. Several campaigns have emerged in response to the new policies of the Trump administration, these including the cessation of funding for family planning and abortion services and the imposition of a ninety-day ban on refugees and other migrants from seven, predominantly Muslim, countries. Websites can help people coalesce, express and exchange ideas, contest competing descriptions and put forward analyses of the problem, intended focus or target, choice of methods, tactics and so on. Two good examples can be seen in the refugee rights movement and the #BlackLivesMatter movement (discussed later in this chapter). Costanza-Chock (2012) helpfully poses the following three questions regarding the group processes and media strategies adopted by social movements: (1) what media platforms, tools and skills are used most widely by movement participants? (Practices); (2) what role do experienced practitioners play in movement media practices? (Expertise); and (3) in what ways does the movement media culture lean toward open or partici-patory, and in what ways toward closed or top-down? (Open/Closed). Keck and Sikkink (2014: ix) emphasize the importance of international networks for both solidarity and strategic reasons:

> where the powerful impose forgetfulness, networks can provide alterna-tive channels of communication. Voices that are suppressed in their own societies may find that networks can project and amplify their concerns into an international arena, which in turn can echo back into their own countries.

However, as Keck and Sikkink (2014: ix) remind us, the proliferation of voices through alternative networks, including those on social media, carries its own problems: "the multiplication of voices is imperfect and selective — for every voice that is amplified, many others are ignored."

Transformative social movements usually confront prevailing orthodox views, unsettle assumptions about what is right and natural, and may appear — at least to the uninitiated — to be radical, even militant (Dickinson and Schaeffer 2015; Munro 2005). Often, the animal rights movement has been vilified as violent and extreme, even though the vast majority of activists engage in non-violent acts of persuasion and protest, including blockades and other expressions of non-cooperation (Munro 2005; see also Glasser 2014). It is not always easy to shrug off reputational issues. With the constant flow of media, negative messages about "the brand" (including misrepresentations) can destroy faith, trust and support. Under neoliberalism, which has infiltrated not just the private sector but also public services and everyday life (see Duvnjak and Fraser 2014; Reiter and Oslender 2015), we are increasingly urged to clarify, market and protect our brand. This includes our brand of argument.

Brands are often conveyed through logos and other shorthanded emblems designed to express value and help distinguish identities. They are also conveyed through the reputations associated with brands, such as whether the brand can be trusted, respected and valued. Advocates, community groups and social movements are also exposed to this injunction to manage their brands. There are two ways to do this: a) sculpt the key message of the group/movement to widen appeal; and b) stage-manage how the brand is to be represented in media. Apart from the argument that such practices have no place in justice movements, there is also the problem of the complexity of the message. Unlike commercial products such as packet soup or novelty flavored toothpaste, the key messages of social justice movements are not easily expressed in a fifteen-second advertisement. Yet, they are necessary for many forms of protest, including the use of banners, street protests and petitions.

Other Dilemmas about Methods and Funding

Since advocacy involves taking a side on behalf of an individual, group or cause, it is inherently bound up with debates about ethics and morality (see Chapters 1, 2 and 3). There is no ethics-free zone. On a collective scale, advocacy requires the negotiation of which issues, problems and/or claims will be prioritized, how membership eligibility and recruitment and processes will be determined, which networks of information and methods of protest will be used and representational issues, such as who gets to speak on behalf of a group or issue and who gets to associate their local events and actions with the wider cause. All these decisions speak to ethics and morality in action.

In recent years, social movements have emerged more as diffuse constellations of mass activity from *community networks* (see Halvorsen 2012), rather than pre-planned or centrally organized. These community networks can precipitate Do-It-Yourself (DIY) activism, or the seemingly random, creative and/or idiosyncratic methods of expressing dissent and pushing for change (Halvorsen 2012). These DIY activities often intersect street protests and banners, both of which are visual displays of protest designed to capture public interest and, in many instances, generate media attention. They may include slogans or clever turns of phrase more likely to be remembered.

Online petitions are now common and, to some extent, have democratized petition practices as they have allowed many more people to sign others' petitions and create their own without leaving home. There are literally thousands of petitions circulating about violence and abuse on social media around the world each day. Not all of them cut through, that is, gain support. Some circulating petitions will be given a few likes on social media, but stop there, without people going onto the petition site, completing their details and then sharing their pledge. Others will hit a cord, that is, resonate with large numbers of people, and sometimes unexpectedly.

Music is an important communication medium and source of inspiration for transformative, collective change. Even soothing-sounding ballads can convey messages of political action. For instance, in "Waiting on the World to Change," John Mayer (2006) sings:

> we see everything that's going wrong, with the world and those who lead it. We just feel like we don't have the means to rise above and beat it ... It's hard to beat the system when we're standing at a distance. So we keep waiting, waiting, waiting on the world to change.

Video activism (also discussed below in relation to the Occupy movement) has much potential for generating public interest and support for social justice issues, particularly now that increasing numbers of people have access to smart phones, which come complete with videorecording and editing software. As Mateos and Gaona (2015) suggest:

> video activism is an audiovisual mode of communicative action that consists in taking possession of discourse itself from the public sphere (occupying it by means of an audiovisual narrative) with the aim of fighting against repressions of a symbolic nature that have biopolitical repercussions on the individual.

Dissent can be expressed through video recordings that challenge traditional beliefs about how the world can and should be. Actual footage of events can verify accounts that might otherwise seem incredible. Anti-animal abuse activist Tim Pachirat (2011) combined undercover participation to expose and record the violence perpetrated in a slaughterhouse that was hidden in plain sight.

As with all mediums and methods of community organizing, web-based methods have limitations. Criticisms have been made about internet-based advocacy being a form of "slactivism" (see Lee and Hsieh 2013), or a way of appearing to care while not expending much energy or commitment at all. Yet, embodied interactions in live events and actions are not always possible, especially for people living in remote areas and/or with mobility or transport difficulties. Rather than placing physical interactions in opposition and superior to virtual communication methods, we take the view that both can be important platforms to raise consciousness, build commitment to issues and mobilize campaigns, while raising much-needed operating funds.

Even if it is modest, community groups and social movements usually need operating funds, if not for labour, it may be for equipment and software, events and renting office and online space. However, funding relationships that are often contracted through funding agreements can pose quandaries. As many oppressed persons know well, accepting money from others, especially in the form of a donation, often comes with strings attached. The same principle applies for community groups and social movements who solicit support through grants, sponsorship and partnership deals and other financial arrangements. Many ethical, practical and legal questions flow from these arrangements, such as what the outside supporters expect to get in return for their money, how much influence they will have over priorities set, methods adopted and language used to represent issues (see Dickinson and Schaeffer 2015).

Noting the widespread transfer of responsibility for social issues from the state to the private sector, Den Hond and De Bakker (2007) advocate for corporate responsibility and for corporations to be a focus of activists' work. Careful negotiations are needed. Whether it is through corporations, state sponsorship or philanthropic organizations, grants usually come with conditions of acceptance of some kind, from focus, target group, methodology, findings dissemination and, more recently, trademark if any commercial opportunities emerge. Being clear about these parameters and conditions up front may help prevent undue influence from funders.

Be warned, however, that some funding deals, if accepted, may sound the death knell for the group. For instance, several years ago, Rio Tinto, a multinational mining conglomerate, offered $130,000 AUD a year to fund a community advocacy centre based at a local university. It was around the time when the company was implicated in a major environmental and human rights disaster in Papua New Guinea (see Marshall 2002). Our best guess told us that it was looking for ways to sanitize its now sullied reputation, so as to resurrect dignity in its own brand. With pressure from the university to hear out the proposal, the community advocacy centre met with the mining representatives sent to do the deal. In our view, the proposal was audacious. In exchange for the money the centre would be renamed The Rio Tinto Human Rights Centre and any programs that followed would be negotiated with the funders. That no such centre eventuated may seem positive — until you learn that the original community advocacy unit was shut down in the process.

Critical Consciousness and Accidental Activism

A wide variety of interactions, including those on electronic forums, can generate alternative ways of seeing, thinking and being (Ollis 2008). In Chapter 3 we noted how *critical consciousness* is a process of growing critical awareness of the political nature of personal problems (and the personal face of politics). When it is tied to a deep awareness of and active opposition to structural inequalities, it is anti-oppressive. As Friere (1970: 47) writes:

> To surmount the situation of oppression, people must first critically recognize its causes, so that through transforming action they can create a new situation, one which makes possible the pursuit of a fuller humanity.

Yet, questions remain: how do we not just engage, but also sustain people in these processes of critical consciousness (see Ayres 2015)? How can we prevent people — especially oppressed groups — resorting to movements of exclusion, where discrimination is not challenged but extolled as a virtue?

There are many pathways into critical consciousness and participation in contemporary social justice movements — all of them valuable. One of them is through formal university study. Another is through more ad-hoc interactions, including those on social media. Social media sites such as Facebook, Twitter, Instagram and Pinterest circulate so many texts (visual, written, audio) that even the most conservative of online participants are likely to be exposed to opposing information and challenges to their cherished precepts (or prized ways of viewing the world). In *Tweets and the Streets*, Gerbaudo (2012) discusses the multiple uses of social media where cyberspaces and physical realities merge (rather than one supplanting the other), generating activities that can disrupt the political evanescence or the vanishing of public exchanges and resistance. Immersion into causes and campaigns through social media is one of the active strategies for both social progressive movements' inspiration for justice and the radical right's incitement of hatred and terror.

Critical consciousness can result from life's circumstances, where people are thrust into issues unexpectedly, sometimes issues that they have otherwise avoided in their lives. Ollis (2008) explains that while activism involves purposive, embodied actions, often infused with passion, anger and a hunger for change, people's initiation into activism can be accidental. Canadian researcher Panitch (2008), for example, examined how mothers of disabled children became accidental activists, challenging prevailing stereotypes about disability and adequacy of care arrangements. For instance, it could happen through personally experiencing domestic violence and the victim-blaming that can follow; being made redundant at work at age 50 and realizing that unemployment was much harder to bear than imagined; adopting a child through an international agency and later finding out that the child is a "paper orphan," that is, falsely documented as an orphan but sold through a human trafficking network (van Doore 2016; see also Chapter 6). Van Doore (2016) noted that global estimates of children living in orphanages and other residential institutions are at 8 million and that many of the children in these facilities are not orphans, but rather sold into orphanages through trafficking rings that make significant profits in the process.

Critical consciousness can emerge through proximity to family, friends and workmates who share similar circumstances, which are not always immediately apparent. For instance, in a small town in South Australia called Port Pirie, there is a lead smelter that has poisoned more than three thousand children in the last decade; poisoning well known to seriously compromise children's cognitive development and produce chronic learning, behavioural and mental health problems into adulthood (see Taylor 2012). Living in Port Pirie, or having friends or relatives there, may precipitate an awareness of environmental issues, especially those relating to air pollution and health problems. However, for some people, including residents, the problem of lead being forty-four times higher in Port Pirie than average may have remained downplayed or dismissed until loved ones are directly affected (Taylor 2012).

Harris (2008) documented the impact of feminist and child rights movements on childcare policies in Australia and the U.S., describing some participants as "accidental philanthropists," or people who do not set out to be so generous to others. Accidental activists go beyond charitable donations. They are people who do not set out or mean to be activists, but find themselves protesting for, or against, something meaningful to them (see Ollis 2008). Often they are people with little or no prior experience protesting; they are ordinary people who have not necessarily studied at university or completed high school, but who take up an issue or cause and try to get traction on it with others. They are people who have not necessarily worked in community organizations, on previous campaigns, or are even associated with people who do so. Among the many possible examples, consider, for instance, the mostly white middle-class older women in Canada who call themselves the Wakefield Grannies, who joined forces with Black, impoverished older women raising their grandchildren in the AIDS-ravaged Soweto more than a decade ago and are still sharing stories, resources, visits and camaraderie in the fight against AIDS, poverty and isolation (Ottawa Women's Council 2014).

Inspiration for social, cultural and personal change can also come through epiphanies (new and important realizations) and turning points, where decisions are made to institute changes of some magnitude. When discrete tasks and actions become systematic and woven into identities, people may, over time, identify as an activist. Practitioners, managers and clients/patients/students alike may experience eye-opening, mind-altering and/or life-changing experiences, which can provide powerful motivations to join or initiate campaigns against violence. Sometimes, it is service users, program participants and/or volunteers who are critically conscious and share their understandings and experiences of violence and abuse with professionals, or at least would do so, if asked and listened to.

The Duty of Care for Others and Ourselves

Welfare, health and education workers inclined towards AOP perspectives deploy most of their energy through the course of their daily interactions, through the ways they view the operations of privilege and oppression in homes, hospitals, classrooms, workplaces and clinics. Some will get involved in more active struggles of resistance, sometimes unexpectedly, spurred on to act by the things that they see in the course of their work. For others, or at other times, there will be epiphanies or turning points that occur, or a nagging call to do more.

If you work in health, welfare or education, at least part of your work requires you to care for others. Broadly speaking, we have a *duty of care* to ensure or try to safeguard the well-being of the people with whom we work. It also calls for us to take action if any of our participants or recipients of service face imminent danger. Some settings make this easier than others, for instance, working in a refugee camp or detention centre compared to working as a therapist in private practice. Similarly, some forms of violence and abuse are easier to respond to than others. As we have explored in earlier chapters, different forms of violence and abuse are not uniformly recognized, condemned or prevented. Some forms, such as poverty and poisoning from pollution, are not widely recognized as abuse.

As AOP workers we must all find ways to see the connections between personal and political abuse and violence without becoming overwhelmed, paralysed and/or consumed with rage. It can take patience and self-discipline to carefully explain your AOP-related insights to others, while still allowing them to process what you have said and still hold different views. Sometimes we fall silent and tired

Many teachers, social workers, police, nurses, doctors, ambulance officers and others work in tough environments, where deprivation levels are high and intergenerational, where there are inadequate public resources to address social problems and where violence and abuse occur regularly in people's lives. It is not surprising that some, if not many, will feel ground down, at least at particular times in their work, by the lack of resources and constraints on responding programmatically to social/health/education problems. Using an appreciative enquiry approach, Wendt, Tuckey and Prosser (2011) focused on the personal domain in their Australian study of social workers and teachers who had been working in tough, outer suburban communities for more than ten years. Participants discussed how their life experiences, ideologies, beliefs, values and other life resources in their personal domain helped them to thrive in their work, not just survive doing it.

It can be tiring, especially if you do not have support, seeing, hearing and thinking about the interconnecting causes of violence and abuse. This includes being kind to yourself and giving yourself time out (whatever this means to you), without allowing your fears or fatigue to become an excuse for inactivity and indifference. Resisting apathy and fatalism is as important to AOP workers as it is to our clients/students/patients and their communities. From personal experience, we can vouch for the health benefits of building a mix of longstanding (historical, ongoing), time-specific (temporal) and diverse alliances. Looking for the other benefits advocacy and activism can bring that are not always apparent from the outside is worth considering the long haul of some campaigns.

We also need to think about our practices of non-violent resistance, including risks and penalties. It is wise to know if gag orders (or legal prohibitions against speaking out) apply, and what the penalties may be for civil disobedience (such as leaking documents or doing undercover video activism) before you engage in such work. Looking for ways around these orders, through loopholes or law-testing strategies, may be a possibility for some. In some contexts, legal advice and support are priorities. More generally, it is wise to determine the space you have to do media work and/or public campaigning, including whether you might be able to offer behind-the-scenes support.

How will you combat others who try to discredit your interest in and commitment to peace and non-violence? Try not to lose energy being shocked when you meet opposition from others who reframe your empathy, compassion and awareness of structural inequalities as evidence that you are soft, immature and/or inexperienced. "One day you will see it my way" is the message many inspired new graduates receive from seasoned, and sometimes twisted, seniors. Staying connected with social justice movements and the host of campaigns done in their name helps to resist these messages and see them as indicative of burnout and/or compassion fatigue and/or the cultural tendency to blame the oppressed for their suffering.

Keeping relatively sane and healthy is required to sustain AOP work. Self-care should not be seen as indulgent, including self-care in our personal lives. At the same time, all responsibility for workers sustaining their own health and well-being relies on more than their personal resilience. It may seem trite to suggest that we try to do what we can when we can, but for socially progressive advocates, especially those fighting violence (endemic and interpersonal), it is a maxim worth remembering.

ILLUSTRATIVE CASE STUDIES

Opportunities to learn from and be inspired by the past are (sadly) plentiful in the history of social justice-inspired struggles against violence and abuse. In the following examples, most of which are internationally based, we explore ideas relating to AOP workers connecting with, supporting and/or being prepared to lead particular social justice movements and campaigns.

Climate Change and Green Movements

The problems facing humans, other species and the environment are multiple, serious and pressing. Environmental activists across issues, fields, modes of practice, species and national boundaries have shown how many disasters still referred to as "natural" are products of *climate change*, which refers to rising atmospheric temperatures across the world, with melting ice and rising sea levels posing serious problems for ecological and human health (see Conca and Dabelko 2014; Keck and Sikkink 2014):

> The threat of global warming must be added other environmental and resource issues: the inevitability of peak oil with its dramatic conse-quences for the global economy; the impending world food crisis, resulting from increasing desertification caused by climate change, from the use of land for bio-fuels and from increased competition for limited food stocks; the overfishing of the oceans, which seems likely to lead to a major shortage of seafood by the middle of the century; increasing scarcity of water, whether for drinking or for agriculture; the dangers of serious pandemics caused by the mutations of viruses in an overpopulated and highly mobile world; and the effect of continuing use of chemicals and pesticides. (Ife 2010: 149)

Also focusing on the implications of climate change on human health, McMichael (2013) studied the global scale of environmental changes, noting the negative impacts of the great and growing gulf between rich and poor (between and within countries) and the acceleration of consumerism and waste production. While concerned about the health risks from the emergence and spread of infec-tious diseases, rising obesity levels and other problems associated with sedentary lifestyles, he pointed out that the rising threats of so-called natural disasters, such as wildfires, droughts and reduced food yields, are crucial to human health.

Environmental advocates and activists working from an intersectional perspec-tive appreciate that climate change, growing poverty, inequality and exploitation work together to deny increasing numbers of people around the world decent living conditions, creating volatile, explosive social contexts. These hardships are not felt equally. Kabir et al. (2015) remind us that countries like Bangladesh are the most vulnerable to climate change and its negative implications for health, including survival. Asking why some people or communities are more affected by disasters than others, Ngoh Tiong (2011) describes the need for social work to protect vulnerable groups, with vulnerability defined as "the degree of internal risk and susceptibility of societies," as well as the level of resistance and resilience to disasters (McEntire 2004). While we prefer the term "oppressed groups" to "vulnerable groups," as it signals the active way in which some groups are disadvantaged, we agree that "poverty and social exclusion are primary causes of vulnerability [and] reduce resilience"; that "the goal is to improve policies and measures to disaster management and recovery" by "building on the strengths of the community ... [and] resilience [that] is the resourcefulness of people, families, and communities, along with the ability to bounce back from calamities" (Ngoh Tiong 2011). Yet, we are equally clear that attention must be given to the underlying causes of natural disasters, especially those related to climate change, which place the heaviest burden on the people who can least afford to manage the loss of housing, income and personal belongings. The Kashmir floods in 2014 are a good example:

> A resident of Gangbugh, Tengpura in Srinagar, Gulshan was at home when the gushing sound created by the flood waters disturbed her sleep in the intervening night of September 6–7. As soon as she opened her eyes, she recalls, she woke up to a disturbing reality — the first floor of her house was completely inundated.
>
> Gulshan's family was rescued and relocated to a relief camp set up in a marriage hall in Sanat Nagar, Srinagar, which is named after famous Urdu poet, Dr. Allama Iqbal. According to the volunteers, over 2,000 people had taken shelter in the relief camp there by then. [Meanwhile] a group of young Kashmiri doctors led by Dr. Zahida and Dr. Sajad Fazili have set up a free medical camp, where flood victims are being treated ... [Yet] The local administration was invisible on the ground for nearly two weeks. There was scarcity of drinking water, no traffic cops on the roads, no municipality workers or sweepers to dispose garbage and all channels of communication had broken down.
>
> ... [Fortunately] Some members of India's National Disaster Response Force (NDRF), Jammu and Kashmir Light Infantry (JAKLI), and other government forces were seen aiding in rescue and relief operations at some places. Also, four army helicopters were seen air-dropping food packets to people trapped in waterlogged areas. *However, the major rescue and relief work was solely being performed by Kashmiri volunteers, young men and local boatmen.* (Geelani 2014, emphasis added)

While set in Kashmir, the above case study illustrates the wider themes of human-environmental interconnectedness and the importance of local, professional, government and informal supports collaborating together in rescue and rebuilding efforts (see Ife 2010).

Abolitionism/Anti-Slavery

Opposition to the violence of enslavement, also referred to as *abolitionism*, has an ancient history and continues today (Schwartz 2013). It is an extreme expression of labour exploitation, forcibly extracted and often involving sexual exploitation (Schwartz 2013). Tilly and Tarrow (2015) describe the convergence of organized labour and civil rights opposition to the slave trade in eighteenth-century Britain and the United States. They were referring to what some now call "old slavery," distinguishing it from "new slavery" (see Brysk and Choi-Fitzpatrick 2012), which is estimated by the United Nations International Labor Organization (UNILO) to be at least twenty-one million current slaves, of which 78 percent are estimated to be in forced manual labour, 22 percent in sex slavery (forced prostitution) and of the total group contains approximately 26 percent children (Free the Slaves 2016).

There are many possible ways for AOP workers to participate in or lend their support to contemporary abolitionist movements. Learn about slavery and abolitionist campaigns, past and present, and understanding the links between poverty, oppression and slavery are entry points. Notice how poverty, labour and sexual exploitation are operating at the local level, in your own cities, towns and workplaces. Support anti-poverty groups far and near that promote systemic, not just individual change, including those that promote universal access to decent healthcare, education, housing and welfare (see Mendes 1997, 2000). Time, money, information and expertise can be donated.

Another way to practice the personal as political (and vice versa) is by refusing to blame individuals for their oppression, poverty and/or enslavement (see Ife 2012; Mendes 1997, 2000, 2012). This sounds simple but is much harder to maintain given so many cultural and organizational invitations and inducements are made to blame victims (Mendes 2000, 2012), sometimes surreptitiously through discourses of resilience and self-responsibility (see Chapter 3). One way to avoid getting swept up in the latest professional intervention for the symptoms of violence and abuse is to keep connected to and focused on the needs of people in poverty and other forms of enslavement — and needs as they express them. For health, welfare and education professionals, it starts with the recognition of where clients/students/patients are at (rather than where we think they should be), and takes seriously the rights of groups (not just individuals) to self-determine:

Empowerment involves providing people with the skills and resources necessary to increase their capacity to determine their own future, and to effectively participate in the life of their community. Participation refers to the right of community members to directly participate in the identification of social problems, and in determining strategies for their resolution. (Mendes 2012: 5)

Across the divide of service provider and receiver, small, practical steps in our everyday life can help us to connect to global campaigns for justice. Attempts to live ethical lives can include seeking out, rather than turning away from information about how we are currently benefiting from the enslavement of others. For many Westerners, this occurs through everyday consumption of coffee, chocolate, meat and dairy, but also clothing, shoes, smart phones, televisions and laptops. All of these items can be traced to the enslavement and oppression of others, from the animal rights abuses committed against livestock, to the exploitation of tea, coffee and chocolate growers' labour. Other possible steps towards living an ethical life include eliminating items or trying to source ethical products and services — aware that they may (and perhaps should) cost more, at least for the most affluent in the world. Ethical purchasing practices are needed at an organizational, not just individual level. Plenty of websites can help, for instance, Ethical Trading Initiative, Respect for Workers Worldwide <http://www.ethicaltrade.org/issues/company-purchasing-practices>.

AOP ethical deliberations extend well beyond purchasing practices. Our commitment to social equality and opposition to the systems of privilege and oppression prompt us to look beyond superficialities when identifying leaders and recognizing the achievements of members whose actions significantly influence whether leaders flourish or fail. Unlike hierarchical organizations, leadership in social justice movements is not usually so revered. It is certainly not something to be ceded or acquiesced to those who make the most noise. For social justice movements to thrive, we must recognize those who sustain the movement, even or especially if they are not deemed worthy of individual mention. Jeffrey (1998) makes this point in relation to "ordinary" women's contribution to abolitionism, which has historically been overlooked. It is important to recognize the politics of voice and the need for oppressed persons, especially those subjected to multiple oppressions, to speak for themselves about important issues, including those relating to heath, welfare and education policies and practices. Showing solidarity with the most devalued and stigmatized groups rather than reproducing hierarchies, cliques and systems of segregation may be challenging, but it is essential (see Conway 2003).

Anti-Apartheid and Refugee Rights Movements

The anti-apartheid movement was designed to protest the violent and intensely oppressive racial segregation of whites from non-whites in South Africa between 1948 and 1994 (see Digby 2013). Internal resistance to apartheid was significant, included trade union activism and was dealt with brutally (Hart 2002). Internal opposition to apartheid was widespread, but sometimes too dangerous to express. It came from Black but also white doctors, lawyers and other professionals, and of course seriously affected who was able to study at university and go on to practice their profession (Digby 2013; Moodley and Kling 2015).

Internationally, the anti-apartheid movement against the regime in South Africa started back in 1959, first in Britain as a consumer boycott, then extending to more systematic economic, arms and sporting embargoes, such as getting South Africa expelled from the Commonwealth Games and boycotted from the Olympic Games (see Hart 2002; Peet 2002). For many trade union organizers, supporting the international struggle against apartheid was a galvanizing force (see Nastovski 2014 on Canadian labour solidarity).

Hart (2002) used the concept of *racial capitalism* to describe the colonization of people of colour in South Africa via apartheid, which involved the systematic, legislated oppression of non-whites, dispossessing them from their land and forcing them to become extremely cheap (exploited) labour:

> Starting in the 1960s, millions of black South Africans were ripped from the land in rural "white" South Africa, and packed into huge relocation townships like Ezakheni on patches of land defined as part of purportedly self-governing "bantustans." (Hart 2002: 2)

In 1994, the African National Congress (ANC) assumed power in South Africa, and remains dominant today. The current South African Government (2016) identifies the following priorities: the extension of education, healthcare, skills and job development, but also police protection for the nearly 53 million residents of the country. However, Peet (2002) takes a more critical stance, explaining that after the first couple of years in office, the ANC moved from a broadly socialist agenda to adopt neoliberal global capitalism, which does not prioritize the health, welfare and education of the local people, but instead has produced widespread and extreme poverty, violence and corruption.

Outside of South Africa, systems of apartheid exist. Some have used the term *apartheid* to describe other discriminatory systems that continue to segregate the privileged from the oppressed. For instance, Rashidi (1996) described the violence of Aryan-European instituted apartheid in India, starting 350 years ago. Massey and Denton (1993) use it to describe the racial segregation of Black and

Hispanic populations and the creation of the underclass in the U.S. It has been used to describe the class and racial struggles over what constitutes legitimate knowledge in Western universities (see Bernal and Villalpando 2002; Da Costa and Philip 2010). Galabuzi (2001) described how Canada's creeping economic apartheid was separating white Canadians from Canadians of colour, calling for national programs for affordable housing, childcare, education and community development, all with anti-racism as a core part. Speaking from the U.S. and commenting on the treatment of women in many Middle Eastern countries, Mayer (2000) argued that, while forms of gender apartheid existed across the world, they were wrongly represented as more benign than racial apartheid. From Australia, Goggin and Newell (2005) showed how social apartheid was occurring between able-bodied and disabled people, through everyday activities that excluded so many groups, such as sensory, mobility and intellectual impairments.

More than twenty years ago, Richmond and Valtonen (1994) noted the emergence of apartheid — or *apart-hood* — for the vast majority of the world's refugees. Many current refugee activists incorporate anti-apartheid arguments in their protests. One of many great examples of protest has been by #Mums4Refugees (2015) in Australia, with their poignant, ninety-six-second video campaign, "Our War on Women," which calls for the end of mandatory detention in Australia and associated policies of holding indefinitely refugees who try to arrive in Australia by boat in off-shore detention. In their 2015 campaign, #Mums4Refugees used animation and the help of local university students to focus on the Islamophobic-inspired violence facing women and children living on the tiny island of Nauru (see Noyes 2015). With so many other refugee rights groups, #Mums4Refugees are voicing their opposition to the system that has effectively created an apartheid between people seeking asylum (many of whom are Muslim) and those who are not; a system that in Australia has removed refugees from public visibility and forced them to languish in hastily made, unhygienic, ill-resourced off-shore detention camps, where they are subjected to ongoing, systematic violence and deprivation (Noyes 2015).

Many other possible applications of the concept of apartheid could be cited, and thinking through the multiple possibilities of application can help to develop insights, especially in relation to the infiltration of insidious (that is, powerful but hard to see) ways people can be segregated from each other. This includes learning about the ways in which apartheid can be instituted or evolve, both now and in the past. Part of the work involves critically analyzing colonization (systemic but also cultural forms) and its legacy, and the negative impacts of global capitalism, which may be understood as colonization by class, religion, gender, ability and race.

The Occupy Wall Street Movement

Making up the Occupy Wall Street movement is a broad alliance of anti-glo-balization activists protesting about poverty and increased inequality. In this movement, workers rights are central. Collectively, this movement includes mass protests, online and in the streets, often culminating in blockades to entry ports of prominent economic forums when they are held in major cities around the world (Halvorsen 2012). This movement against the oppression and violence of poverty is also described as "We are the 99 percent," which refers to the vast majority of the world's population with little to no control over most of the world's resources as distinct from the 1 percent of super rich who own and control most of the world's resources (see Chapters 3 and 4).

A key strategy and communication method in the Occupy Wall Street movement has been through video activism, which provides a powerful channel for protests that are materially based but also symbolic and discursive (Askanius 2013; Mateos and Gaona 2015). Askanius (2013) provides a taxonomy of video activism used in the Occupy movement:

1. *mobilization videos* that deliberately incite political action;
2. *witness videos* that show lived experiences of violence, abuse and in-equality;
3. *documentation videos* that plainly identify and describe issues, goals and steps taken to redress injustice;
4. *archived radical videos* that provide members with historical inspiration; and
5. *political mash-ups,* which involve members amalgamating texts, images and other materials in their videos.

While these methods of video activism have been related to the Occupy move-ment, they have broader possibilities for AOP workers interested in exploring different ways to mobilize for change and allow people to incorporate their own DIY methods in the process (see Costanza-Chock 2012).

The Global Call to Action Against Poverty

The Global Call to Action Against Poverty (GCAP) is a worldwide movement to engage diverse international communities in serious attempts to end poverty, now so extreme that "the world's 85 richest people are worth as much as the poorest 3.5 billion (half the globe's population)" (GCAP 2016). Using impassioned language, they seek extensive, systemic change on a global scale:

> GCAP works for social justice, against a backdrop of obscene inequality, both within and between countries. We envision a world where economies

create prosperity for all and not a select few, where governments, people and the private sector respect and treasure the planet so that it will be habitable not just for us but for generations to come. (GCAP 2016)

GCAP's mission statement appreciates intersecting oppressions and the need for inclusion of diversity:

We, the GCAP movement, will not rest until we defeat the underlying and structural causes that impoverish and exclude large sections of the population, including women, indigenous peoples, minorities, children, youth, persons with different abilities, people of different sexual orientations, workers, dalits [members of lower castes in Indai] and displaced persons, amongst others. (GCAP 2016)

GCAP (2016) identify themselves as "one of the largest civil society networks with National Coalitions and Constituency Groups in more than eighty countries" and are proud to have the support of freedom fighter and past (ANC) South African President Nelson Mandela, who has described it as central to past anti-slavery and anti-apartheid movements.

GCAP comprises a network of temporal, voluntary alliances, made up of diverse forms of organizations to achieve particular purposes, making these alliances complex, unstable and difficult to coordinate, generating frustrations for some (see Mati 2009). As discussed earlier in this chapter, while democratic processes can be messy and cumbersome, they have value and should not be replaced with competitive individualism and market versions of efficiency.

Disability Rights Movements and Improving Care

Across the world there have been many disability rights movements that have generated collective campaigns to recognize the many forms of suffering and rights abuses experienced by people with disabilities (see Panitch 2008). The diverse collection of groups that make up a movement intersect countries and often criss-cross health conditions, diagnoses, prognoses, as well as fields and modes of practice. Campaigns for the rights of those afflicted with various physical health conditions (such as motor neuron disease) sit beside campaigns for the rights of people diagnosed with mental illness, including psychiatric survivors, that is, people who have survived the trauma of forced psychiatric treatment (see Pelka 2012). Underlying these campaigns is steadfast opposition to the discrimination and exclusion of people with disabilities (see Sayce 2000).

In Chapter 6 we discussed how disabling social, cultural and physical environments can be. Often pity, if not contempt, is shown to people with disabilities, through attitudes and patronizing, demeaning interactions, including those that remain invisible to those without disabilities or able-bodied people unaccustomed to empathizing with others who do have disabilities. Then there is the routine indifference, which can sometimes feel like an impermeable wall, shown by systems (run by people) largely blind to the ways systems, policies and practices block or sabotage opportunities for people with disabilities. Writing about the disability rights movement in India, Mehrotra (2011) describes how hard it has been to shake disablism in the country, noting that the movement has struggled to register its presence across India, in spite of its self-help ethic and the support periodically provided by other social justice groups, such as women's groups and international aid organizations. India is not alone, however. Across the world, disability rights activists must confront able-bodied people's ignorance of and/or indifference to disabled rights (see Sayce 2000).

Many strategies are deployed to deal with this indifference, to break through the wall of silence and disinterest, including but not limited to: (a) reminders of the existing legal rights of disabled people; (b) support from allies; and (c) disabled people creatively expressing their experiences. Reminders of existing legal rights possessed by disabled people may be used to leverage attention. Article 29 of the United Nation's Convention on the Rights of Persons with Disabilities, is often cited because it is a global document that confirms equality of political rights, including the right to vote and run for election, for all adults, including those with intellectual disabilities living in Kenya, England and Wales (Redley et al. 2012). Government policy makers, private businesses and the general public may be reminded that special protections are already afforded children and people with disabilities under the United Nations conventions on human rights. These protections are in place to support their life chances and address the disadvantages they are likely to face, including an increased risk of poor health and poverty (Taylor-Robinson, Whitehead and Barr 2014). Cross-alliances and support from others sustains campaigns and ongoing activism, as Callus and Farrugia (2016) discuss in relation to disabled children's rights work. Finally, disabled people creatively express their experiences, through art, music, dance and theatre. So extensive are these artistic activities that Swain and French (2000) refer to the "disabled arts movement." This movement has done much to esteem participants, recognize their creative talents and raise community awareness of some of the problems they face, including problems that could be solved if abled-bodied people were to give more than passing interest and support (see Swain and French 2000).

Across borders, ages and conditions, disability rights movements continue to share an interest in, and deep commitment to, the way care is understood and provided to people with disabilities, in family homes and paid care facilities, irrespective of whether they are state-run or sponsored, or privately owned and operated (see Stroman 2003). Australian researcher, Cummins (2001), conducted a study on the subjective well-being of people caring for severely disabled family members in their family homes and found that this group of primary caregivers faced high risks of developing high levels of stress and the symptoms of clinical depression, which explained their self-reports of low quality of life. Among other recommendations, Cummins (2001) called for urgent public expenditure on respite care and other supported care arrangements — for the health and safety of both caregivers and care recipients.

Challenges to institutionalized care has come in many forms, with isolation, abuse and neglect often cited as reasons for shutting down particular care homes (Sayce 2000; Stroman 2003). Yet, as disabled rights activists are well aware, deinstitutionalization alone is not the answer. As suggested above, campaigns are still underway to get quality residential support for particular cohorts of disabled people, at least for periods of time, such as when they are critically ill and/or in the final phases of life. For the rest of the time, stable, affordable housing is required (among other needs) but remains elusive for many, particularly as countries privatize housing and leave their citizens to negotiate their needs through private markets (see Fraser and Taylor 2016; Mendes 2012).

The Women's Movement and Reclaim the Night

Well documented in large bodies of literature are the waves of feminism and variety of women's movements that have existed over recent centuries, including many women's peace activist groups (see Dickinson and Schaeffer 2015). Most associated with the second wave of feminism, the women's movements of the 1960s to the 1980s campaigned hard to have formerly private matters, such as domestic violence and child abuse, recognized as public issues (Fraser 2008). It was the time in the West where women's refuges from domestic violence were being initiated, and when the Reclaim the Night/Take Back the Night marches surged in popularity.

Each year around the world Reclaim the Night (RTN), also referred to as Take Back the Night, marches take place to raise awareness of the many forms of violence perpetrated against women and children, mostly by men. RTN is also a long-term protest against the cultural expectation that women and children maintain night curfews (off the streets and other public places) or be held liable for any violence inflicted against them (see Chan 2004; Mackay 2015). Placards, songs, costumes and chants are common parts of the process, often with celebrations held after the march and speeches are over.

Street marches protesting culturally and systemically embedded beliefs and practices are not easy, especially claims that are seen to be "radical" or "militant," such as RTN's argument that women should be safe to walk the streets in whatever clothing they choose (see Chan 2004; Mackay 2015). Physically engaging diverse groups of women to be prepared to walk down the street chanting "No means no" can be difficult in this era where mainstream media tells us that gender equality has arrived and that women are not interested in feminism, if not actively alienated from it. With this, managing disputes within RTN has also been necessary; from charges of racism relating to chosen routes taken for the march and treatment of Black women who oppose the protest (see Mackay 2015), to debates about whether men should be allowed to march and, if so, whether they need to march at the back so as not to displace women's leadership in the movement.

There are also questions to be raised about the impact of such marches on laws and public policy making. Our view is that there is no single point of influence, nor a linear dynamic of one event or group being entirely responsible for progressive changes. Many dynamics operate together to effect change. Just as positive, egalitarian attitudes and behaviours don't always flow on from each other, nor is there one identifiable site responsible for large-scale change. From an AOP perspective, the priority is not to disaggregate these changes but to look for ways to forge links between compatible alliances and sustain the momentum for protest. Interesting and engaging ways of maintaining the interest of diverse protestors are required, as many LGBTIQ communities understand all too well.

LGBTIQ Rights and Pride

Across the world and to varying degrees, basic human rights have long been denied people identified as lesbian, gay, bisexual, transgendered, intersex and/or queer (LGBTIQ). Several international campaigns are currently underway, from those relating to equal marriage and other intimacy rights, to safety in schools and workplaces, to those associated with professional sports players (professional football players, for instance) or LGBTIQ members serving in the military or as police and other emergency response officers.

International LGBTIQ alliances have been impressive, especially in times of crises requiring urgent responses, such as those relating to HIV/AIDS; young LGBTIQ people feeling suicidal from homophobic bullying; and the rise of hate crimes, including large scale massacres like the recent mass shooting at the Florida gay nightclub and the assassination of a prominent magazine editor and gay rights activists in Bangladesh (see Smith 2016; Syed 2016).

Gay pride is a hallmark of so much LGBTIQ activism, and gay pride marches (including gay Mardi Gras) provide sites for resistance to homophobia and heteronormativity. These marches allow for the public enactment of pride, rather than the private internalization of shame, which is why Johnson and Waitt (2015) classify gay pride marches as forms of *emotional activism*. For many participants, it is the emotional connectedness to the movement that propels many to travel great distances to attend, as de Jong describes (2015) in "Dykes on Bikes and the Long Road to Mardi Gras."

From an AOP perspective, LGBTIQ pride in all forms (including marches) are worth supporting because they promote the rights of diverse populations to live freely, where they are able to make their sexual identities public without the fear of violence and abuse being perpetrated against them (see Montgomery and Stewart 2012). Recently, Justin Trudeau was the first Canadian Prime Minister to lead the Toronto Gay Pride March and was widely acclaimed for participating (see Braithwaite 2016). This was not because his involvement has transformed the socio-political landscape for LGBTIQ populations in Canada, but because it was an implicit vote of confidence in the LGBTIQ movement, a public affirmation of LGBTIQ rights and campaigns and a gesture of solidarity across the straight–queer divide.

The Trudeau story reminds us that small steps and gestures of openness and support can be helpful. For AOP workers it is often possible to reach out, through liaising with queer organizations on LGBTIQ issues or displaying rainbow stickers or posters in your organization to signal that it is queer friendly. More systematic but still local actions are also helpful, such as providing LGBTIQ-specific program options welcoming the input from LGBTIQ students/clients/ patients about services and actively soliciting their feedback on service anomalies and gaps.

As it is with any oppressed group, if you are not a member (in this case, LGB-TIQ) then your efforts are best channeled into being an ally. The good news is that several benefits usually accrue to allies. According to those who participated in a study conducted by Rostosky et al. (2015), being a heterosexual ally generated increased knowledge and awareness in LGBTIQ issues, a sense of belonging and the satisfaction that can come from using social privilege for the benefit of others who are being treated unfairly.

Black Lives Matter

Black Lives Matter is a call to action to protest the dehumanizing experiences Black people face in the U.S. and elsewhere. One of the events that precipitated this campaign occurred in 2012 after Trayvon Martin's murderer, George Zimmerman, was acquitted for killing 17-year-old Trayvon, and Trayvon himself was (posthumously) placed on trial for his own murder (see <http://blacklivesmatter.com/about/>). This campaign has received much public attention, tragically because so many deaths have occurred recently at the hands of police.

As indicated below, Black Lives Matter's analyses of violence and abuse are explicitly intersectional, and founding members Patrisse Cullors, Opal Tometi and Alicia Garza are unapologetic about their intentions to move beyond reformism, that is, small incremental reforms that largely leave untouched systemic racism, classism, sexism, disablism and ageism:

It goes beyond the narrow nationalism that can be prevalent within Black communities, which merely call on Black people to love Black, live Black and buy Black, keeping straight cis Black men in the front of the movement while our sisters, queer and trans and disabled folk take up roles in the background or not at all.

Black Lives Matter affirms the lives of Black queer and trans folks, disabled folks, black-undocumented folks, folks with records, women and all Black lives along the gender spectrum. It centers those that have been marginalized within Black liberation movements. It is a tactic to (re)build the Black liberation movement. <http://blacklivesmatter.com/about/>

Current Black Lives Matter campaigns connect direct violence with cultural and structural violence. This includes examining the state violences of: Black poverty; the widespread incarceration and genocide of Black people; the burden of disease for Black women who experience the state violence of massive under-support and over-surveillance; the heteropatriarchal oppression experienced by Black queer and trans folks "that disposes of us like garbage and simultaneously fetishizes us and profits off of us"; the labour exploitation of undocumented Black immigrants; the objectification and enslavement of Black girls in times of conflict and war; and the white supremacist and eugenics-oriented denigration of Black people with disabilities "and different abilities" <http://blacklivesmatter.com/about/>.

Black Lives Matter is an example of how a social movement often deploys a range of creative methods to increase the reach of their message, solicit interest in issues and encourage commitment to action. Storytelling, personal testimonies and other politicized accounts of individual experience are common to many social movements, and on their website they call for audio-recorded submissions from Black people where they are asked to "imagine a world where Black life is valued by everyone." These stories will form an online public story bank and be exhibited along with artwork, which has long been a source of inspiration and engagement for a great range of campaigns and social movements (see <http://art.blacklivesmatter.com/blackfuturesmonth/>).

Yet, caution must be taken to not romanticize this movement, which, like all others, battles with its own struggles and misconceptions. This includes the misconceptions that it is a leaderless movement without an agenda that hates white people and police officers, has no respect for elders and is unconcerned about Black-on-Black crime, discussed on a special page, "11 Major Misconceptions About the Black Lives Matter Movement" (<http://blacklivesmatter.com/11-major-misconceptions-about-the-black-lives-matter-movement/>).

Even if you do not participate in Black Lives Matter campaigns directly, there are plenty of other practical contributions that can be made to anti-racist health, welfare and education practice. For instance, this may include critically analyzing the use of science to justify ongoing racial discrimination through racial profiling in policing and some health and welfare programs (see Da Costa and Philip 2010). Since poverty is so unevenly experienced by Black communities around the world, AOP workers might also look for ways to extend whatever services or expertise they have to those who cannot afford to pay market rates for services.

CONCLUSION

Social movements and community responses to violence and abuse have been considered in this chapter. We noted that violence and abuse are emotionally charged topics that can elicit intense emotions, producing passion and compassion that can motivate us into action, but also feelings of rage, anxiety and depression that often need to be processed. Because of the AOP focus of this book, the challenges associated with community organizing for the purposes of peace and non-violence have also been foregrounded, and practice notes incorporated.

Illustrative examples were used to provide snapshots of the great variety of advocacy and activism work from the past and currently, their different goals, methods, approaches and interpretations of success. These examples show how advocating for socially just change has often included raising awareness and promoting social and cultural attitudinal changes, organizing community events and mass protests that produce feelings of solidarity and pride, but also press for important changes to laws, policies and social practices. The most important point of this chapter was to highlight how responses to violence and abuse come not just from professionals but cross sections of people, for specific purposes, who collectively agitate for change, and with whom AOP practitioners may form important alliances.

9. INDIVIDUAL AND THERAPEUTIC RESPONSES

- How do individual victims of violence and abuse get constituted?

- What is the Duluth Model and how does it relate to attempts to hold violent perpetrators accountable?

- How might an AOP worker view other therapeutic responses in victim and perpetrator programs?

Anti-oppressive perspectives emphasize structural power relations and social change. This does not, however, override the need for individual, therapeutic responses to abuse and violence. The potency of AOP lies in its striving to bring together a passion for social justice with a deep connection with, and accountability to, those people and groups most affected. We must recognize the embedded nature of violence in and throughout our everyday lives and the complex contingencies of our investment(s) in the violent status quo. A critical stance is needed in relation to the ways that we think about — and respond to — diverse experiences of violence. By acknowledging that these overlap with experiences of inequality and oppression, AOP practice seeks to avoid "replicating disempowering dynamics" by "adopting a critically reflective response" (Connolly and Harms 2015: 164) grounded in compassion and respect for humanity.

VICTIMS OF ABUSE AND VIOLENCE

One of the more confronting aspects of working with abuse and violence is its very human messiness. More often than not, the people and situations encountered will not fit easily within broader ideas about right and wrong, innocence and evil, victim and perpetrator. This is not to say that people do not victimize others, nor to imply that abuse and violence can ever be justified or deserved. Rather, it draws our attention to the shifting and intersectional dynamics of power such that victims are also perpetrators, often simultaneously and vice versa. This is a confronting recognition that can disrupt our sense of order regarding the existence of clear boundaries between the so-called good and bad people of the world. Again, this does not imply that violence should ever be excused on the basis of prior experiences of victimization. It does, however, trouble the assumption that is it possible to draw a straightforward distinction between victim and perpetrator and their respective needs. Most importantly, it makes clear that there is no "ideal" victim or perpetrator; no matter our preconceptions about how victims behave or the kinds of things that they say and are concerned about, for example, the people that we meet are unlikely to match up. As discussed in Chapter 4, this reflects both the conservative politics of neoliberalism characterized by social division and hierarchy — of us and them — and the deep morality associated with ideas about what constitutes a "real" or "worthy" victim.

The idea that abused women are "passive participants in their own intimate relationships" has traditionally underpinned the delivery of domestic violence services (Cavanagh 2003: 230). In neglecting the complexities discussed above, victim services may be missing the mark by both assuming a "uniformity in women's responses to violence" and failing to "consider men's responses to their use of violence" (230). Fundamental to AOP is the need to engage with diverse perspectives — especially those frequently silenced or invalidated — while considering issues of voice, identity and agency. We need to be "attentive to the strategies of resistance which women deploy in order to stop/reduce the violence and abuse ... [as they can] ... contextualise women's responses within the sphere of intimate, interactive relationships" (Cavanagh 2003: 246). Our principles and practices need to be informed by, and accountable to, women's "interpretations of their responses to abuse" (246). Space needs to be given to different perspectives and priorities regarding family and relationships more generally, including a genuine respect for women's hopes and desires for their relationships in and beyond their families. While challenging in practice, AOP requires us to establish "more flexible and sensitive" ways of working with victims "who desire a both/and solution — continuing the relationship but keeping safe" (Milner and Jessop 2003: 139).

Responding to the Needs of Victims of Direct Violence

As we have argued throughout this book, structural and cultural violences have many casualties. Experiences of oppression are broad and diverse and may manifest in people internalizing their marginalization. This makes responding to the needs of victims challenging, requiring that we keep searching for ways to connect with all who are violated. Experiences of *direct violence* are equally diverse and the people victimized are a heterogeneous group with needs that are "disparate and complex" (Bricknell, Boxall and Andrevski 2014: 1). As a result, it is difficult to speak about victims' needs in anything other than very general terms. Also, the ways in which victims react to violence, and express their service/support needs, depends on a range of factors including age, socio-economic status, prior experiences of victimization, pre-existing coping strategies, knowledge and familiarity with available services and so on.

Across these differences, we can say that the impact of direct violence for those victimized can be both significant and wide ranging. Attending to physical/bodily injuries may be the most immediate priority, but victims may also experience other ongoing symptoms of ill health (Bricknell, Boxall and Andrevski 2014: 7). The psychological impacts can also be substantial, with victims more likely to face a range of mental health issues such as depression and anxiety, difficulty sleeping and symptoms of post-traumatic stress disorder. Broader impacts may include relationship stress and/or break down and social isolation, as well as the financial implications of having to take time off work, the costs associated with attending court and other appointments, medical treatment expenses and so on. Participation in the court process — when this occurs — is also widely recognized as especially difficult for victims, with many reporting their experience of this as "confronting and distressing," intimidating and potentially re-traumatizing (Bricknell, Boxall and Andrevski 2014: 7).

The support needs of victims of direct violence include but are not limited to issues relating to health and medical care, communication with/from police, personal/emotional support, counselling, legal advice, financial assistance, affordable and decent housing and other safety concerns. Strengths and solution-based therapeutic approaches, explored in more depth later in this chapter, are recognized as especially relevant to work with victims of direct violence. Drawing out stories of strength and resilience reflects the symbolic significance of the term "survivor" as opposed to "victim." Such interventions aim to help survivors "create resistance to oppression by subverting the problem, [and] setting boundaries and relationship styles that resist oppressive or violent behaviour in their relationships" (Payne 2014: 258; see also Milner 2001).

Male Victims of Direct Violence

Statistics show, pretty consistently, that adult men are more likely than adult women to be the victims of direct violence, specifically that which is "non-sexual [and] non-domestic" (Bricknell, Boxall and Andrevski 2014: ix). Overwhelmingly, though, much of the existing research on violence has centred on women's experiences of sexual and domestic violence. Male victims are, in many respects, "largely missing from broader discussions around the impact of violent offences on victims and their subsequent support needs" (Bricknell, Boxall and Andrevski 2014: ix). Research designed to address this knowledge gap is required, bearing in mind that male victims' experiences of violence are "complicated by traditional notions of masculinity" (8), and men's willingness to name their experiences *as* violence and themselves as victims. Reflecting on men as victims adds another dimension of complexity to our thinking about service responses for victims of violence and abuse. Whether men's victimization relates to their experiences as adults and/or in their family of origin (as children), there are societal barriers — including gendered norms and assumptions regarding strength and vulnerability — that get in the way of recognizing men's needs in this regard.

Acknowledging and exploring men's "genuine experiences of victimisation" (Vlais 2014: 7) can be valuable in men's behaviour-change work. Nonetheless, while service providers can be "allies to men in their attempts to change" by "nurturing rapport, trust and emotional safety," that violence intervention work is not "about *doing therapy*" (7, emphasis in original):

> for many men, the most potent contributor to their "victim stance," and their feelings of righteous anger, is when their partner, children or others act or fail to act in ways that the man expects, with these expectations being unfair, unjust and fuelled by male entitlement and privilege. Doing therapy runs the risk of marginalising the vital work needed to address this latter sense of perceived/felt victimisation that is based on men's recruitment into exercising patriarchal power and thinking ... Rather [it is essential that men] take responsibility for these emotions, not draw on their male privilege and entitlement to use these emotions as an excuse to choose violence. (Vlais 2014: 7–8)

Direct Abuse Disclosures Involving Family or Caregivers

To the uninformed and inexperienced, it can seem obvious that if someone is abusing you, you tell others to get help. People may hypothesize to themselves and others, often quite adamantly, saying things like "if you don't speak up how can you expect anything to change?" They might say or imply, "that's what I'd do it if happened to me," "I can tell you now I wouldn't be keeping quiet about it" and so on. If only it were that simple.

There are many reasons why disclosing direct abuse can be so difficult. Perpetrators may induce secrecy in victims, including through calculated threats directed at family members and pets. Perpetrators may also threaten further or more extensive abuse if victims tell others. They may tell victims that they imagined the abuse, deserved it and/or that no one will believe them anyway. Even without such overt pressure, victims may fear that they will not be believed, often with good reason. All forms of abuse undermine the self-worth and self-esteem of victims, providing fertile ground for the internalization of shame and self-blame. As discussed throughout this book, victims are silenced and blamed in so many ways — sometimes intentionally, sometimes not — including through comments such as:

- "It's your word against theirs."
- "We have no indication that person has ever behaved like that with anyone else."
- "If it did happen the way you say it did, then why didn't you say something earlier?"
- "But didn't you go back to him/her later on? Why would you, if you were being abused?"
- "If it were so bad, why do you still say you love them?"
- "If the Catholic/Anglican/United Church did that to you why are you still in their congregation?"

Disclosing direct abuse can be especially challenging when those perpetrating it are family members. Victims may not know what to expect and whether or not they will be believed or supported, and may fear the consequences of doing so: of getting in trouble, of the family breaking up, of having to move house or talk to the police and so on (see Alaggia 2005). Trust, respect, authority, loyalty and the expectation of gratitude can all get in the way of disclosing direct abuse, especially if this involves sexual violation (see London et al. 2005). Complicating matters is that not all relationships in which abuse occurs are *only, and always,* abusive. Love and abuse can, and does, coexist (Fraser 2008). Abusers may intermittently show care and regard for victims, for example, by complimenting and praising them, buying special presents, doing fun activities such as swimming or playing basketball, offering special favours and so on (see Fraser 2008). Relationships that are experienced as both abusive and pleasurable, affirming and degrading, are especially difficult to navigate.

The issues associated with disclosing direct abuse are influenced not just by age, but also by gender, sexuality, class, ability and religion (see Priebe and Svedin 2008). The very young and elderly, and especially people with disabilities, may find this additionally challenging where the abuse involves relatives or caregivers who provide practical day-to-day support. In this context, reluctance to disclose should never be interpreted as evidence of consent, nor of the inability to conceptualize what is happening as abuse; rather, this reflects the very limiting contexts in which many people live. Victims may be very aware of their (lowly) place in the system, as well as their own households, and the little control that they have over their income, housing and other important life matters. Importantly, not all victims can be confident that disclosing abuse will improve their circumstances; they face very real risks including eviction, abandonment, humiliation, loss of access and/or resources and further abuse and violence.

RESPONDING TO PERPETRATORS OF DIRECT VIOLENCE

Perpetrator responses commonly vary according to the type of (direct) violence. In contrast to generic violences (such as that between men), domestic violence is understood as gendered violence (see Chapter 5) and positioned as a distinct behaviour requiring particular models of intervention (discussed further later in this chapter). In contrast, non-domestic violence intervention largely occurs in the justice/correctional setting — largely in response to criminal violence — and is, most often, designed for and targeted at male offenders. In this context, programs range from more generic, relatively short anger management programs to intensive and longer term specialist interventions reserved for abnormal (excessive or un-controllable) violent behaviour(s). As discussed in Chapter 7, interventions designed to improve decision making mistakenly suggest that we choose how to behave on the basis of costs and benefits analysis ("rational choice" theories), while also assuming that non-violent behaviour is inherently good and rewarding. Among other problems, this focus on individual choice deflects attention away from wider patterns of inequality and injustice, specifically those structural and cultural violences that shape the experience of oppression. It is our position that, to be consistent with AOP principles, interventions must consider all forms of violence, not just direct violence. Within the parameters of social justice, all sorts of responses should be canvassed in order to ensure that not only is the diversity among perpetrators recognized, but also the overlap between perpetrators and victims acknowledged.

A Note on Culture and Perpetrator Interventions

Many perpetrator interventions have their origins in narrowly defined, scientific, positivist bodies of knowledge that (wrongly) assume that "methods that are found to be effective within one culture are likely to be universally valid and generalizable across different groups" (Day 2003: 4). As observed by Day (2003: 6), however, notions of universality are "at best culturally determined, and at worst, oppressive." For example, psychology-based interventions such as cognitive behavioural therapies (discussed later) tend to "emphasise individual factors and de-emphasise contextual or cultural factors" (4). Even programs specifically designed for cultural groups tend to use standard content that has been modified by adding in (what are assumed to be) culturally relevant issues and material. Sometimes — but not always — these programs are "delivered by a counsellor of the same cultural group with ties to the cultural community" (Mackay et al. 2015: 5). Exceptions exist, but these tend to be localized and are often not sufficiently resourced or developed to be sustainable in the longer term. Indigenous peoples the world over have been especially poorly served in this respect.

In the excerpt below, Cunneen and Rowe discuss the situation for Indigenous Australians; the issues they raise though are likely to have broader relevance for all colonized countries:

> Indigenous programs start with the collective Indigenous experience. Inevitably, that involves an understanding of the cumulative harms and long-term outcomes of colonisation, including genocidal policies and practices; the loss of lands; the disruptions of culture; the changing of traditional roles of men and women; the collective loss and sorrow of the removal of children; and relocation of communities. Criminal offending is not only understood as an outcome of disadvantage and marginalisation: it is also linked to non-economic deprivation "such as damage to identity and culture, as well as trauma and grief" (Aboriginal and Torres Strait Islander Social Justice Commissioner 2002: 136).
>
> Individual harms and wrongs are placed within a social context. On the one hand, offenders are dealt with as individuals responsible for their own actions: their pain and the forces that propel them to harmful behaviour towards themselves and others are confronted. On the other hand, they are understood within a collective context of the experience of Indigenous peoples in the dominant non-Indigenous society. The explanatory context — the explanation for behaviour — is within the collective experiences of Indigenous peoples. Healing is not simply about addressing individualised offending behaviour. It is fundamentally about addressing trauma.

... Individual and collective grief and loss become core issues that programs need to address rather than focusing on criminogenic need. Mainstream programs simply ignore the nexus between oppression and liberation, between collective grief and loss and individual healing. Indigenous healing programs start from this nexus: they begin with understanding the outcomes and effects of longer-term oppression, and move from there towards the healing of individuals. (Cunneen and Rowe 2014: 59–60)

Perpetrator Intervention Programs and Accountability

Intervention programs for perpetrators of domestic violence are widely used across the world. While programs differ substantially in their approach and content, most are designed to target the behaviour, attitudes and beliefs of perpetrators (Mackay et al. 2015: 5). Domestic violence perpetrator intervention programs may be voluntary or court-mandated, community or custodial, however, the vast majority are group based.

Perspectives on understanding and intervening in domestic violence are quite polarized. There is a discernible split between those that emphasize the individual/psychological and those who focus on the broader socio-political context (Laing 2002). Correspondingly, while most mainstream psychological approaches conceptualize domestic violence in terms of incidents and events, socio-political approaches (compatible with AOP), are more likely to see this as a process of domination and control. Reflecting their diverse theoretical underpinnings, different program models may emphasize socio-political factors, personal dysfunction, learned behaviour, behavioural deficits and/or psychopathy (Laing 2002).

Interestingly, whereas non-domestic violence intervention is generally associated with specialist psychological expertise, domestic violence is understood as gendered violence and more commonly undertaken by the "applied knowledge" professions (Rose, O'Malley and Valverde 2006), including social workers, probation officers, and community health/welfare workers. This distinction probably reflects the essentialist tendency in mainstream psychology to conceptualize gender as sex difference and an "independent variable," implying a causal link between biological sex and violent behaviour (Anderson 2005: 863).

Responses to violence, whether domestic or non-domestic, increasingly emphasize individual responsibility and choice — or "perpetrator accountability." The term "accountability" is used in different, sometimes contradictory, ways. For example, to be held accountable invokes the moral imperative that individuals acknowledge their wrong-doing and face the (generally punitive) consequences. Accountability also refers to the integrity of practitioners and, in particular, to ensuring that their work with perpetrators is both transparent and accountable to victims of violence, their experiences and immediate/ongoing safety. References to accountability further point to the responsibility of the broader community to expose and address violence. The extract below nicely captures the interrelatedness of these dimensions of accountability:

> perpetrator accountability is about all parts of the system working together. It is not about excluding, or excusing, violent and controlling men. It is not simply about locking people up, and certainly not about letting them off the hook. First and foremost, accountability means making victims of family violence safe. It means keeping the perpetrator firmly in view, not isolating him or propelling him from scrutiny. It means leveraging the authority of the justice system and whatever stake in conformity the perpetrator has to ensure that he complies with the law. It means measuring the right things. It means keeping not only the violence and its user visible but also the system's response. It means every part of the system bearing responsibility and the victim setting the pace. Just as importantly, it means coming to terms with the fact that family violence is core business in the legal system and has to be treated — and funded — as such. At its simplest, perpetrator accountability is about widening our gaze to include individuals who use family violence — bringing them squarely into the spotlight; making them responsible for their own behaviour, certainly; but *all* of us accountable for how the community steps up to meet it. (Centre for Innovative Justice 2015: 88)

Domestic Violence Programs: Models and Approaches

The rest of this chapter provides an overview of key program approaches and/or principles in domestic and family violence intervention. Those considered here include psychoeducational, psychotherapeutic and cognitive behavioural programs, as well as those based upon narrative, strengths-based and solution-focused principles. This list is not exhaustive; not only are there are other programs out there, but, importantly, the actual interventions on offer may not fit easily within any one category, instead drawing on various programs/models. Many practitioners, including those delivering domestic violence programs, talk about taking an eclectic (theoretical) approach to practice. The problem with this "overly pragmatic approach of 'taking a bit from here, and a bit from there'" (Vlais 2014: 1), though, is that it risks "falling into the trap of unsystematic 'technical eclecticism,' where the underlying philosophies and values of the program become inconsistent and confused … and its integrity and coherency become watered down" (1).

Psychoeducational Programs:
The Duluth Coordinated Community Response

The Duluth Coordinated Community Response, also known as the "Duluth Model" is probably the most widely recognized model of domestic violence perpetrator intervention. According to Dobash et al. (2000: 48), it is "generally acknowledged to be one of the most successful community-based projects for violent men anywhere in the world." The Duluth Domestic Abuse Intervention Project (DAIP), to which it refers, was established in the early 1980s in North America to develop an integrated community and multi-agency response to violence against women and children (see Pence and Paymar 1993). The aim was for a "coordinated community response" and of "law enforcement, criminal and civil courts, and human service providers working together to make communities safer for victims" (Paymar and Barnes 2011: 10). The Duluth Model emphasized the need for perpetrators — men — to be actively held accountable for their violent behaviour. At the time, this represented a significant shift in ways of thinking about men's violence. Similarly innovative — and of particular relevance to AOP students and practitioners — was the Duluth model's notion of community responsibility, specifically that the "onus of intervention" should fall on the community rather than on "isolated victims" (Gadd 2004: 175). The Duluth Model consists of a series of psychoeducational sessions, but was never intended to be just a group program. Rather, it sought to address systemic issues, such as those concerning policing, appropriate arrests and prosecutions:

> The Duluth Model is not a treatment program, but rather a coordinated response by community institutions that holds offenders accountable for their behaviour while ensuring that victims are protected from ongoing violence. The core elements of the Duluth Model are:
>
> 1. Written policies that centralize victim safety and offender accountability
> 2. Practices that link intervening practitioners and agencies together
> 3. An entity that tracks and monitors cases and assesses data
> 4. An interagency process that brings practitioners together to dialogue and resolve problems
> 5. A central role in the process for victim advocates, shelters, and battered women
> 6. A shared philosophy about domestic violence
> 7. A system that shifts responsibility for victim safety from the victim to the system. (Paymar and Barnes 2011: 10)

The Duluth Model is underpinned by a broadly feminist understanding of domestic abuse and violence as a primary means by which men exercise power and control over women. Importantly, it shifted the focus from physical assault, more narrowly, to the broader spectrum and dynamics of abuse — the "constellation of violence as women experience it" (Wilson 2003: 3). Working from the premise that violence is learned — that men are not just "born this way" — the Duluth Model calls for perpetrators to interrogate their sense of entitlement and reflect on the benefits derived from their use of violence. For instance, the aim of the group program, Creating a Process of Change for Men Who Batter, is to "immerse [men] in critical thinking and self-reflection" while engaging them "in a dialogue about their beliefs" (Paymar and Barnes 2011: 11). Skill development through "role-playing and other exercises" is also prioritized so that "participants become aware of alternatives to violence" (11). The Duluth Model is probably best known for its power and control wheel (Figure 3), developed for use in its perpetrator programs as a way of graphically representing the "lived experience of women who live with a man who beats them" (DAIP 2011). Their equality wheel (Figure 4) — an especially useful tool for AOP practice — was subsequently developed to "describe the changes needed for men ... to move from being abusive to a non-violent partnership" (DAIP 2011).

Criticisms of the Duluth Model include that it is "too confrontational in its approach" (McMaster and Gregory 2003: 23) and potentially shaming to men. Such a confrontational style, it is argued, "inadvertently models coercion and control, rather than demonstrating trusting and cooperative relationships," thereby limiting "treatment effectiveness" (Baker 2011: 200). The model's feminist underpinnings — in particular, linking men's violence to societal gender norms, is variously seen as both its greatest strength and its greatest weakness. With respect to the latter, some critics have interpreted this as suggesting "all men want to dominate women" (Paymar and Barnes 2011: 10) and argue that this is not useful nor likely to be culturally appropriate for engaging diverse groups of men.

As with other perpetrator programs, perspectives on the effectiveness of the Duluth Model vary. Even those evaluations showing a "very modest success rate" have been "hard to substantiate," given low completion (and high drop-out) rates (Milner 2004: 81). Nonetheless, while it may not be possible to prove that the Duluth Model is more effective than other interventions (Mackay et al. 2015: 6), it is important that we do not overlook the broader elements of the approach, that is, its value as a coordinated community response. Its emphasis on the system, rather than isolated perpetrator programs, is what distinguishes the Duluth Model from other interventions and ensures its relevance to AOP perspectives.

Figures 3 & 4: The Duluth power and control and equality wheels

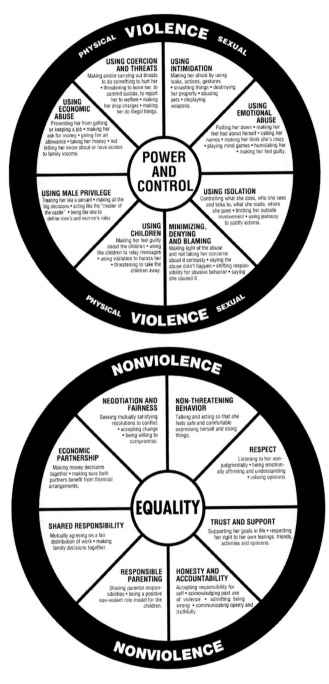

Source: Domestic Abuse Intervention Programs <www.theduluthmodel.org>.

Cognitive Behavioural Approaches

Cognitive-behavioural approaches, while broad and diverse, share a common focus on the "interdependence of thoughts, feelings and behaviour" (McMaster and Gregory 2003: 20) within the context of "people's problem behaviours" (Payne 2014: 150). Cognitive behavioural approaches, more commonly referred to as CBT (cognitive behavioural therapy), focus on individual problems, deficits, solutions and outcomes. They are ordinarily underpinned by a commitment to positivist knowledge and evidence — that is, the assumption that there exists "universal knowledge which is relevant in every culture" (Payne 2014: 153).

From a cognitive behavioural perspective, violent behaviour is generally understood as the outcome of an individual's thoughts (or perceptions) and feelings about a situation, thus the focus for intervention is identifying, tracking and ultimately modifying "unhelpful thinking patterns" (McMaster and Gregory 2003: 21). Depending on the practitioner, this might involve challenging ideas about "male entitlement and victim blame" (Laing 2002: 5) or a more narrow focus on idiosyncratic or "dysfunctional" patterns of thinking. CBT has consequently been criticized for its individualist, short-term focus and its emphasis on individual deficits. Its failure to acknowledge that individual problems are, largely, the "manifestations of oppressive social structures" (Payne 2014: 153) means that it has limited appeal and relevance for AOP.

More person-centred approaches to CBT do exist, however, and have more potential for anti-oppressive practice. For example, motivational interviewing and mindfulness training may be usefully integrated with AOP work, especially if combined with a harm-reduction focus and strengths perspective. Care must always be taken, though, to ensure that work with individuals is flexible and dynamic; that program objectives and adherence to a "detailed manual of action" are not prioritized over the needs and interests of participants (Payne 2014: 165).

Anger Management Programs

Anger management (AM) programs, on the whole, exemplify core CBT principles in their emphasis on "anger as the impetus for violence" (McMaster and Gregory 2003: 19). Participants are encouraged to identify their "early warning signs" and are taught specific techniques, such as "time out" and self-talk, to "interrupt the tension building and replace these with more appropriate behaviours" (19). AM programs are generally short (four to six sessions) and relatively low key, delivered in a non-confrontational and neutral manner. They are routinely (and frequently) run in correctional and other institutional settings, with some participants attending and completing the program on multiple occasions. The focus on anger is underpinned by two interlinked assumptions: firstly, that violence is the "expression of angry impulses" (Howells et al. 2002: 1); and secondly, that violence arises from "skills deficits" (Laing 2002: 5). Both of these are problematic for AOP, especially in the context of family/domestic violence, not least because coordinated community responses including "linked partner contact" are unlikely to be in place (Respect 2015: 17).

Morran (2003: 5) observes that men "can be routinely violent without necessarily being angry [and that] mind games, financial control and isolation are not about anger, they are about power." It is also the case that anger, even intense and explosive anger, does not inevitably result in violent behaviour. Emphasizing anger management as the "problem" wrongly implies that violence is somehow "caused by external forces, and therefore *beyond* the control of the perpetrator, rather than something which is used instead to *exert* control" (Centre for Innovative Justice 2015: 34, emphasis in original). Even more problematic is the tendency for AM programs to assume that victims bear at least some responsibility for "provoking the anger and thus the abuse" (Laing 2002: 5). Widespread popular and professional attachment to the idea that anger and violence go together is critical and is particularly hard to break, despite the lack of supporting evidence. While AM programs may well be useful in other respects, there is little evidence to support their effectiveness in the context of violence; the overall impact of AM programs for violence prevention is "small" and lacking in "real clinical significance" (Howells et al. 2002: 3).

Moral Reasoning: The Moral Reconation Program

Moral Reconation Therapy (MRT) also utilizes a cognitive behavioural approach in its emphasis on the "changes in cognitions [that] lead to changes in behaviour" (Ferguson and Wormith 2013: 3). Unlike more conventional CBT programs, however, it is uniquely focused on *moral* reasoning. The MRT group program is highly structured and delivered in accordance with a facilitator manual and participant workbook that aims to "influence how offenders think about moral issues and make moral judgments" (4). Facilitators of the program must have completed accredited training and be recognized as "MRT certified." As a deficit-oriented model, MRT assumes that there is something wrong with, or lacking in people who commit offences. This translates into a focus on individual change, achieved through group work that confronts "individual beliefs, attitudes and behaviours" and reinforces "positive behaviour and habits [and] positive identity formation," while developing "frustration tolerance" and "higher stages of moral reasoning" (Ferguson and Wormith 2013: 4).

Showing little recognition of structural and cultural violence, nor any of the ways in which oppressed groups are over-regulated and over-policed, educational psychologists Gregory Little and Kenneth Robinson (1998: 135) developed MRT on the basis of their belief that offenders "enter treatment with low levels of moral development, strong narcissism, low ego/identity strength, poor self-concept, low self-esteem, inability to delay gratification, relatively strong defence mechanisms, and relatively strong resistance to change and treatment." Accordingly, the goal of intervention, in the MRT view, is to "move offenders from a lower, hedonistic level of moral reasoning (pleasure vs. pain) to a higher level where social rules and others become important" (Ferguson and Wormith 2013: 3). Drawing upon Kohlberg's stages of moral development, MRT:

> lies at the crossroads between ethics and psychology, where issues such as moral reasoning, moral responsibility, psychological egoism, and moral character are featured. Most offenders are not psychiatrically disabled, amoral, or hopeless psychopaths … Rather, their moral development was somehow stunted at a lower, more child-like stage of development. However, with the proper treatment, many offenders can resume their natural development. Although MRT emphasizes the passions and formal moral reasoning, the latter is preeminent. Formal moral reasoning is the avenue whereby offenders modify beliefs, identify distorted thinking, and gain control over their passions. (Ferguson and Wormith 2013: 21–22)

"Bringing peace to relationships" is an adaptation of the MRT program for use with perpetrators of domestic violence. While the program is a little longer (twenty-four to twenty-six sessions as compared to twelve to sixteen sessions) and includes some additional content, it applies the same principles and strategies as the standard MRT program, aiming to challenge "inappropriate thought processes" and develop "positive" skills. A participant workbook with associated group and homework activities is central to the program:

> the participants present their homework during the group sessions and move through the 12 stages in accordance to the standards of their homework and testimonies. Group facilitators and fellow group members vote on the standards of homework and testimonies. Length of the program for the participants depends on standards of the homework presented, compliance and engagement. Should the homework not reach the expected performance level the participant would need to repeat the required step. (Corrections SA 2011)

The critiques made of CBT apply equally to MRT; critics observe that MRT is highly individualistic, "rationalistic" and ethnocentric (Ferguson and Wormith 2013: 22). Grounded in Western ideals of independence, free will and personal responsibility, MRT narrowly focuses on individuals as the origin of social problems, overemphasizing individual agency and neglecting the social-structural context for these problems. Its narrow understanding of morality and tendency for programs and facilitators to be prescriptive and didactic means that it is largely incompatible with AOP principles.

Strengths-Based Perspectives

Strengths-based perspectives, closely aligned with solution-focused and narrative approaches, can be clearly distinguished from other therapeutic interventions on the basis of their focus on a client's strengths rather than the problems that they face. Positioned as optimistic, positive and future-oriented, the relationship — or therapeutic alliance — between client and practitioner is seen as pivotal with strong emphasis on collaboration, non-judgement and "unconditional positive regard" (Payne 2014: 262). Described by Connolly and Harms (2015: 135) as "story-telling theories," they are centrally concerned with the ways in which the "stories we live by" impact upon "human well-being and identity" (135). In emphasizing the transformative potential of stories, key areas for work include giving voice to "our own internalised stories" so that we may understand how these influence the way we live our lives — "how we think, feel and act" — and, ultimately change or "re-author" these stories to "enable more positive and rewarding life outcomes" (Connolly and Harms 2015: 135).

Strengths, solution and narrative approaches are closely connected and motivated by a shared belief in people's capacity to change and a commitment to uncovering stories of strength and resilience. Each approach, nonetheless, represents a distinct perspective. Fundamental to the strengths-based perspective is the "belief that people have strengths and are motivated towards well-being and optimal functioning" (Connolly and Harms 2015: 138). Solution-focused approaches place more emphasis on identifying exceptions — those times when the problem was "dealt with or experienced differently" — which are seen as providing "insight into new ways of being" (148). Narrative therapy, discussed next, goes further, seeking to provide "options for the telling and retelling of preferred stories of people's lives" (Milner and Jessop 2003: 129).

Strengths and solution-focused approaches have an "important place" (Vlais 2014: 10) in AOP work with perpetrators of violence. Solution-focused men's groups, for example, may help "group members construct new discourses and strategies" (McMaster and Gregory 2003: 31) by building on and extending the "competencies that they already have" and promoting a "greater sense of agency" (29). Applied to men's behaviour change work, key aspects of a strengths or solution-focused approach include: "separating the man from the behaviour"; "assuming that there is something more to the man than his behaviour"; "unearthing men's existing, or latent, ethics and motivations ... honourable intentions, goals and needs"; and helping men to "identify existing or previous strategies that have been useful in choosing non-violence" (Vlais 2014: 9–10). This last point — the discovery of exceptions — is considered especially important because it "enables the identification of the beginnings of a solution in the violent person's current repertoire" (Milner and Jessop 2003: 129).

Strengths approaches are problematic, however, if not integrated with intersectional analyses of power relations and grounded in a thorough understanding of class, race and gender politics. Programs that lack clear lines of accountability to the experiences of victims are potentially dangerous. In terms of effectiveness, evidence indicates that programs that combine a strengths focus with a coordinated, multi-agency domestic violence response are most effective, with "lower drop-out rates, higher completion rates, [and] longer term reduction in violence" (Milner 2004: 92).

Narrative Approaches

In contrast to cognitive behavioural approaches, the narrative approach is underpinned by the idea that, as humans, we construct stories — or narratives — to make sense of our experiences. As a "respectful, non-blaming approach" to practice, it seeks to centre "people as the experts in their own lives" and separate "problems" from people (Dulwich Centre n.d.). Developed originally by Michael White and David Epston, narrative therapy is concerned with the "telling and retelling of preferred stories of people's lives" (Milner and Jessop 2003: 129).

A distinction is made between dominant stories, as the "primary means of interpreting reality" (O'Connor et al. 2004: 28), and "alternate stories," which are drawn upon less frequently. The problems people seek help for are understood as "embedded in a dominant narrative that robs the person/s of success." Narrative therapy aims to "discover unique outcomes," that is, those times when that "problem didn't exist and/or was 'defeated' by client/s" (O'Connor et al. 2004: 28). Discovering and co-constructing alternative stories about the self and others can be empowering. Identified through conversations between therapist and client, "unique outcomes" become the building blocks for developing alternate stories. Narrative therapists focus on "moments of success" because they build "personal agency" (O'Connor et al. 2004: 28).

Narrative therapy approaches have been especially influential in the field of perpetrator intervention, specifically men's behaviour change programs. In viewing violence as a problem that is separate from people who use it (known as "externalization"), narrative practices focus on the "skills, competencies, beliefs, values, commitments and abilities" (Dulwich Centre n.d.) that can enable men to "reduce the influence" of violence in their lives.

Interestingly, McMaster and Gregory (2003: 26) refer to the narrative approach as "restraint theory" or "restraint-based practice" in recognition of its core focus on what stops people from behaving badly and/or changing their behaviour. Unlike the problem-focused approaches discussed earlier, narrative approaches are especially attentive to social and cultural dynamics as constraints on behaviour, including, for example, gendered beliefs, ideas and traditions about male entitlement, privilege and so on. Externalizing men's "internalised stories," particularly those of "misogyny and woman-blaming" (Milner and Jessop 2003: 129), provides a way to explore the social/structural context of gender and violence, bringing together the personal and the political.

Alan Jenkins' (1990) *Invitations to Responsibility: The Therapeutic Engagement of Men Who Are Violent and Abusive* is perhaps the most widely known and highly regarded application of narrative ideas to violence intervention. In Jenkins' (1997: 44) explanation:

> Men who enact violence tend to engage with a range of ideas, preoccupations and thinking practices that are self-righteous, blaming, vengeful and contemptuous about other individuals or subcultures. Some invest in sexually exploitative preoccupations, which are increasingly self-centred and insensitive to the actual feelings and experience of others. It is these thinking patterns that create a context for violence and abuse. In my work with men who enact violence or abuse I have found that they tend to "work themselves up" with these self-righteous, blaming and vengeful preoccupations. They "intoxicate themselves" with a range of ideas, a range of attributions of blame, and give themselves a range of permissions to hurt other people.
>
> Violence and abusive behaviour are the result of active choices which are informed by sequences of self-centred preoccupation, rationalisation and justification. These ideas and preoccupations are in turn informed by dominant cultural ideologies, which relate to beliefs about entitlement, privilege and power and expectations of deference and submission from those regarded as inferior or of lesser status.

Jenkins argues that, to be effective, work with men who perpetrate violence and abuse must seek to open up possibilities for responsibility taking and accountability by, "tak[ing] violence out of a context of pathology and into a broader context that examines the ways in which ideology informs behaviour, and invites personal choice and personal responsibility" (Jenkins 1997: 44).

The narrative emphasis on the practitioner–client relationship as essentially collaborative, and the importance of multiple opportunities for mutual learning and reflection is especially significant for AOP practice. In contrast to more confrontational and/or pathologizing approaches, the aim is to engage clients in purposeful conversations in which they are invited to explore "their beliefs about their use of violence and [the] 'cultural' stories [that] support these beliefs" (Milner and Jessop 2003: 139).

Restorative Justice

Restorative justice (RJ) approaches are generally talked about in terms of "repairing the harm" within the context of an understanding of crime (or direct forms of violence) as "fundamentally a violation of people and interpersonal relationships" (Cunneen and White 2011: 357). While a broad range of restorative approaches exist, commonly these share an emphasis on social inclusiveness, providing "symbolic and practical solution[s] to actual harms" (369) and positioning victims and community as central to the process. In practice, restorative justice is concerned with the bringing together of offenders, victims and community stakeholders for the purpose of interactive discussion and negotiation. Emphasis is placed on offender accountability and hearing — and validating — the voice of the victim regarding the impact and harm caused by the offence.

The use of RJ as a response to domestic violence has been a topic of debate for some time. Examples of domestic violence programs with a restorative focus can be found throughout the U.K., Europe, North America and Australia. However, its appropriateness in cases of domestic violence remains controversial and has not, as yet, been taken up more broadly. The appeal of RJ in responding to domestic violence is that it can, potentially, provide a safe space in which victims can "tell their story," where they can have their experience "heard and acknowledged." It can be used to promote "genuine accountability, rather than denial, on the part of the perpetrator" (Centre for Innovative Justice 2015: 76). Restorative processes can offer a "way of subverting the logic of violence itself by giving voice and validation to those violence seeks to silence" (Hamill and Marshall 2015: 3). They may be especially valuable for those victims who choose not to involve the criminal justice system, but nonetheless desire a response and/or seek specific outcomes. For example, this could better address the needs of victims "who do not want to see, or cannot afford to have, their partners incarcerated, but simply want their partner to acknowledge and take responsibility for their behaviour" (77).

Critics of restorative justice, however, highlight the potential for "further abuse and manipulation" given that domestic violence usually constitutes an ongoing pattern of behaviour, involving "cycles in which violence is followed by apparent remorse and reconciliation," rather than isolated acts. Its potential to re-privatize domestic violence is another significant concern. Diverting domestic violence cases away from the criminal justice system may, for example, be seen as repositioning this as interpersonal conflict and risks re-traumatizing victims without regard for their immediate and ongoing safety.

Still relevant today, this excerpt from Edwards and Sharpe (2004: 22) nicely summarises the "state of play" regarding restorative justice:

> Based on the literature available at this point, it appears that restorative justice holds theoretic promise as an intervention in domestic violence, offering victims and offenders something they typically have been unable to get through other approaches: a choice of avenues for how to meet particular needs, including the potential for a focused dialogue about the violence that one partner has perpetrated on the other ... Yet the complex dynamics of violence between intimate partners makes the dynamics of restorative justice in that context more complex as well ... Informed consent and unencumbered participation are more difficult to assess and ensure; preparation becomes more crucial and more challenging; unseen dangers can be laced through the parties' dialogue. Violence puts a relationship on unstable ground, and a dialogue about that violence and its effects may then also rest on unstable ground ... [There is a pressing need for] more research, more consultation and dialogue, and an unwavering commitment to listening and responding to the needs of those impacted by domestic violence.

"THE LINK" AND ANIMALS-ASSISTED INTERVENTIONS

Advances have been made in recent decades with regard to understanding the links between human and animal violence. Shorthanded as "The Link," this diverse collection of work examines how humans may express malevolence through the abuse of domestic animals, human partners and children. The Link proposes the close interconnection of four fields of violence and abuse: (1) animal abuse; (2) child maltreatment; (3) domestic violence; and (4) elder abuse (National Link Coalition 2016). In several countries (but not yet Australia), the cross reporting of human and animal abuse is taking place, recognizing the intersecting and cumulative harms of violence for human and animal victims/survivors.

Alongside The Link, Animal-Assisted Interventions (AAIs) have made their way into many health, welfare and education services. AAIs are deliberate, goal-directed attempts to incorporate animals into therapeutic processes that are designed to address some kind of *human* issue or problem (Kruger and Serpell 2006). While there is no reason that the term AAI cannot include the work one group of non-humans does for one another that is purposeful, emotionally attuned and therapeutically oriented, in its mainstream use AAI places humans at the centre of the receipt of care from other animals.

There are many possible applications of AAIs and dogs, in particular, are regularly employed. Guide dogs for people with visual impairments have a long history, and are well known. Perhaps less known are the many other programs, such as those involving returned soldiers diagnosed with post-traumatic stress, in which dogs play a major role in re-entry to community life. Dogs are also being used in Reading Buddies programs in which, instead of reading to a human, children sit beside a dog — whose handler is nearby — and read. Many children find this not just comforting but also a safe space to practice their reading without the fear of human criticism. Paws in Prison programs aim to contribute to the rehabilitation of prisoners by involving them in the rehabilitation of cats and dogs, and various Greyhound Adoption programs exist to socialize ex-racing dogs for domestic life.

For all of the potential benefits of AAIs, however, Kruger and Serpell (2006: 25) note that the human–animal studies area is diverse and contested, "lacking a unified, widely accepted or empirically supported theoretical framework for explaining how and why relationships are potentially therapeutic." There are broad differences in philosophy and ethics: for instance, in the Americans with Disabilities Act of 1990, "service animals are typically viewed *as tools* rather than treatments and thus do not constitute an animal assisted intervention as we define the term" (Kruger and Serpell 2006: 25).

Comfort dog programs such as K9support are now being used to assist victims/ survivors of sexual abuse to give court testimonies. Young and old alike report the comfort associated with giving their statement in the presence of a dog rather than a support person (Booker 2016). The potential problem of such programs, however, is the way in which canine comfort can be assumed to be a human entitlement rather than gift of care. This may sound far-fetched, but remember that the idea of comfort can obscure abuse, as seen through the experiences of "comfort women" in Asia. The term "comfort women" refers to the approximately 200,000 Asian women that were forced by the Japanese government into brothels designed to sexually serve Japanese military during the Asian and Pacific War (1937–1945). Many of the women were from Korea, at that time a colony of Japan, young and unmarried. The testimony of former comfort women in the 1990s was a significant trigger for public recognition of — and subsequent protest regarding — rape in war, especially the systematic rape of women under the guise of comforting men (Min 2003).

The ethical legitimacy of AAIs rests on humans' preparedness to recognize animals not as possessions or tools but as sentient beings, with their own needs and interests (Legge 2016; Taylor et al. 2016). This ethical stance begins with us posing serious questions about the conventional ways in which we distinguish humans from (other) animals, ways that, in effect, deny human animality — our connectedness to other species and our place in the whole world (see Legge 2016; Hamilton and Taylor 2013). Such artificial separations block our understanding of, for instance, the complexity of interspecies relationships and the insidious ways in which species of animals are placed on a hierarchy by humans who position themselves at its pinnacle (see Hamilton and Taylor 2013).

CONCLUSION

Work with family and domestic violence is one of the "few areas of practice where the individual and the social, the psychological and the political are so closely entwined" (Humphries and Tsantefski 2013: 177). Vlais (2014: 19), for example, conceptualizes domestic violence-perpetrator work as a "non-violent social justice struggle" and argues that those who choose to work with men must "act in solidarity with those affected by men's violence." In this sense, perpetrator interventions are compatible with AOP;

> while the welfare, dignity and wellbeing of the men in the programs matter, and while there are potentially real gains for men if they work hard through the program … [this] work is primarily about assisting women's existing resistance, struggle and strivings for dignity. (Vlais 2014: 19)

AOP-oriented perpetrator work takes seriously the complex relations of power, oppression and privilege and, in particular, the "intersectionalities that affect men's [and women's] experiences" (Vlais 2014: 19). This recognizes:

> some, perhaps many, participants in perpetrator programs … have experienced oppression in other ways — based on social class, ethnicity, sexual identity or disability. While these cannot be seen as an excuse for their use of violence, helping men to understand their struggles and resistance for dignity in the face of these experiences might be important, in some cases, for helping them to understand the effects of their violence and controlling behaviours on their family. (Vlais 2014: 19)

10. CLOSING COMMENTS

Throughout this book we have shown that violence and abuse occur directly, but also through structures and cultures. Our discussion has deliberately included violence that is denied, trivialized or discounted. We have stressed the need to understand violence and abuse in relation to the intersections of oppression and privilege. As many of us experience both oppression and privilege, we must pick our way through the web of complexities that make up our often mixed identities, as women or men, white people or people of colour, disabled and/or ageing, straight, trans, gay and/or queer or members of different socio-economic locations, all of which affect our life chances, burden of disease and ways of seeing the world.

Our rationale for responding to violence is based on the principles of peace and non-violence, however difficult this can be. Throughout this book we have stressed the challenging nature of AOP work. Working across differences requires the shelving of ego-driven motivations and hosing down of self-righteous indignation. Professionally, it calls for us to work across disciplines and boundaries, for example, ambulance officers with nurses, doctors and social workers, teachers with police, youth workers with drug treatment staff, and across the borders of professional, sub-professional and administrative. Collectively, we amount to more than our immediate roles, tasks and identities and, together, we can contribute to practices that are not (as) oppressive. This is particularly important as neoliberalism permeates entire health, welfare and education networks, leading to a shift in focus away from the needs of people and towards matters of cost reduction and efficiency.

From an AOP perspective, we take the often difficult and confronting view that even the most violent person can change. In Chapter 6 we stressed the importance of rights being extended to all, including people who have committed brutal acts, cruel deeds and even atrocities. By virtue of being human and a member of our global society, every person must be afforded value. This means that *perpetrators of direct violence cannot be ignored.* Doing so leaves current and future victims at risk and, importantly, denies perpetrators the opportunity for change. To quote forensic psychiatrist and violence expert James Gilligan (cited in Aponte 2011), who has worked for many years with violent offenders in the U.S. prison system, "there's nobody who [we should] regard as hopeless." Change — individual, social, cultural and structural — is the oxygen of AOP practice. While we accept that it is possible that there are violent perpetrators who are unable or unwilling to change, we consider this the vast minority. Neither do we hold the view that people are born bad, rather we take seriously the profound privileges associated with our vantage point.

Understanding violence and abuse from an AOP perspective requires that we look beyond acts and incidents — whether individual or collective — for context and meaning. It means asking different — and tough — questions. A commitment to AOP represents a commitment to critical questioning through which we seek to disrupt the "logic of hierarchical and oppositional social relations" (Greig 2002) that underlies all abuse and violence.

Collectively, we must commit to facilitating the difficult and confronting conversations required to produce fair, responsive and helpful services. We know the benefits of collectivizing the experiences of abuse victims/survivors. Approached with caution, there may be equal benefits to collectivizing the experiences of perpetrators. While this complexifies, rather than simplifies what (we think) we know about abuse and violence, it also enables us to extend our understanding of the interconnections between the personal and the political. Material conditions, especially the conditions of deprivation, cannot, however, be ignored. As Gilligan (1996: 238) argues, the most effective way to increase violence is to "widen the gap between the rich and the poor." This is a strategy being practiced "on a worldwide scale, among the increasingly impoverished nations of the third world," and one that we should expect to "culminate in increasing levels of violence, all over the world."

We have argued for AOP work to include problematizing and democratizing the production and valuing of knowledge about violence and abuse. Personal, not just professional or expert knowledge is important, this including the insights gained through lived experience and especially those of groups battling multiple forms of oppression. We must ensure that subordinated groups are provided with respectful spaces in which to voice their experiences, recognizing — and accepting — that these might also cause dominant and privileged groups to feel uncomfortable (Crichlow 2015).

Acknowledging our shared responsibility for social justice implies a commitment to "challenge one another and call one another to account for what [we] are doing or not doing" (Young 2006: 130). This does not mean descending into endless circular, indulgent discussions of personal politics or group dynamics. Instead it means being willing to temporarily shelve our need for comfort and affirmation, especially those of us who are multi-privileged (for instance if we are white, able-bodied, middle-class professionals). Whatever our role or status, AOP work is grounded in beliefs about equality and justice and the imperative to confront power, privilege and oppression. As Delpit (1995, cited in Crichlow 2015: 195, emphasis added) reminds us:

> we do not really see through our eyes or hear through our ears, *but through our beliefs.* To put our beliefs on hold is to cease to exist as ourselves for a moment — and that is not easy. It is painful as well, because it means turning yourself inside out, giving up your own sense of who you are, and being willing to see yourself in the unflattering light of another's angry gaze.

BIBLIOGRAPHY

Aboriginal and Torres Strait Islander Social Justice Commissioner. 2002. HREOC *Social Justice Report 2002*. <https://www.humanrights.gov.au/sites/default/files/content/social_justice/sj_report/sjreport02/Social_Justice_Report02.pdf> viewed 30 April 2014.

ABS (Australian Bureau of Statistics). 2010. *4714.0 — National Aboriginal and Torres Strait Islander Social Survey, 2008*. Canberra: Australian Bureau of Statistics, ACT <http://www.abs.gov.au/AUSSTATS/abs@.nsf/Lookup/4714.0Main+Features122008?OpenDocument>.

____. 2013a. *Cat. No. 4906.0 — Personal Safety, Australia, 2012*. Canberra: Australian Bureau of Statistics. <http://www.abs.gov.au/ausstats/abs@.nsf/Lookup/4906.0Explanatory+Notes12012>.

____. 2013b. *Cat. No. 3238.0.55.001 — Estimates of Aboriginal and Torres Strait Islander Australians, June 2011*. Canberra, Australian Bureau of Statistics. <http://www.abs.gov.au/ausstats/abs@.nsf/mf/3238.0.55.001>.

Acheson, Louise. 1993. "Depression or Oppression?" *Archives of Family Medicine*, 2, 5: 475.

Adams, Robert, Lena Dominelli, and Malcolm Payne (eds.). 2009. *Critical Practice in Social Work*. Palgrave Macmillan.

Adelman, Madelaine, Edna Erez, and Nadera Shalhoub-Kevorkian. 2003. "Policing Violence Against Minority Women in Multicultural Societies: 'Community' and the Politics of Exclusion." *Police & Society*, 7: 103–131.

Adelman, Madelaine, Hilary Haldane, and Jennifer R. Wies. 2012. "Mobilizing Culture as an Asset: A Transdisciplinary Effort yo Rethink Gender Violence." *Violence Against Women*, 18, 6: 691–700.

Agozino, Biko. 2000. "What Is Institutionalised? The Race-Class-Gender Articulation of Stephen Lawrence." In G. Mair and R. Tarling (eds.), *The British Criminology Conference: Selected Proceedings* (Vol. 3). Liverpool: British Society of Criminology Conference.

AIHW (Australian Institute of Health and Welfare). 2011. "Australian Burden of Disease Study, Impact and Causes of Illnesses and Deaths in Australia." <http://www.aihw.gov.au/WorkArea/DownloadAsset.aspx?id=60129555176>.

Alaggia, Ramona. 2005. "Disclosing the Trauma of Child Sexual Abuse: A Gender Analysis." *Journal of Loss and Trauma*, 10, 5: 453–470.

Aldama, Arturo J. 2003. *Violence and the Body: Race, Gender and the State.* Bloomington, IN: Indiana University Press.

Ali, Tazeen Saeed, Gunnhildur Arnadottir, and Asli Kulane. 2013. "Dowry Practices and Their Negative Consequences from a Female Perspective in Karachi, Pakistan: A Qualitative Study." *Health*, 5, 7A4: 84–91.

Aljazeera Human Rights. 2016. "Syria's War: Calls for Truce to get Aid into Aleppo." 22 Aug. <http://www.aljazeera.com/news/2016/08/syria-war-calls-truce-aid-aleppo-160821052204413.html> Retrieved 2 Sept., 2016.

Allan, June, Bob Pease, and Linda Briskman. 2009. *Critical Social Work: Theories and Practices for a Socially Just World.* Crows Nest, NSW: Allen & Unwin.

Altman, Jon. 2007. "The Howard Government's Northern Territory Intervention: Are Neo-Paternalism and Indigenous Development Compatible?" Centre for Aboriginal Economic Policy Research, Topical Issue No. 16/2007. <http://caepr.anu.edu.au/sites/default/files/Publications/topical/Altman_AIATSIS.pdf> Viewed 19 May 2015.

Anastasiou, Dimitris, and James. M. Kauffman. 2013. "The Social Model of Disability: Dichotomy Between Impairment and Disability." *Journal of Medicine and Philosophy*, 38, 4: 441–459.

Anaya, James. 2010. "Observations on the Northern Territory Emergency Response in Australia. United Nations Special Rapporteur on the situation of human rights and fundamental freedoms of indigenous people, February 2010." <http://www.ncca.org.au/files/Natsiec/NTER_Observations_FINAL_by_SR_Anaya_.pdf>.

Anderson, Benedict. 1983. *Imagined Communities: Reflections on the Origins and Spread of Nationalism.* London: Verso.

Anderson, Kirsten L. 2005. "Theorizing Gender in Intimate Partner Violence Research." *Sex Roles*, 52, 11/12: 853–865.

Androff, David.K. 2010. "Truth and Reconciliation Commissions (TRCs): An International Human Rights Intervention and Its Connection to Social Work." *British Journal of Social Work*, 40, 6: 1960–1977.

ANROWS (Australia's National Research Organisation for Women's Safety). 2015. "Violence against Women in Australia: Additional Analysis of the Australian Bureau of Statistics' Personal Safety Survey, 2012." *Horizons Research Report*, Issue 1.

Ansello, Edward F. 1978. "Ageism—The Subtle Stereotype." *Childhood Education*, 54, 3: 118–122.

Aponte, Rebecca. 2011. "James Gilligan on the Psychology and Treatment of Violent Offenders." <https://www.psychotherapy.net/interview/gilligan-violence#section-the-point-of-it-all>

Arias, Ileana. 2004. "Report from the CDC. The Legacy of Child Maltreatment: Long-Term Health Consequences for Women." *Journal of Women's Health*, 13, 5: 468–473.

Ashworth, Peter D., M. Ann Longmate, and Paul Morrison. 1992. "Patient Participation: Its Meaning and Significance in the Context of Caring." *Journal of Advanced Nursing*, 17, 12: 1430–1439.

Askanius, Tina. 2013. "Online Video Activism and Political Mash-Up Genres." *Journal of Journalism Media and Cultural Studies*, 4.

Australian Human Rights Commission. 2015. *National Prevalence Survey of Age Discrimination in the Workplace.* Sydney, AHRC.

Australian Indigenous HealthInfoNet. 2015. "Overview of Australian Indigenous Health Status, 2014." <http://www.healthinfonet.ecu.edu.au/health-facts/overviews>.

Ayres, Jeffrey. M. 2015. "Framing Collective Action Against Neoliberalism: The Case of the Anti-Globalization Movement." *Journal of World-Systems Research,* 10, 1: 11–34.

Ayres, Sarah, and Alex Marsh. 2013. "Reflections on Contemporary Debates in Policy Studies." *Policy & Politics,* 41, 4: 643–663.

Babu, Gopalan Retheesh, and Bontha Veerraju Babu. 2011. "Dowry Deaths: A Neglected Public Health Issue in India." *International Health,* 3: 35–43.

Bacchi, Carol Lee. 2000. "Policy as Discourse: What Does it Mean? Where Does it Get Us?" *Discourse: Studies in the Cultural Politics of Education,* 21, 1: 45–57.

____. 2009. *Analysing Policy: What's the Problem Represented to Be?* Frenchs Forest, NSW: Pearson.

Baines, Donna (ed.). 2006. *Doing Anti-Oppressive Practice: Building Transformative, Politicized Social Work.* Winnipeg: Fernwood Publishing.

____ (ed.). 2011. *Doing Anti-Oppressive Practice: Social Justice Social Work.* Fernwood.

Baines, Donna, and Ian Cunningham. 2015. "Care Work in the Context of Austerity." *Competition and Change,* 19, 3: 183–193.

Baines, Donna, Ian Cunningham, and Heather Fraser. 2011. "Constrained by Managerialism: Caring as Participation in the Voluntary Social Services." *Economic and Industrial Democracy,* 32, 2: 329–352.

Baines, Sue, and Jane Edwards. 2015. "Considering the Ways in Which Anti-Oppressive Practice Principles Can Inform Health Research." *The Arts in Psychotherapy,* 42: 28–34.

Baker, Garth. 2011. "Effective Programmes for Men Who Use Family Violence." In Ken McMaster and David Riley (eds.), *Effective Interventions with Offenders: Lessons Learned.* Aotearoa, NZ: HMA and Steele Roberts (Chapter 9).

Barak, Gregg, Paul Leighton, and Allison Cotton. 2014. *Class, Race, Gender, and Crime: The Social Realities of Justice in America.* MD: Rowman and Littlefield.

Barrientos, Armando. 2013. "Does Vulnerability Create Poverty Traps?" In A. Shepherd and J. Brunt (eds.), *Chronic Poverty.* Palgrave Macmillan UK.

Bass, Ellen, and Laura Davis. 2002. *The Courage to Heal: A Guide for Women Survivors of Child Sexual Abuse.* Random House.

BBC News. 2016. "Syria: The Story of the cConflict." <http://www.bbc.com/news/world-middle-east-26116868> retrieved Sept 2, 2016.

Beaverstock, Jonathan V., Philip Hubbard, and John R. Short. 2004. "Getting Away With it? Exposing the Geographies of the Super-Rich." *Geoforum,* 35, 4: 401–407.

Beck, Aaron T. 1999. *Prisoners of Hate: The Cognitive Basis of Anger, Hostility, and Violence.* New York: HarperCollins Publishers.

Bentley, Tyrone, and Cathy S. Widom. 2009. "A 30-Year Follow-Up of the Effects of Child Abuse and Neglect on Obesity in Adulthood." *Obesity,* 17, 10: 1900–1905.

Bernal, Dolores Delgado, and Octavio Villalpando. 2002. "An Apartheid of Knowledge in Academia: The Struggle over The 'Legitimate' Knowledge of Faculty of Color." *Equity and Excellence in Education,* 35, 2: 169–180.

Berndtson, A.E., A. Fagin, S. Sen, D.G. Greenhalgh, and T.L. Palmieri. 2014. "White

Phosphorus Burns and Arsenic Inhalation: A Toxic Combination." *Journal of Burn Care & Research*, 35, 2: e128–e131.

Bessant, Judith, and Rob Watts. 2002. *Sociology Australia,* 2nd edition. Crows Nest, NSW: Allen & Unwin.

Bettcher, Talia Mae. 2014. "Transphobia. [Postposttranssexual: Key Concepts for a Twenty-First-Century Transgender Studies]." *TSQ: Transgender Studies Quarterly*, 1, 1–2: 249–251.

Bevington, Douglas, and Chris Dixon. 2005. "Movement-Relevant Theory: Rethinking Social Movement Scholarship and Activism." *Social Movement Studies*, 4, 3: 185–208.

Bhadoriya, Rakesh Singh. 2016. "Dowry Deaths in India." Lex Hindustan website. July 22. <http://lexhindustan.com/uncategorized/dowry-deaths-in-india/>.

Black, Sandra E., Paul. J. Devereux, Petta Lundborg, and Kaveh Majlesi. 2015. *Poor Little Rich Kids? The Determinants of the Intergenerational Transmission of Wealth* (No. w21409). National Bureau of Economic Research.

Bloch, Francis, and Vijayendra Rao. 2002. "Terror as a Bargaining Instrument: A Case Study of Dowry Violence in Rural India." *The American Economic Review*, 92, 4: 1029–1043.

Boghossian, Paul. 2001. "What Is Social Construction?" *Times Literary Supplement*, 5108. 23 Feb.

Booker, Chloe. 2016. "Meet the Dog at Centre of Push for Comfort Dogs for Abuse Victims in Victoria's Courts." *The Age*. <http://www.theage.com.au/victoria/meet-the-dog-at-centre-of-push-for-comfort-dogs-for-abuse-victims-in-victorias-courts-20160814-gqs9dx.html> retrieved 5 Sept, 2016.

Boothby, Neil, Jennifer Crawford, and Jason Halperin. 2006. "Mozambique Child Soldier Life Outcome Study: Lessons Learned in Rehabilitation and Reintegration Efforts." *Global Public Health*, 1, 1: 87–107.

Boston, Jonathan, and Simon Chapple. 2014. *Child Poverty in New Zealand*. Bridget Williams Books.

Boston Globe. 2017. "A Timeline of Trump's Immigration Ban." <https://apps.bostonglobe.com/news/nation/graphics/2017/01/travel-ban/> retrieved 10 Feb. 2017.

Boughton, Bob, Donna Ah Chee, Jack Beetson, Deborah Durnan, and Jose Charla Leblanch. 2013. "An Aboriginal Adult Literacy Campaign Pilot Study in Australia uUsing 'Yes I Can'." *Literacy and Numeracy Studies*, 21, 1: 5.

Bourdieu, Pierre, and Lois Wacquant. 2002. *An Invitation to Reflexive Sociology*. Cambridge: Policy Press.

Boushel, Margaret. 1994. "The Protective Environment of Children: Towards a Framework for Anti-Oppressive, Cross-Cultural and Cross National Understanding." *British Journal of Social Work*, 24, 2: 173–190.

Braithwaite, Alyssa. 2016. "Justin Trudeau Leads the Way at Toronto Pride Parade." *SBS News*, July 5. <http://www.sbs.com.au/topics/sexuality/agenda/article/2016/07/05/justin-trudeau-leads-way-toronto-pride-parade>.

Braithwaite, John, and Kathleen Daly. 1994. "Masculinities, Violence and Communitarian Control." In T. Newburn and B. Stanko (eds.), *Just Boys Doing Business: Men, Masculinity and Crime*. London: Routledge.

Braun, Lundy, Melanie Wolfgang, and Kay Dickersin. 2013. "Defining Race/Ethnicity and Explaining Difference in Research Studies on Lung Function." *European Respiratory Journal*, 41, 6: 1362–1370.

Braun, Virginia. 2009. "'The Women Are Doing it for Themselves': The Rhetoric of Choice and Agency around Female Genital Cosmetic Surgery." *Australian Feminist Studies*, 24, 60: 233–249.

Breckenridge, Jan. 1999. "Subjugation and Silences: The Role of Professions in Silencing Victims of Sexual and Domestic Violence." In J. Breckenridge and L. Laing (eds.), *Challenging Silence: Innovative Responses in Sexual and Domestic Violence*. St Leonards: Allen & Unwin.

Bricknell, Samantha, Hayley Boxall, and Hannah Andrevski. 2014. "Male Victims of Non-Sexual and Non-Domestic Violence: Service Needs and Experiences in Court." AIC *Reports: Research and Public Policy Series,* 126. Canberra, Australian Institute of Criminology, ACT.

Bridgman, Peter, and Glyn Davis. 2014. *The Australian Policy Handbook*, 3rd edition. Sydney: Allen & Unwin.

Broom, Dorothy. 2008. "Hazardous Good Intentions? Unintended Consequences of the Project of Prevention." *Health Sociology Review,* 17, 2: 129–140.

Brough, M. 2007. "National Emergency Response to Protect Aboriginal Children in the NT." Media release, 21 June. Department of Families, Community Services and Indigenous Affairs, Canberra, Australia. <http://www.formerministers.dss.gov.au/3581/emergency_21june07/> viewed 20 May 2014.

Brown, Alex, and Ngiare Brown. 2007. "The Northern Territory Intervention: Voices from the Centre of the Fringe." *Medical Journal of Australia*, 187, 11/12: 621–623.

Brown, David. 2005. "Continuity, Rupture or Just More of the 'Volatile and Contradictory'?: Glimpses of New South Wales' Penal Practice Behind and Through the Discursive." In J. Pratt, D. Brown, S. Hallsworth, and W. Morrison (eds.), *The New Punitiveness: Trends, Theories, Perspectives*. Devon, UK: Willan Publishing.

Brown, Leslie, and Susan Strega. 2005. *Research as Resistance: Critical, Indigenous and Anti-Oppressive Approaches*. Toronto: Canadian Scholars' Press.

Bruffee, Kenneth A. 1986. "Social Construction, Language and the Authority of Knowledge: A Bibliographic Essay." *College English*, 48, 8: 773–790.

Brysk, Alison, and Austin Choi-Fitzpatrick (eds.). 2012. *From Human Trafficking to Human Rights: Reframing Contemporary Slavery*. University of Pennsylvania Press.

Bufkin, Sarah. 2015. "Forced Sterilisation of the Disabled in Australia Doesn't Seem to Be Going Anywhere." 19 Feb. <http://www.bustle.com/articles/65104-forced-sterilization-of-the-disabled-in-australia-doesnt-seem-to-be-going-anywhere>.

Bull, Melissa. 2010. *Punishment and Sentencing: Risk, Rehabilitation and Restitution*. South Melbourne, Victoria: Oxford University Press.

Bumiller, Kristin. 2008. *In an Abusive State: How Neoliberalism Appropriated the Feminist Movement Against Sexual Violence*. Durham, NC: Duke University Press.

Bussell, Helen, and Deborah Forbes. 2002. "Understanding the Volunteer Market: The What, Where, Who and Why of Volunteering." *International Journal of Nonprofit and Voluntary Sector Marketing*, 7, 3: 244–257.

Butler, Robert N. 1989. "Dispelling Ageism: The Cross-Cutting Intervention." *The Annals of the American Academy of Political and Social Science*: 138–147.

____. 2009. "Combating Ageism." *International Psychogeriatrics,* 21, 2: 211.

Bylander, Maryann, and John Kydd. 2008. "Violence to Children, Definition and Prevention of." *Encyclopedia of Violence, Peace, & Conflict,* 2nd edition. Academic Press, Elsevier.

Byrne, Paul. 2013. *Social Movements in Britain.* Routledge.

Calhoun, Avery, Maureen G.Wilson, and Elizabeth Whitmore. 2014. "Activist Resistance in Neoliberal Times: Stories from Canada." *Critical and Radical Social Work,* 2, 2: 141–158.

Call, Christine R., and Judith C. Nelsen. 2007. "Partner Abuse and Women's Substance Problems from Vulnerability to Strength." *Affilia, Women and Social Work,* 22, 4: 334–346.

Callus, Anne-Marie, and Ruth Farrugia. 2016. *The Disabled Child's Participation Rights.* Routledge.

Campion-Smith, Bruce. 2014. "Suicide Claims More Soldiers than Those Killed by Afghan Combat." *The Star News Canada.* <https://www.thestar.com/news/canada/2014/09/16/suicide_claims_more_soldiers_than_those_killed_by_afghan_combat.html>.

Carlton, Rosemary, Julia Krane, Simon Lapierre, Cindy Richardson and Susan Strega (eds.), 2013. *Failure to Protect: Moving Beyond Gendered Responses.* Winnipeg, Fernwood Publishing.

Carson, Ed, and Lorraine Kerr. 2014. *Australian Social Policy and the Human Services.* Port Melbourne, Victoria: Cambridge University Press.

Cavanagh, Kate. 2003. "Understanding Women's Responses to Domestic Violence." *Qualitative Social Work,* 2, 3: 229–249.

Centre for Innovative Justice. 2015. "Opportunities for Early Intervention: Bringing Perpetrators of Family Violence into View." March 2015. Melbourne, Victoria: RMIT University. <http://mams.rmit.edu.au/r3qx75qh2913.pdf>.

Chan, Beatrice. 2004. "Reclaim the Night." Paper presented at *Social Movements in Action* conference, University of Sydney.

Chapman, Simon. 2013. *Over Our Dead Bodies: Port Arthur and Australia's Fight for Gun Control.* Sydney University Press.

Chowdhury, Farah Deeba. 2010. "Dowry, Women and Law in Bangladesh." *International Journal of Law, Policy and the Family,* 24, 2: 198–221.

Clarke, John, and Allan Cochrane. 1998. "The Social Construction of Social Problems." In E. Saraga (ed.), *Embodying the Social: Constructions of Difference.* London: Routledge

Cline, Austin. 2016. "How Religion, Religious Groups, and Beliefs Are Privileged." *About Religion.* <http://atheism.about.com/od/churchstate/p/ReligiousPriv.htm> retrieved 2 Sept., 2016.

CNN.com. 2015. "Trump Mocks Reporter with Disability." Nov. 25. <http://edition.cnn.com/videos/tv/2015/11/26/donald-trump-mocks-reporter-with-disability-berman-sot-ac.cnn> retrieved 13 Feb 13, 2017.

Coker, Donna, and Ahjane Macquoid. 2015. "Why Opposing Hyper-Incarceration Should Be Central to the Work of the Anti-Domestic Violence Movement." *University of Miami Race & Social Justice Law Review,* 5, 2. <http://repository.law.miami.edu/umrsjlr/vol5/iss2/30>.

Coldrey, Barry. 1999. "Good British Stock: Child and Youth Migration to Australia." Research Guide Number 11. Canberra: National Archives of Australia. <http://guides.naa.gov.au/good-british-stock/>.

Colic-Peisker, Val, and Farida Tilbury. 2008. "Being Black in Australia: A Case Study of Intergroup Relations." *Race & Class,* 49, 4: 38–56.

Collett, DeShana, and Tamara Bennett. 2015. "Putting Intimate Partner Violence on Your Radar." *Journal of the American Academy of Physician Assistants*, 28, 10: 24–28.

Collins, Randall. 2009. "Social Movements and the Focus of Emotional Attention." In J. Goodwin, J.M. Jasper, and F. Polletta (eds.), *Passionate Politics: Emotions and Social Movements*. University of Chicago Press.

Commonwealth of Australia. 2001. "Lost Innocents: Righting the Record — Report on Child Migration." Canberra: Senate Standing Committee on Community Affairs, ACT. <http://www.aph.gov.au/Parliamentary_Business/Committees/Senate/Community_Affairs/Completed_inquiries/1999-02/child_migrat/report/index>.

____. 2004. "Forgotten Australians: A Report on Australians Who Experienced Institutional or Out-of-Home Care as Children." Canberra: Senate Standing Committee on Community Affairs, ACT. <http://www.aph.gov.au/~/media/wopapub/senate/committee/clac_ctte/completed_inquiries/2004_07/inst_care/report/report_pdf.ashx>.

____. 2008. "Northern Territory Emergency Response: Report of the NTER Review Board, 14 Oct 2008." <http://apo.org.au/system/files/551/apo-nid551-81416.pdf> viewed 15 May 2015.

____. 2009. *Future Directions for the Northern Territory Emergency Response — Discussion Paper*. Canberra: Department of Families, Housing, Community Services and Indigenous Affairs, ACT.

Comunello, Francesca, and Giuseppe Anzera. 2012. "Will the Revolution Be Tweeted? A Conceptual Framework for Understanding the Social Media and the Arab Spring." *Islam and Christian–Muslim Relations*, 23, 4: 453–470.

Conca, Ken, and Geoffrey Dabelko (eds.). 2014. *Green Planet Blues: Critical Perspectives on Global Environmental Politics*. Boulder, CO: Westview Press.

Connell, Raewyn W. 2000. *The Men and the Boys*. St Leonards, NSW: Allen & Unwin.

____. 2007. "Masculinities, Power, and the Epidemic: Messages of Social Research." International symposium, "Politicising Masculinities: Beyond the personal," 15–18 October, 2007, Dakar, Senegal. <http://www.bridge.ids.ac.uk/docs/Connell_epidemic.doc>.

____. 2014. *Gender and Power: Society, the Person and Sexual Politics*. John Wiley & Sons.

Connolly, Marie, and Louise Harms. 2015. *Social Work: From Theory to Practice*, 2nd edition. Melbourne, Victoria: Cambridge University Press.

Conway, J. 2003. "Civil Resistance and the Diversity of Tactics in the Anti-Globalization Movement: Problems of Violence, Silence, and Solidarity in Activist Politics." *Osgoode Hall Law Journal*, 41: 505.

Cornish, Lisa. 2014. "South Australia's Most Dangerous Suburbs." *Sunday Mail,* 12 Jan. <www.adelaidenow.com.au/news/south-australia/south-australias-most-dangerous-suburbs/story-fni6uo1m-1226799849382>.

Corrections SA. 2011. "September in Corrections." Newsletter, 5 (September). Department for Correctional Services, Adelaide, South Australia. <http://www.corrections.sa.gov.au/newsletters/2011/September/>.

Costanza-Chock, Sasha. 2012. "Mic Check! Media Cultures and the Occupy Movement." *Social Movement Studies*, 11, 3–4: 375–385.

Crichlow, Wesley. 2015. "Critical Race Theory: A Strategy for Framing Discussions Around

Social Justice and Democratic Education." Paper presented at the Higher Education in Transformation Conference, Dublin, 31 May–1 April. <http://arrow.dit.ie/st2/6/> viewed 25 Aug. 2016.

Crowe, Laura, and Peter Butterworth. 2016. "The Role of Financial Hardship, Mastery and Social Support in the Association Between Employment Status and Depression: Results from an Australian Longitudinal Cohort Study." *BMJ Open*, 6, 5: e009834. <http://bmjopen.bmj.com/content/6/5/e009834>.

Cummins, Robert. A. 2001. "The Subjective Well-Being of People Caring for a Family Member with a Severe Disability at Home: A Review." *Journal of Intellectual and Developmental Disability*, 26, 1: 83–100.

Cunneen, Chris, and Rob White. 2011. *Juvenile Justice: Youth and Crime in Australia*, 4th edition. South Melbourne, Victoria: Oxford University Press.

Cunneen, Chris, and Simone Rowe. 2014. "Changing Narratives: Colonised Peoples, Criminology and Social Work." *International Journal for Crime, Justice and Social Democracy*, 3, 1: 49–67.

Curry, G. David. 2008. "Law and Violence." *Encyclopedia of Violence, Peace, & Conflict*, 2nd edition. Academic Press, Elsevier.

Da Costa, Beatriz, and Kavita Philip. 2010. *Tactical Biopolitics: Art, Activism, and Technoscience*. MIT Press.

DAIP. 2011. "Wheel Gallery." Domestic Abuse Intervention Programs: Home of the Duluth Model. <http://www.theduluthmodel.org/training/wheels.html>.

Dalrymple, Jane, and Beverley Burke. 2006. *Anti-Oppressive Practice: Social Care and the Law*. London: McGraw-Hill Education.

Dalton, Tony, Mary Draper, Wendy Weeks, and John Wiseman. 1996. *Making Social Policy in Australia: An Introduction*. Sydney: Allen & Unwin.

Danish Bilharziasis Laboratory for the World Bank, People's Republic of Bangladesh. 2004. "Disability in Bangladesh, A Situational Analysis." <http://siteresources.worldbank.org/DISABILITY/Resources/Regions/South%20Asia/DisabilityinBangladesh.pdf>.

Davidovic, Mladen, Zorana Djordjevic, Predrag Erceg, Nebojsa Despotovic, and Dragoslav P. Milosevic. 2007. "Ageism: Does It Exist Among Children?" *The Scientific World Journal*, 7: 1134–1139.

Davis, Tracy, and Laura M. Harrison. 2013. *Advancing Social Justice: Tools, Pedagogies, and Strategies to Transform Your Campus*. San Francisco: John Wiley & Sons.

Dawe, Sharon, Sally Frye, David Best, Derran Moss, Judy Atkinson, Chris Evans, Mark Lynch, and Paul Harnett. 2007. *Drug Use in the Family: Impacts and Implications*. Report prepared for Australian National Council on Drugs, Canberra, ACT. ISBN: 9781877018169.

Day, Andrew. 2003. "Reducing the Risk of Reoffending in Australian Indigenous Offenders: What Works for Whom?" *Journal of Offender Rehabilitation*, 37, 2: 1–15.

____. 2015. "Working with Perpetrators of Domestic Violence to Change Their Behaviour." *InPsych*, 37, 5. <https://www.psychology.org.au/inpsych/2015/october/day/>.

Day, Kirsten. 2008. "Being Feared: Masculinity and Race in Public Space." In S. Farrall and M. Lee (eds.), *Fear of Crime: Critical Voices in an Age of Anxiety*. London: Routledge-Cavendish.

de Jong, Anna. 2015. "Dykes on Bikes and the Long Road to Mardi Gras." *The Conversation*,

5 March: 1–3.

Deal, Mark. 2007. "Aversive Disablism: Subtle Prejudice toward Disabled People." *Disability & Society*, 22, 1: 93–107.

Deleuze, Gilles. 1994. *Difference and Repetition*. Columbia: Columbia University Press.

Delpit, Lisa. D. 1995. *Other People's Children: Cultural Conflict in the Classroom*. New York: W.W. Norton.

Den Hond, Frank, and Frank G. De Bakker. 2007. "Ideologically Motivated Activism: How Activist Groups Influence Corporate Social Change Activities." *Academy of Management Review*, 32, 3: 901–924.

Dhillon, Preeti, and Laishram Ladusingh. 2013. "Working Life Gain from Gain in Old Age Life Expectancy in India." *Demographic Research*, 28: 733–762.

Dickinson, Torry D., and Robert K. Schaeffer. 2015. *Transformations: Feminist Pathways to Global Change*. Routledge.

Digby, Anne. 2013. "Black Doctors and Discrimination under South Africa's Apartheid Regime." *Medical History*, 57, 02: 269–290.

Dobash, Rebecca, Russell Dobash, Kate Cavanagh, and Ruth Lewis. 2000. *Changing Violent Men*. Thousand Oaks, CA: Sage.

Dominelli, Lena. 1996. "Deprofessionalizing Social Work: Anti-Oppressive Practice, Competencies and Postmodernism." *British Journal of Social Work*, 26, 2: 153–175.

____. 2012a. *Green Social Work: From Environmental Crises to Environmental Justice*. Polity.

____. 2012b. "Claiming Women's Places in the World: Social Workers' Roles in Eradicating Gender Inequalities Globally." *Handbook of International Social Work: Human Rights, Development, and the Global Profession*, 63.

____. 2016. "Poverty Alleviation in a Globalized World: A Feminist Perspective." In S. Wendt and N. Moulding (eds.), *Contemporary Feminisms in Social Work Practice*. Routledge.

Dominelli, Lena, and Jo Campling. 2002. *Anti-Oppressive Social Work Theory and Practice*. Palgrave Macmillan.

Donovan, Catherine, and Marianne Hester. 2010. "I Hate the Word 'Victim': An Exploration of Recognition of Domestic Violence in Same Sex Relationships." *Social Policy and Society*, 9: 279–289.

Doucette, Jeremy, Bryanne Harris, and Peter Jaffe. 2014. "Educating Canadians on the Health Risks of Corporal Punishment and Safe and Effective Alternatives." *Health Tomorrow: Interdisciplinarity and Internationality*, 2, 1.

Doyal, Lesley. 2000. "Gender Equity in Health: Debates and Dilemmas." *Social Science & Medicine*, 51, 6: 931–939.

Drabsch, Talina. 2004. "Indigenous Issues in New South Wales." Background Paper No. 2/04. NSW: NSW Parliamentary Library Research Service.

Drucker, Peter. F. 1984. "Converting Social Problems into Business Opportunities: The New Meaning of Corporate Social Responsibility." *California Management Review*, 26, 2: 53–63.

Dulwich Centre. n.d. "What Is Narrative Therapy?", <http://dulwichcentre.com.au/what-is-narrative-therapy/> viewed 15 September 2016.

Duvnjak, Angella, and Heather Fraser. 2014. "Targeting the 'Hard to Reach': Re/producing Stigma?" *Critical and Radical Social Work*, 1, 2: 167–182.

Dyer, Richard. 1997. *White*. London: Routledge.

Dysart-Gale, Deborah. 2010. "Social Justice and Social Determinants of Health: Lesbian,

Gay, Bisexual, Transgendered, Intersexed, and Queer Youth in Canada." *Journal of Child and Adolescent Psychiatric Nursing*, 23, 1: 23–28.

Eardley, Tony. 1995. "Violence and Sexuality." In Susan Caffrey and Gary Mundy (eds.), *The Sociology of Crime and Deviance: Selected Issues.* Greenwich University Press.

Easton, Scott. D. 2013. "Disclosure of Child Sexual Abuse among Adult Male Survivors." *Clinical Social Work Journal*, 41, 4: 344–355.

Eckhardt, Christopher, Christopher Murphy, Daniel Whitaker, Joel Sprunger, Rita Dykstra, and Kim Woodard. 2013. "The effectiveness of Intervention Programs for Perpetrators and Victims of Intimate Partner Violence." *Partner Abuse*, 4, 2: 196–231.

Edwards, Alan, and Susan Sharpe. 2004. "Restorative Justice in the Context of Domestic Violence: A Literature Review." Alberta, Canada, Mediation and Restorative Justice Centre. <https://s3.amazonaws.com/mrjc/restorative_justice_DV_Lit_Review.pdf>.

Emerson, Eric, and Alan Roulstone. 2014. "Developing an Evidence Base for Violent and Disablist Hate Crime in Britain: Findings from the Life Opportunities Survey." *Journal of Interpersonal Violence*, 0886260514534524.

Emslie, Carol, Damien Ridge, Sue Ziebland, and Kate Hunt. 2006. "Men's Accounts of Depression: Reconstructing or Resisting Hegemonic Masculinity?" *Social Science & Medicine*, 62, 9: 2246–2257.

Engle, Lauren. B. 2004. *The World in Motion: Short Essays on Migration and Gender.* Geneva: World Health Organization.

Eriksson, Maria, Linnéa Bruno, and Elisabet Näsman. 2013. "Privilege and Marginalization." In *Domestic Violence, Family Law and School.* Palgrave Macmillan UK.

Evans, Susan. P. 2008. "Promoting the 'Good' Relationship: Recognising Moral Dimensions in Violence Prevention Education." PhD thesis, University of Western Sydney, NSW, NSW.

Falkenström, Fredrik, Fredrik Granström, and Rolf Holmqvist. 2013. "Therapeutic Alliance Predicts Symptomatic Improvement Session by Session." *Journal of Counseling Psychology*, 60, 3: 317.

Farmer, Paul E., Bruce Nizeye, Sara Stulac, and Salmaan Keshavjee. 2006. "Structural Violence and Clinical Medicine." *PLoS Medicine*, 3, 10: e449. <http://doi.org/10.1371/journal.pmed.0030449>.

Fater, Kerry, and Jo Ann Mullaney. 2000. "The Lived Experience of Adult Male Survivors Who Allege Childhood Sexual Abuse by Clergy." *Issues in Mental Health Nursing*, 21, 3: 281–295.

Faulkner, David. 2004. "Probation and Citizenship in an Uncertain Society." *Vista: Perspectives on Probation*, 8, 1: 9–17.

Fawcett, Barbara, Gail Goodwin, Gabrielle Meagher, and Ruth Phillips. 2010. *Social Policy for Social Change.* South Yarra, Victoria: Palgrave Macmillan.

Ferguson, Iain, and Michael Lavalette. 2006. "Globalization and Global Justice: Towards a Social Work of Resistance." *International Social Work*, 49, 3: 309–318.

____. 2013. "Crisis, Austerity and the Future(s) of Social Work in the UK." *Critical and Radical Social Work*, 1, 1: 95–110.

Ferguson, Leon Myles, and Stephen Wormith. 2013. "A Meta-Analysis of Moral Reconation Therapy." *International Journal of Offender Therapy and Comparative Criminology*, 57, 9: 1076–1106.

Findlay, Carly. 2016. "Why Did the Mass Murder of 19 Disabled People in Japan

Barely Rate?" *Sydney Morning Herald*, Aug 2. <http://www.smh.com.au/lifestyle/news-and-views/opinion/why-did-the-mass-murder-of-19-disabled-people-in-japan-barely-rate-20160801-gqiphz.html> retrieved 23 August, 2016.

FitzRoy, Lee. 2001. "Violent Women: Questions for Feminist Theory, Practice And Policy." *Critical Social Policy*, 21, 1: 7–34.

Flaherty, Emalee G., Jeannette M. Perez-Rossello, Michael A. Levine, et al. 2014. "Evaluating Children with Fractures for Child Physical Abuse." *Pediatrics*, 133, 2: 477–489.

Flood, Michael. 2001. "Men's Collective Anti-Violence Activism and the Struggle for Gender Justice." *Development*, 44, 3: 42–47.

____. 2015. "Work with Men to End Violence Against Women: A Critical Stocktake." *Culture, Health & Sexuality*, 17 (sup2): 159–176.

Flores, Thomas Vincent. 2012. "The Continuum of Violence and Peace: Applying a Contemplative Framework for Turning the Problem into the Solution." *Practical Matters*, 5. <http://practicalmattersjournal.org/2012/03/01/continuum-of-violence-and-peace/>.

FORWARD. 2012. *Female Genital Mutilation: Frequently Asked Questions: A Campaigner's Guide for Young People*. London, UK, Foundation for Women's Health, Research and Development. <http://www.forwarduk.org.uk/wp-content/uploads/2014/12/Forward_-FGM-FAQ.pdf>.

Foucault, Michel. 1985. *The Use of Pleasure: History of Sexuality* (Vol. 2). New York: Vintage.

____. 2007. *The Politics of Truth*. New York: Semiotext(e).

Fozdar, Farida, Raelene Wilding, and Mary Hawkins. 2009. *Race and Ethnic Relations*. South Melbourne: Oxford University Press.

Fraser, Heather. 2004. "Doing Narrative Research: Analysing Personal Stories Line by Line." *Qualitative Social Work*, 3, 2: 179–201.

____. 2005. "Four Different Approaches to Community Participation." *Community Development Journal*, 40, 3: 286–300.

____. 2008. *In the Name of Love, Women's Narratives of Love and Abuse*. Toronto: Women's Press.

Fraser, Heather, and Christine Craik. 2009. "Women and Violence." In J. Allen, B. Pease, and L. Briskman (eds.), *Critical Social Work*, 2nd edition. South Melbourne: Allen & Unwin.

Fraser, Heather, and Nik Taylor. 2016. *Neoliberalization, Universities and the Public Intellectual: Species, Gender and Class and the Production of Knowledge*. London: Palgrave.

____. 2017. "In Good Company: Women, Companion Animals, and Social Work." *Society & Animals*, 25: 341–361.

Free the Slaves. 2016. "Our Model for Freedom." <http://www.freetheslaves.net/our-model-for-freedom/community-based-causal-model/>.

French Sally, and John Swain. 2004. "Whose Tragedy? Towards a Personal Non-Tragedy View of Disability." In J. Swain, S. French, C. Barnes and C. Thomas (eds.), *Disabling Barriers — Enabling Environments*, 2nd edition. London: Sage.

Friere, Paulo. 1970. *Pedagogy of the Oppressed*. New York: Continuum.

Frohmader, Carolyn. 2013. "Dehumanised: The Forced Sterilisation of Women and Girls with Disabilities in Australia." WWDA Submission to the Senate Inquiry into the involuntary or coerced sterilisation of people with disabilities in Australia. Tasmania, Women With Disabilities Australia. <http://wwda.org.au/wp-content/

uploads/2013/12/WWDA_Sub_SenateInquiry_Sterilisation_March2013.pdf>.

Gadd, David. 2004. "Evidence-Led Policy or Policy-Led Evidence? Cognitive Behavioural Programmes for Men Who Are Violent towards Women." *Criminal Justice*, 4, 2: 173–197.

Galabuzi, Grace-Edward. 2001. *Canada's Creeping Economic Apartheid*. Toronto: CSJ Foundation for Research and Education.

Galtung, Johan. 1990. "Cultural Violence." *Journal of Peace Research*, 27, 3: 291–305.

Gangoli, Geetanjali. 2006. "Engendering Genocide: Gender, Conflict and Violence." *Women's Studies International Forum*, 29, 5: 534–538.

Gates, Trevor G., and Jessica L. Sniatecki. 2016. "Tolerating Transphobia in Substance Abuse Counseling: Perceptions of Trainees." *Human Service Organizations: Management, Leadership & Governance*: 1–17.

GCAP (Global Call to Action Against Poverty). 2016. "Our Mission." <http://www.globaleducationmagazine.com/global-call-action-poverty-gcap/>.

Geelani, Gowhar. 2014. "Jammu and Kashmir: An Eyewitness Account of Tragedy and Valour." *Daily News and Analysis*, 27 September. <http://www.dnaindia.com/analysis/comment-jammu-and-kashmir-floods-an-eye-witness-account-of-tragedy-and-valour-2021883>.

Gerbaudo, Paolo. 2012. *Tweets and the Streets: Social Media and Contemporary Activism*. Pluto Press.

Gershoff, Elizabeth. T. 2002. "Corporal Punishment by Parents and Associated Child Behaviors and Experiences: A Meta-Analytic and Theoretical Review." *Psychological Bulletin*, 128, 4: 539–579.

Gilligan, Carol. 1977. "In a Different Voice: Women's Conceptions of Self and of Morality." *Harvard Educational Review*, 47, 4: 481–517.

Gilligan, James. 1997. *Violence: Reflections on a National Epidemic*. New York: Vintage Books.

Glasser, Carol S. 2014. "The Radical Debate: A Straw Man in the Movement?" In N. Taylor and R. Twine (eds.), *The Rise of Critical Animal Studies: From the Margins to the Centre* (Vol. 125). Routledge.

Goffman, Erving. 2009 [1963]. *Stigma: Notes on the Management of Spoiled Identity*. New York: Simon and Schuster.

Goggin, Gerard, and Christopher Newell. 2005. *Disability in Australia: Exposing a Social Apartheid*. UNSW Press.

Gonzales, Ernest, Christina Matz-Costa, and Nancy Morrow-Howell. 2015. "Increasing Opportunities for the Productive Engagement of Older Adults: A Response to Population Aging." *The Gerontologist*, 55, 2: 252–261.

Goodley, Dan. 2013. "Dis/entangling Critical Disability Studies." *Disability & Society*, 28, 5: 631–644.

Government of India. 2014. *Crime in India 2014*. National Crime Records Bureau, Ministry of Home Affairs, New Delhi. <http://ncrb.gov.in/index.htm>.

Greenberg, Max A., and Michael A. Messner. 2014. "Before Prevention: The Trajectory and Tensions of Feminist Antiviolence." In M. Segal and V. Demos (eds.), *Gendered Perspectives on Conflict and Violence: Part B*. Bingley, UK: Emerald Group Publishing Ltd.

Greenleaf, Arie T., and Joseph M. Williams. 2009. "Supporting Social Justice Advocacy: A Paradigm Shift Towards an Ecological Perspective." *Journal for Social Action in Counseling and Psychology*, 4, 2: 1–14.

Greig, Alan. 2002. "Political Connections: Men, Gender and Violence." <http://www.alangreig.net/wp-content/uploads/2017/01/Political-Connections-2.pdf> viewed 27 July 2017.

Greig, Alastair, Frank Lewins, and Kevin White. 2003. *Inequality in Australia*. Cambridge, UK: Cambridge University Press.

Grenier, Amanda. 2007. "Constructions of Frailty in the English Language, Care Practice and the Lived Experience." *Aging & Society*, 27: 425–445.

Grönvik, Lars. 2009. "Defining Disability: Effects of Disability Concepts on Research Outcomes." *International Journal of Social Research Methodology*, 12, 1: 1–18.

Grossman, Nienke. 2007. "Rehabilitation or Revenge: Prosecuting Child Soldiers for Human Rights Violations." *Georgetown Journal of International Law*, 38.

Guardian. 2015. "The Counted, People Killed by Police in the US." <http://www.theguardian.com/us-news/ng-interactive/2015/jun/01/the-counted-police-killings-us-database>.

Guo, Chao, and Gregory D. Saxton. 2013. "Tweeting Social Change: How Social Media Are Changing Nonprofit Advocacy." *Nonprofit and Voluntary Sector Quarterly*, 0899764012471585.

Gutberlet, Jutta. 2012. *Recovering Resources-Recycling Citizenship: Urban Poverty Reduction in Latin America*. Ashgate Publishing.

Habibis, Daphne, and Maggie Walter. 2009. *Social Inequality in Australia: Discourses, Realities & Futures*. South Melbourne: Oxford University Press.

Hall, Nathan. 2013. *Hate Crime*. Routledge.

Hall, Nathan, Abbee Corb, Paul Giannasi, and John Grieve. 2014. *The Routledge International Handbook on Hate Crime*. Routledge.

Halvorsen, Sam. 2012. "Beyond the Network? Occupy London and the Global Movement." *Social Movement Studies*, 11, 3–4: 427–433.

Hamill, Chrissy, and Chris Marshall. 2015. "Family Violence, the Law and Restorative Justice: Summary of Conference Proceedings and Practitioner Workshop, 7–8 May 2015." *Occasional Papers in Restorative Justice Practice*, 2. School of Government, Victoria University, Wellington, NZ. <http://www.victoria.ac.nz/sog/researchcentres/chair-in-restorative-justice>.

Hamilton, Lindsay, and Nik Taylor. 2013. *Animals at Work: Identity, Politics and Culture in Work with Animals*. Brill.

Hamm, Brigitte I. 2001. "A Human Rights Approach to Development." *Human Rights Quarterly*, 23, 4: 1005–1031.

Harris, Ian M., and Mary Lee Morrison. 2012. *Peace Education*. McFarland.

Harris, Nonie. 2008. "Radical Activism and Accidental Philanthropy: The Impact of First Wave Feminist Activism on the Later Construction of Child Care Policies in Australia and the United States of America." *Women's Studies International Forum*, 31, 1: 42–52. Pergamon.

Hart, Gillian Patricia. 2002. *Disabling Globalization, Places of Power in Post-Apartheid South Africa*. Berkeley: University of California Press.

Haseler, Stephen. 2000. *The Super-Rich*. London: Palgrave Macmillan.

Hausdorff, Jeffrey M., Becca R. Levy, and Jeanne Y. Wei. 1999. "The Power of Ageism on Physical Function of Older Persons: Reversibility of Age-Related Gait Changes." *Journal of the American Geriatrics Society*, 47, 11: 1346–1349.

Hazlehurst, David. 2001. "Networks and Policy Making: From Theory to Practice in Australian Social Policy." Discussion Paper No. 83. <https://openresearch-repository. anu.edu.au/bitstream/1885/41750/3/No83Hazlehurst.pdf> viewed 15 May 2015.

Hearn, Jeff. 1996. "Men's Violence to Known Women: Historical, Everyday and Theoretical Constructions by Men." In B. Fawcett, B. Featherstone, J. Hearn, and C. Toft (eds.), *Violence and Gender Relations: Theories and Interventions.* London: Sage Publications.

Hearn, Jeff, and Linda McKie. 2010. "Gendered and Social Hierarchies in Problem Representation and Policy Processes: 'Domestic Violence' in Finland and Scotland." *Violence Against Women,* 16, 2: 136–158.

Hearn, Jeff, and Antony Whitehead. 2006. "Collateral Damage: Men's 'Domestic' Violence to Women Seen Through Men's Relations with Men." *Probation Journal,* 53, 1: 38–56.

Henman, Paul, and Greg Marston. 2008. "The Social Division of Welfare Surveillance." *Journal of Social Policy,* 37, 02: 187–205.

Hennessy, Allan. 2016. "The Japan Stabbing Is Not Just Terrorism – It's a Hate Crime that Disabled People like Me Live in Fear of." *The Independent,* 27 July. <http://www. independent.co.uk/voices/japan-stabbing-terrorism-satoshi-uematsu-disabled-hate-crime-people-live-in-fear-a7157841.html> retrieved 23 Aug 2016.

Herman, Judith Lewis. 2013. "PTSD as a Shame Disorder." In *European Journal of Psychotraumatology,* 4. RIPVAGEN 7, JARFALLA, SE-175 64, Sweden: Co-Action Publishing.

Historical Institutional Abuse Inquiry for Northern Ireland. 2014. <https://www.hiainquiry. org> retrieved 27 July 2016.

Hochschild, Arlie Russell. 1990. "Ideology and Emotion Management: A Perspective and Path for Future Research." In T.D. Kemper (ed.), *Research Agendas in the Sociology of Emotions.* Albany, NY: SUNY Press.

Hodgson, Douglas. 1993. "Sex Tourism and Child Prostitution in Asia: Legal Responses and Strategies." *Melb. UL Rev.,* 19: 512.

Hofmann, Stefan G., Anu Asnaani, Imke J. Vonk, Alice T. Sawyer, and Angela Fang. 2012. "The Efficacy of Cognitive Behavioral Therapy: A Review of Meta-Analyses." *Cognitive Therapy and Research,* 36, 5: 427–440.

Holderhead, Sheradyn, and Lauren Novak. 2016. "DV: The Real Numbers." Adelaide *Sunday Mail:* 1–2.

Hollander, Jocelyn A. 2001. "Vulnerability and Dangerousness: The Construction of Gender through Conversation about Violence." *Gender and Society,* 15, 1: 83–109.

Holmes, Mary. 2009. *Gender and Everyday Life.* Oxon: Routledge.

Home Office. 2015. "Coercive or Controlling Behaviour Now a Crime." News story. UK, Home Office/Karen Bradley MP. 29 December. <https://www.gov.uk/government/ news/coercive-or-controlling-behaviour-now-a-crime>

Hood, Christopher. 1991. "A Public Management for All Seasons?" *Public Administration,* 69, 1: 3–19.

Hooper, Fred. 2016. "Joan Webb Just Turned 90 and Is about to Graduate with a PhD." *ABC News Online.* <http://www.abc.net.au/news/2016-08-16/joan-webb-just-turned-90-about-to-graduate-with-phd/7748002> retrieved 18 Aug, 2016.

Hopkins, Rosemary. 2013. "Staying Human: Experiences of a Therapist and Political Activist." In Jeffrey Cornelius-White, Renate Motschnig-Pitrik, and Michael Lux (eds.),

Interdisciplinary Applications of the Person-Centered Approach. New York: Springer.

Horton, Paul. 2011. "School Bullying and Social and Moral Orders." *Children & Society,* 25, 4: 268–277.

Howe, Adrian. 2008. *Sex, Violence and Crime: Foucault and the 'Man' Question.* Oxon: Routledge-Cavendish.

Howells, Kevin, Andrew Day, Susan Bubner, Susan Jauncey, Paul Williamson, Ann Parker, and Karen Heseltine. 2002. "Anger Management and Violence Prevention: Improving Effectiveness." *Trends & Issues in Criminal Justice,* 227.

Huda, Shahnaz. 2006. "Dowry in Bangladesh: Compromising Women's Rights." *South Asia Research,* 26, 3: 249–268.

Human Rights Watch. 2016. World Report 2016: Australia. <https://www.hrw.org/world-report/2016/country-chapters/australia>.

____. 2011. "Sterilization of Women and Girls with Disabilities: A Briefing Paper." <https://www.hrw.org/news/2011/11/10/sterilization-women-and-girls-disabilities>.

Hume, Mo. 2007. "Unpicking the Threads: Emotion as Central to the Theory and Practice of Researching Violence." *Women's Studies International Forum,* 30, 2: 147–157.

Humphries, Cathy, and Menka Tsantefski. 2013. "Children in the Midst of Family and Domestic Violence." In Fiona Arney and Dorothy Scott (eds.), *Working with Vulnerable Families: A Partnership Approach,* 2nd edition. Port Melbourne: Cambridge University.

Hutchison, Jacqueline S. 2015. "Anti-Oppressive Practice and Reflexive Lifeworld-Led Approaches to Care: A Framework for Teaching Nurses about Social Justice." *Nursing Research and Practice.*

IFAW. 2016. "IFAW campaigning for the Universal Declaration for Animal Welfare." Sydney, NSW: International Fund for Animal Welfare. <http://www.ifaw.org/australia/our-work/political-advocacy/udaw-universal-declaration-animal-welfare> viewed 10 February 2016.

Ife, Jim. 2010. "Human Rights and Social Justice." *Ethics and Value Perspectives in Social Work:* 148–159.

____. 2012. *Human Rights and Social Work: Towards Rights-Based Practice.* South Melbourne, Victoria: Cambridge University Press.

____. 2016. "Human Rights and Social Work: Beyond Conservative Law." *Journal of Human Rights and Social Work,* 1, 1: 3–8.

IFSW. 2012. "Ageing and Older Adults, Introduction." <http://ifsw.org/policies/ageing-and-older-adults/>.

ILO (International Labour Organization). 1999. "C182—Worst Forms of Child Labour Convention (No. 182)." *Convention Concerning the Prohibition and Immediate Action for the Elimination of the Worst Forms of Child Labour.* <http://www.ilo.org/dyn/normlex/en/f?p=NORMLEXPUB:12100:0::NO::P12100_ILO_CODE:C182> accessed 18 July 2016.

INSTRAW. 2001. "Racism, Class and Masculinity: The Global Dimensions of Gender-Based Violence." CSW 2001 Panel Sponsored by INSTRAW & UNICEF, 5 April.

Jeffrey, Julie Roy. 1998. *The Great Silent Army of Abolitionism: Ordinary Women in the Antislavery Movement.* Univ. of North Carolina Press.

Jenkins, Alan. 1990. *Invitations to Responsibility: The Therapeutic Engagement of Men Who Are Violent and Abusive.* Adelaide, SA: Dulwich Centre Publications.

____. 1997. "Alcohol and Men's Violence: An Interview with Alan Jenkins." *Dulwich Centre Newsletter*, 2 & 3: 43–47. Special issue — New perspectives on 'Addiction.' <http://dulwichcentre.com.au/articles-about-narrative-therapy/deconstructing-addiction/alcohol-and-mens-violence/>.

____. 2003. "Alcohol and Men's Violence." In C. White (ed.), *Responding to Violence: A Collection of Papers Relating to Child Sexual Abuse and Violence in Intimate Relationships*. Adelaide, SA: Dulwich Centre Publications.

Jewkes, Rachel. 2002. "Intimate Partner Violence: Causes and Prevention." *The Lancet*, 359, 9315: 1423–1429.

Johnson, Margaret Ellen. 2015. "Changing Course in the Anti-Domestic Violence Legal Movement: From Safety to Security." *Villanova Law Review*, 60, 1.

Johnston, Lynda, and Gordon Waitt. 2015. "The Spatial Politics of Gay Pride Parades and Festivals: Emotional Activism." In M. Tremblay and D. Paternotte (eds.), *The Ashgate Research Companion to Lesbian and Gay Activism*. Routledge.

Jones, Michelle. 2004. "'A Fight about Nothing': Constructions of Domestic Violence." PhD thesis, University of Adelaide, South Australia.

Junger, Marianne, Lynette Feder, Joy Clay, Sylvana M. Côté, David P. Farrington, Kate Freiberg, Vicente Garrido Genovés et al. 2007. "Preventing Violence in Seven Countries: Global Convergence in Policies." *European Journal on Criminal Policy and Research*, 13, 3–4: 327–356.

Junger, Marianne, Lynette Feder, Joy Clay, Sylvana Cote, David Farrington, et al. 2007. "Preventing Violence in Seven Countries: Global Convergence in Policies." *European Journal on Criminal Policy and Research*, 13, 3/4: 327–356.

Kabir, Md Iqbal, Md Bayzidur Rahman, Wayne Smith, Mirza Afreen Fatima Lusha, and Abdul Hasnat Milton. 2015. "Child Centred Approach to Climate Change and Health Adaptation Through Schools in Bangladesh: A Cluster Randomised Intervention Trial." *PloS one*, 10, 8: e0134993.

Kangas, Ann, Huma Haider, and Evie Fraser. 2014. "Gender: Topic Guide." Revised edition with E. Browne. Birmingham, UK: Governance and Social Development Resource Centre (GSDRC), University of Birmingham. <http://www.gsdrc.org/topic-guides/gender/>.

Keck, Margaret. E., and Kathryn Sikkink. 2014. *Activists Beyond Borders: Advocacy Networks in International Politics*. Cornell University Press.

Kemshall, Hazel. 2003. *Understanding Risk in Criminal Justice*. Berkshire: Open University Press.

Kendall, Francis E. 2002. "Understanding White Privilege." <https://www.cpt.org/files/Undoing%20Racism%20-%20Understanding%20White%20Privilege%20-%20Kendall.pdf> viewed 9 January 2016.

____. 2013. *Understanding White Privilege: Creating Pathways to Authentic Relationships across Race*, 2nd edition. New York: Routledge.

Kessaris, Terry Ngarritjan. 2006. "About Being Mununga (Whitefella): Making Covert Group Racism Visible." *Journal of Community & Applied Psychology*, 16: 347–362.

Khan, Alam, and Mario Arturo Ruiz Estrada. 2015. "The Effects of Terrorism on Economic Performance: The Case of Islamic State in Iraq and Syria (ISIS)." *Quality & Quantity*: 1–17.

Khan, Alaptagin, Hannah C. McCormack, Elizabeth A. Bolger, Cynthia E. McGreenery, Gordana Vitaliano, Ann Polcari, and Martin H. Teicher. 2015. "Childhood Maltreatment, Depression, and Suicidal Ideation: Critical Importance of Parental and Peer Emotional Abuse During Developmental Sensitive Periods in Males and Females." *Frontiers in Psychiatry*, 6: 42.

Khosla, Natalia, and Sean McElwee. 2016. "White Privilege Has Enormous Implications for Policy — But Whites Don't Think It Exists." Salon online, 12 Sept. 2016. <http://www.salon.com/2016/09/11/white-privilege-has-enormous-implications-for-policy-but-whites-dont-think-it-exists/>.

Kim, Byung-Soo, Dong-Woo Lee, Jae Nam Bae, Sung Man Chang, et al. 2014. "Impact of Illiteracy on Depression Symptomatology in Community-Dwelling Older Adults." *International Psychogeriatrics*, 26, 10: 1669–1678.

Kinder, John. M. 2015. *Paying with Their Bodies: American War and the Problem of the Disabled Veteran*. University of Chicago Press.

Kohlberg, Lawrence. 1971. "Stages of Moral Development." *Moral Education* 1: 23–92.

Kosberg, Jordan I., and Juanita L. Garcia. 2013. *Elder Abuse: International and Cross-Cultural Perspectives*. Routledge.

Koutsoukis, Jason. 2015. "India Burning Brides and Ancient Practice Is on the Rise." *Sydney Morning Herald*, 31 January 2015. <http://www.smh.com.au/world/india-burning-brides-and-ancient-practice-is-on-the-rise-20150115-12r4j1.html>.

Krieger, Nancy. 2003. "Does Racism Harm Health? Did Child Abuse Exist Before 1962? On Explicit Questions, Critical Science, and Current Controversies: An Ecosocial Perspective." *American Journal of Public Health*, 93, 2: 194–199.

Kruger, Katherine A., and James A. Serpell. 2006. "Animal-Assisted Interventions in Mental Health: Definitions and Theoretical Foundations." In Aubrey Fine (ed.), *Handbook on Animal Assisted Therapy, Theoretical Foundations and Guidelines For Practice*, 2nd edition. San Diego: Academic Press.

Kumar, Deepa. 2012. *Islamophobia and the Politics of Empire*. Chicago: Haymarket Books.

Lacroix, Marie, Michael Baffoe, and Marilena Liguori. 2015. "Refugee Community Organizations in Canada: From the Margins to the Mainstream? A Challenge and Opportunity for Social Workers." *International Journal of Social Welfare*, 24, 1: 62–72.

Laing, Lesley. 2002. "Responding to Men Who Perpetrate Domestic Violence: Controversies, Interventions and Challenges." *Australian Domestic & Family Violence Clearinghouse, Issues Paper*, 7. Sydney, NSW: University of New South Wales.

Langley, Jackie. 2001. "Developing Anti-Oppressive Empowering Social Work Practice with Older Lesbian Women and Gay Men." *British Journal of Social Work*, 31, 6: 917–932.

Lazzarino, Antonio I., Mark Hamer, Emmanuel Stamatakis, and Andrew Steptoe. 2013. "Low Socioeconomic Status and Psychological Distress as Synergistic Predictors of Mortality from Stroke and Coronary Heart Disease." *Psychosomatic Medicine*, 75, 3: 311–316.

Lee, Murray. 2001. "The 'Fear of Crime' and Governance: A Genealogy of the Concept of 'Fear of Crime' and its Imagined Subjects." PhD thesis, University of Western Sydney, Hawkesbury.

Lee, Yu Hao, and Gary Hsieh. 2013. "Does Slacktivism Hurt Activism? The Effects of Moral Balancing and Consistency in Online Activism." In *Proceedings of the SIGCHI Conference on Human Factors in Computing Systems*. New York: ACM.

Legge, Melissa Marie. 2016. "The Role of Animal-Assisted Interventions in Anti-Oppressive Social Work Practice." *British Journal of Social Work*, 46, 7.

Lemish, Dafna, and Varda Muhlbauer. 2012. "'Can't Have It All': Representations of Older Women in Popular Culture." *Women & Therapy*, 35, 3–4: 165–180.

Lenski, Gerhard Emmanul. 1966. *Power and Privilege: A Theory of Social Stratification.* UNC Press Books.

Leonard, William, Anne Mitchell, Marian Pitts, and Sunil Patel. 2008. *Coming Forward: The Underreporting of Heterosexist Violence and Same Sex Partner Abuse in Victoria.* Monograph Series No. 69. Melbourne: The Australian Research Centre in Sex, Health and Society, La Trobe University.

Liebling, Alison, and Elizabeth Stanko. 2001. "Allegiance and Ambivalence: Some Dilemmas in Researching Disorder and Violence." *British Journal of Criminology*, 41: 421–430.

Lindert, Jutta, Ondine S. von Ehrenstein, Rachel Grashow, Gilad Gal, Elmar Braehler, and Marc G. Weisskopf. 2014. "Sexual and Physical Abuse in Childhood Is Associated with Depression and Anxiety over the Life Course: Systematic Review and Meta-Analysis." *International Journal of Public Health*, 59, 2: 359–372.

Linn, James Weber, and Anne Firor Scott. 1935. *Jane Addams: A Biography*. University of Illinois Press.

Little, Gregory, and Kenneth Robinson. 1988. "Moral Reconation Therapy: A Systematic, Step-by-Step Treatment System for Treatment Resistant Clients." *Psychological Reports*, 62: 135–151.

Lohan, Maria. 2007. "How Might We Understand Men's Health Better? Integrating Explanations from Critical Studies on Men and Inequalities in Health." *Social Science & Medicine*, 65, 3: 493–504.

London, Kamala, Maggie Bruck, Stephen Ceci, and Daniel Shuman. 2005. "Disclosure of Child Sexual Abuse: What Does the Research Tell Us about the Ways that Children Tell?" *Psychology, Public Policy, and Law*, 11, 1: 194–226.

Lopes, Rodrigo T., Miguel M. Gonçalves, Paulo P. Machado, Dana Sinai, et al. 2014. "Narrative Therapy Vs. Cognitive-Behavioral Therapy for Moderate Depression: Empirical Evidence from a Controlled Clinical Trial." *Psychotherapy Research*, 24, 6: 662–674.

Mackay, Erin, Althea Gibson, Huette Lam, and David Beecham. 2015. "Perpetrator Interventions in Australia: Key Findings and Future Directions." *Compass: Research to Policy and Practice*, November. Sydney, Australia's National Research Organisation for Women's Safety (ANROWS).

Mackay, Finn. 2015. "From Brussels to Leeds, San Francisco, Delhi: The Global March of Reclaim the Night." In *Radical Feminism*. Palgrave Macmillan UK.

MacMillan, Harriet L., Masako Tanaka, Eric Duku, Tracy Vaillancourt, and Michael H. Boyle. 2013. "Child Physical and Sexual Abuse in a Community Sample of Young Adults: Results from the Ontario Child Health Study." *Child Abuse & Neglect*, 37, 1: 14–21.

Mahoney, Martha. 1994. "Victimisation or Oppression? Women's Lives, Violence and Agency." In Martha Fineman and Roxanne Mykitiuk (eds.), *The Public Nature of Private Violence: The Discovery of Domestic Abuse*. New York: Routledge.

Makris, Una E., Robin T. Higashi, Emily G. Marks, Liana Fraenkel, et al. 2015. "Ageism, Negative Attitudes, and Competing Co-Morbidities — Why Older Adults May Not

Seek Care for Restricting Back Pain: A Qualitative Study." BMC *Geriatrics*, 15, 1: 1.

Marshall, Will. 2002. "Australian Mining Giant Leaves Environmental Disaster in Papua New Guinea." *World Socialist Website*. <https://www.wsws.org/en/articles/2002/04/png-a09.html> retrieved 16 Aug 2016.

Mason, Gail. 2006. "Symposium. The Spectacle of Violence: Homophobia, Gender and Knowledge. The Book at a Glance." *Hypatia*, 21, 2: 174–177.

Massey, Douglas S., and Nancy A. Denton. 1993. *American Apartheid: Segregation and the Making of the Underclass*. Harvard University Press.

Mateos, Concha, and Carmen Gaona. 2015. "Video Activism: A Descriptive Typology." *Global Media Journal*. <http://www.globalmediajournal.com/open-access/video-activism-a-descriptive-typology.php?aid=62532> retrieved 16 Aug, 2016.

Mati, Jacob. M. 2009. "A Cartography of a Global Civil Society Advocacy Alliance: The Case of the Global Call to Action Against Poverty." *Journal of Civil Society*, 5, 1: 83–105.

Matthews, Nancy A. 2000. "Generic Violence Prevention and Gendered Violence: Getting the Message to Mainstream Audiences." *Violence Against Women*, 6, 3: 311–331.

Mattsson, Tina. 2014. "Intersectionality as a Useful Tool Anti-Oppressive Social Work and Critical Reflection." *Affilia*, 29, 1: 8–17.

Mayer, Ann Elizabeth. 2000. "Benign Apartheid: How Gender Apartheid Has Been Rationalized." UCLA *Journal of International Law & Foreign Affairs*, 5: 237.

Mayer, John. 2006. *Waiting on the World*. JohnmayerVEVO. <https://www.youtube.com/watch?v=oBIxScJ5rlY> retrieved 5 Sept. 2016.

McCowan, Tristan. 2013. *Education as a Human Right: Principles for a Universal Entitlement to Learning*. A&C Black.

McDonald, John. 2005. "Neo-Liberalism and the Pathologising of Public Issues: The Displacement of Feminist Service Models in Domestic Violence Support Services." *Australian Social Work*, 58, 3: 275–284.

McDonald, Peter, and Mikki Coleman. 1999. "Deconstructing Hierarchies of Oppression and Adopting a 'Multiple Model' Approach to Anti-Oppressive Practice." *Social Work Education*, 18, 1: 19–33.

McEntire, David A. 2004. "Development, Disasters and Vulnerability: A Discussion of Divergent Theories and the Need for Their Integration." *Disaster Prevention and Management: An International Journal*, 13, 3: 193–198.

McHoul, Alec, and Wendy Grace. 1993. *A Foucault Primer: Discourse, Power and the Subject*. Carlton, Victoria: Melbourne University Press.

McIntosh, P. 2015. "Extending the Knapsack: Using the White Privilege Analysis to Examine Conferred Advantage and Disadvantage." *Women & Therapy*, 38, 3–4: 232–245.

McKie, Linda. 2006. "Sociological Work on Violence: Gender, Theory and Research." *Sociological Research Online*, 11, 2. <http://www.socresonline.org.uk/11/2/mckie.html>.

McLaughlin, Katie. 2005. "From Ridicule to Institutionalization: Anti-Oppression, the State and Social Work." *Critical Social Policy*, 25, 3: 283–305.

____. 2015. "Politics as Social Work." *Social Work in a Global Context: Issues and Challenges*, 39, 40.

McLaughlin, Kenneth. 2005. "From Ridicule to Institutionalization: Anti-Oppression, the State and Social Work." *Critical Social Policy*, 25, 3: 283–305.

McMaster, Ken, and Daryl Gregory. 2003. "Introduction." In K. McMaster and A. Wells (eds.), *Innovative Approaches to Stopping Family Violence*. Wellington, New Zealand: Steele Roberts.

McMaster, Ken, and David Riley. 2011. "Introduction." In K. McMaster and D. Riley (eds.), *Effective Interventions with Offenders: Lessons Learned*. Aotearoa, NZ, HMA and Steele Roberts.

McMichael, Anthony J. 2013. "Globalization, Climate Change, and Human Health." *New England Journal of Medicine*, 368, 14: 1335–1343.

Medina, Jameelah X. 2011. "Body Politicking and the Phenomenon of 'Passing.'" *Feminism & Psychology*, 21, 1: 138–143.

Mehrotra, Nilika. 2011. "Disability Rights Movements in India: Politics and Practice." *Economic & Political Weekly*, 46, 6: 65–72.

Meinck, Franziska, Lucie D. Cluver, Mark E. Boyes, and Lodrick D. Ndhlovu. 2015. "Risk and Protective Factors for Physical and Emotional Abuse Victimisation amongst Vulnerable Children in South Africa." *Child Abuse Review*, 24, 3: 182–197.

Mendes, Philip. 1997. "Blaming the Victim: The New Assault on the Welfare State." *Journal of Economic & Social Policy*, 2, 1: 41.

____. 2000. "Eliminating Welfare Dependency Not Poverty: A Critical Analysis of the Howard Government's Welfare Reform Review." *Policy Organisation and Society*, 19, 2: 23–38.

____. 2003. "Australian Neoliberal Think Tanks and the Backlash Against the Welfare State." *Journal of Australian Political Economy*, 51: 29–56.

____. 2008. *Australia's Welfare Wars Revisited: The Players, the Politics and the Ideologies*. Sydney, NSW: University of New South Wales Press.

____. 2012. "Australia's Income Security System and the Abandonment of Equity." In *Address to Social Policy Connections Forum*. <http://www.socialpolicyconnections.com.au/wp-content/uploads/2012/08/pmendes-equity-aug12.pdf>.

Meyer, David S., and Nancy Whittier. 1994. "Social Movement Spillover." *Social Problems*, 41, 2: 277–298.

Michalowski, Raymond. 1985. *Order, Law, and Crime* New York: Random House.

Middleton, Warwick, Pam Stavropoulos, Martin J. Dorahy, Christa Krüger, et al. 2014. "Institutional Abuse and Societal Silence: An Emerging Global Problem." *Australian and New Zealand Journal of Psychiatry*, 48, 1: 22–25.

Mies, Maria. 1991. "Women's Research or Feminist Research? The Debate Surrounding Feminist Science and Methodology." In Mary Margaret Fonow and Judith A. Cook (eds.), *Beyond Methodology: Feminist Scholarship as Lived Research*. Indiana University Press.

Miller, Peter, and Nikolas Rose. 2008. *Governing the Present: Administering Economic, Social and Personal Life*. Cambridge: Polity Press.

Milner, Jan. 2001. *Women and Social Work: Narrative Approaches*. Basingstoke: Palgrave Macmillan.

____. 2004. "From 'Disappearing' to 'Demonized': The Effects on Men and Women of Professional Interventions Based on Challenging Men Who Are Violent." *Critical Social Policy*, 24, 1: 79–101.

Milner, Jan, and Dorothy Jessop. 2003. "Domestic Violence: Narrative and Solutions."

Probation Journal, 50, 2: 127–141.

Min, Pyong Gap. 2003. "Korean 'Comfort Women': The Intersection of Colonial Power, Gender, and Class." *Gender & Society,* 17, 6: 938–957.

Mitra, Rahul, and Vikram Doctor. 2016. "Passing in Corporate India: Problematizing Disclosure of Homosexuality at the Workplace." In Thomas Köllen (ed.), *Sexual Orientation and Transgender Issues in Organizations.* New York: Springer.

Montgomery, Samantha A., and Abigail J. Stewart. 2012. "Privileged Allies in Lesbian and Gay Rights Activism: Gender, Generation, and Resistance to Heteronormativity." *Journal of Social Issues,* 68, 1: 162–177.

Moodley, Keymanthri, and Sharon Kling. 2015. "Dual Loyalties, Human Rights Violations, and Physician Complicity in Apartheid South Africa." AMA *Journal of Ethics,* 17, 10: 966–972.

Moore, Henrietta. 1994. *A Passion for Difference: Essays in Anthropology and Gender.* Bloomington: Indiana University Press.

Morgan, David. 1987. "Masculinity and Violence." In Mary Maynard and Jalna Hanmer (eds.), *Women, Violence and Social Control.* London: Macmillan.

Morley, Chris, Selma Macfarlane, and Phil Ablett. 2014. *Engaging with Social Work: A Critical Introduction.* Port Melbourne: Cambridge University Press.

Morran, David. 2003. "Men and Their Violence: Terrifying Others and Afraid of Themselves. The Experience of Group-Work with Men Who Are Violent." Bradford Reducing Anger & Violent Emotions (BRAVE). <http://www.brave-project.org/menandtheirviolence.pdf>.

Mullaly, Bob. 2007. *The New Structural Social Work: Ideology, Theory, Practice.* Toronto: Oxford University Press.

____. 2010. *Challenging Oppression and Confronting Privilege.* Ontario: Oxford University Press.

Mums4Refugees. 2015. <https://twitter.com/mums4refugees>.

Munro, Lyle. 2005. "Strategies, Action Repertoires and DIY Activism in the Animal Rights Movement." *Social Movement Studies,* 4, 1: 75–94.

Naffine, Ngaire. 1997. *Feminism & Criminology.* St Leonards, NSW: Allen & Unwin.

Nastovski, Katherine. 2014. "Workers Confront Apartheid: Comparing Canadian Labor Solidarity Campaigns against South African and Israeli Apartheid." *Working USA,* 17, 2: 211–237.

National Link Coalition. 2016. "What Is the Link?" <http://nationallinkcoalition.org/what-is-the-link>.

Nayak, Meghana, and Jennifer Suchland. 2006. "Gender Violence and Hegemonic Projects." *International Feminist Journal of Politics,* 8, 4: 467–485.

Nelson, Todd D. 2005. "Ageism: Prejudice against Our Feared Future Self." *Journal of Social Issues,* 61, 2: 207–221.

____. 2016. "Promoting Healthy Aging by Confronting Ageism." *American Psychologist,* 71, 4: 276.

Nepstad, Sharon Erickson. 2011. "Nonviolent Resistance in the Arab Spring: The Critical Role of Military–Opposition Alliances." *Swiss Political Science Review,* 17, 4: 485–491.

Nerenberg, Lisa. 2000. "Developing a Service Response to Elder Abuse." *Generations,* 24, 2: 86.

Newfoundland and Labrador Violence Prevention Unit. 2015. "Defining Violence and Abuse." <http://www.gov.nl.ca/VPI/types/>.

Ngo, Bic, and K. Kumashiro. 2014. *Six Lenses for Anti-Oppressive Education: Partial Stories, Improbable Conversations*. New York: Peter Lang.

Ngoh Tiong, T. 2011. "Disaster Management and Recovery: Concepts, Models and Process." *Australian Association of Social Workers North Queensland and Queensland Biennial Conference*. <http://www.aasw.asn.au/document/item/3008>.

Nittle, Nadra, K. 2016. "What Is the Definition of Passing for White?" <http://racerelations. about.com/od/understandingrac1/g/Definition-Of-Passing.htm>.

Nolan, Brian, Wiemer Salverda, Daniele Checchi, Ive Marx, et al. (eds.). 2014. *Changing Inequalities and Societal Impacts in Rich Countries: Thirty Countries' Experiences*. Oxford University Press.

Norman, Jane. 2016. "Domestic Violence Ad Campaign to Focus on 'Influencers' in Bid to Change Attitudes." *ABC News Online*. <http://www.abc.net.au/news/2016-04-20/ dv-campaign-to-focus-on-influencers/7340120> retrieved 13 Feb 2017.

Norman, Rosana E., Munkhtsetseg Byambaa, Rumna De, Alexander Butchart, et al. 2012. "The Long-Term Health Consequences of Child Physical Abuse, Emotional Abuse, and Neglect: A Systematic Review and Meta-Analysis." *PLoS Med*, 9, 11: e1001349.

Noske, Barbara. 1997. "Speciesism, Anthropocentrism, and Non-Western Cultures." *Anthrozoös* 10, 4: 183–190.

Noyes, Jenny. 2015. "Powerful Video Calls on the Australian Government to End its 'War' on Refugee Women." *Daily Life,* Nov 2. <http://www.dailylife.com.au/dl-people/ powerful-video-calls-on-the-australian-government-to-end-its-war-on-refugee-women-20151102-gkp0zh.html>.

Nzira, Viola, and Paul Williams. 2009. *Anti-Oppressive Practice in Health and Social Care*. London, Sage.

O'Connor, Thomas, Andrea Davis, Elizabeth Meakes, Ruth Pickering, and Martha Schuman. 2004. "Narrative Therapy Using a Reflective Team: An Ethnographic Study of Therapists' Experiences." *Contemporary Family Therapy*, 26, 1: 23–39.

O'Neill, Brenda, and Elisabeth Gidengil (eds.). 2013. *Gender and Social Capital*. Routledge.

Office of the Registrar General and Census Commissioner, India New Delhi. 2013. *Census of India, 2011 Data on Disability*. <http://www.languageinindia.com/jan2014/ disabilityinindia2011data.pdf>.

OHCHR, UNAIDS, and UNECA UNDP. 2008. "Eliminating Female Genital Mutilation." *An Interagency Statement*. Geneva: WHO. <http://www.un.org/womenwatch/daw/csw/ csw52/statements_missions/Interagency_Statement_on_Eliminating_FGM.pdf>.

Ollis, Tracey. 2008. "The 'Accidental Activist': Learning, Embodiment and Action." *Australian Journal of Adult Learning*, 48, 2: 316.

Ottawa Women's Council. 2014. "Congratulations: Wakefield Grannies Celebrate 10th Anniversary!" *Facebook* page. <https://www.facebook.com/permalink.php?story_fbi d=1530708120481851&id=1399743136911684>.

Pachirat, Timothy. 2011. *Every Twelve Seconds: Industrialized Slaughter and the Politics of Sight*. New Haven and London: Yale University Press.

Padilla, Mark B., Ernesto Vásquez del Aguila, and Richard G. Parker. 2007. "Globalization, Structural Violence, and LGBT Health: A Cross-Cultural Perspective." In Illan Meyer and Mary Northridge (eds.), *The Health of Sexual Minorities: Public Health Perspectives on Lesbian, Gay, Bisexual and Transgender Populations*. New York: Springer.

Palombi, Barbara. 2012. "Women with Disabilities: The Cultural Context of Disability, Feminism, Able-Bodied Privilege, and Microaggressions." In C. Zerbe Enns and E. Nutt Williams (eds.), *The Oxford Handbook of Feminist Counseling Psychology*. Oxford University Press.

Panitch, Melanie. 2008. *Disability, Mothers, and Organization: Accidental Activists*. Routledge.

Paymar, Michael, and Graham Barnes. 2011. "Countering Confusion about the Duluth Model." Domestic Abuse Intervention Programs: Home of the Duluth Model (Research on the Duluth Model and Domestic Violence). <http://www.theduluthmodel.org/pdf/CounteringConfusion.pdf>.

Payne, Malcolm. 2007. *What Is Professional Social Work?* Chicago, IL: Lyceum Books.

____. 2014. *Modern Social Work Theory*, 4th edition. Basingstoke: Palgrave Macmillan.

Pearson, Adam R., John F. Dovidio, and Samuel L. Gaertner. 2009. "The Nature of Contemporary Prejudice: Insights from Aversive Racism." *Social and Personality Psychology Compass*, 3, 3: 314–338.

Pease, Bob. 1999. "The Politics of Men's Health Promotion." *Just Policy*, 15: 29–35.

____. 2010. *Undoing Privilege: Unearned Advantage in a Divided World*. London: Zed Books.

____. 2011. "Men in Social Work: Challenging or Reproducing an Unequal Gender Regime?" *Affilia, Journal of Women and Social Work*, 26, 4: 406–418.

Pease, Bob, and Michael Flood. 2008. "Rethinking the Significance of 'Attitudes' in Challenging Men's Violence Against Women." *Australian Journal of Social Issues*, 43, 4: 547–562.

Peet, Richard. 2002. "Ideology, Discourse and the Hegemony of Geography: From Socialists to Neoliberal Development in Post-Apartheid South Africa." *Antipode*, 34, 1: 74.

Pelka, Fred. 2012. *What We Have Done: An Oral History of the Disability Rights Movement*. University of Massachusetts Press.

Pence, Ellen, and Michael Paymar. 1993. *Education Groups for Men Who Batter: The Duluth Model*. New York: Springer.

Perry, Barbara. 2001. *In the Name of Hate: Understanding Hate Crimes*. Psychology Press.

Perry, Barbara, and Shaheed Alvi. 2012. "'We Are All Vulnerable'. The In Terrorem Effects of Hate Crimes." *International Review of Victimology*, 18, 1: 57–71.

Phillips, Janet, and Penny Vandenbroek. 2014. "Domestic, Family and Sexual Violence in Australia: An Overview of the Issues." Parliamentary Library, Research paper Series, 2014-15. <http://parlinfo.aph.gov.au/parlInfo/download/library/prspub/3447585/upload_binary/3447585.pdf;fileType=application/pdf>.

Phillips, Peter, and Kimberly Soeiro. 2012. *The Global 1%: Exposing the Transnational Ruling Class*. Sonoma State University, Project Censored.

Ploeg, Jenny, Lynne Lohfeld, and Christine A. Walsh. 2013. "What Is 'Elder Abuse'? Voices from the Margin: The Views of Underrepresented Canadian Older Adults." *Journal of Elder Abuse & Neglect*, 25, 5: 396–424.

Pollock, Sue, Agllias Kylie, and Anne Stubley. 2005. "A Gendered Invitation?" *Women Against Violence: An Australian Feminist Journal*, 18: 65–71.

Powell, Anastasia, and Sue Ellen Murray. 2008. "Children and Domestic Violence: Constructing a Policy Problem in Australia and New Zealand." *Social & Legal Studies*,

17, 4: 453–473.

Powell, Fred W. 2001. *The Politics of Social Work.* Sage.

Powell, Kenneth E., James A. Mercy, Alex E. Crosby, Linda L. Dahlberg, and Thomas R. Simon. 2008. "Public Health Models of Violence and Violence Prevention." *Encyclopedia of Violence, Peace, & Conflict,* 2nd edition. Academic Press, Elsevier.

Presser, Lois. 2013. *Critical Issues in Crime and Society: Why We Harm.* New Brunswick, NJ: Rutgers University Press.

Price, Joshua. 2012. *Structural Violence: Hidden Brutality in the Lives of Women.* Ithaca, NY: University of New York Press.

Priebe, Gisela, and Carl Göran Svedin. 2008. "Child Sexual Abuse Is Largely Hidden from the Adult Society: An Epidemiological Study of Adolescents' Disclosures." *Child Abuse & Neglect,* 32, 12: 1095–1108.

Privileged, Uncensored. "What Is Able-Bodied Privilege?" <https://privilegeuncensored. wordpress.com/what-is-able-bodied-privilege-3/#sdfootnote1sym> retrieved 25 Aug. 2016.

Puzan, Elayne. 2003. "The Unbearable Whiteness of Being (in Nursing)." *Nursing Inquiry,* 10, 3: 193–200.

Rashidi, Runoko. 1996. "Apartheid in India." *The Gaither Reporter,* 3, 7: 61.

Ray, Larry. 2011. *Violence in Society.* London, UK: Sage Publications.

Redley, Marcus, E. Maina, A. Keeling, and P. Pattni. 2012. "The Voting Rights of Adults with Intellectual Disabilities: Reflections on the Arguments, and Situation in Kenya and England and Wales." *Journal of Intellectual Disability Research,* 56, 11: 1026–1035.

Reiter, Bernd, and Ulrich Oslender. 2015. *Bridging Scholarship and Activism.* Michigan State University Press.

Respect. 2015. "Respect Briefing Paper: Evidence Base for Interventions with Domestic Violence Perpetrators." <http://respect.uk.net/wp-content/uploads/2015/03/Respect-FULL-briefing-paper-Evidence-base-for-interventions-with-domestic-violence-perpetrators-Jan-2015.pdf> viewed 10 September 2016.

Richmond, Anthony H., and Kathleen Valtonen. 1994. "Global Apartheid: Refugees, Racism, and the New World Order." *Refuge: Canada's Journal on Refugees,* 14, 6.

Richmond, Katy. 2002. "The Gendered Self." In Peter Beilharz and Trevor Hogan (eds.), *Social Self, Global Culture: An Introduction to Sociological Ideas,* 2nd edition. South Melbourne: Oxford University Press.

Riggs, Damien W., Heather Fraser, Nik Taylor, Tania Signal, and Catherine Donovan. 2016. "Domestic Violence Service Providers' Capacity for Supporting Transgender Women: Findings from an Australian Workshop." *British Journal of Social Work,* 46. 8.

Ringrose, Jessica, and Emma Renold. 2010. "Normative Cruelties and Gender Deviants: The Performative Effects of Bully Discourses for Girls and Boys in School." *British Educational Research Journal,* 36, 4: 573–596.

Robertson, Steve. 2007. *Understanding Men and Health: Masculinities, Identity and Well-Being.* Berkshire: Open University Press.

Rojek, Chris. 2012. *Social Work and Received Ideas.* Routledge.

Romo, Rafael D., Margaret I. Wallhagen, Lindsey Yourman, Christie C. Yeung, et al. 2013. "Perceptions of Successful Aging Among Diverse Elders with Late-Life Disability." *The Gerontologist,* 53, 6: 939–949.

Rose, Nikolas. 1999. *Governing the Soul: The Shaping of the Private Self,* 2nd edition. London: Free Association Books.

Rose, Nikolas, Pat O'Malley, and Mariana Valverde. 2006. "Governmentality." *Annual Review of Law and Social Science,* 2: 83–104.

Rosero-Bixby, Luis, and William H. Dow. 2016. "Exploring Why Costa Rica Outperforms the United States in Life Expectancy: A Tale of Two Inequality Gradients." *Proceedings of the National Academy of Sciences,* 113, 5: 1130–1137.

Ross, Stuart, and Kenneth Polk. 2006. "Crime in the Streets." In A. Goldsmith, M. Israel and K. Daly (eds.), *Crime and Justice: A Guide to Criminology,* 3rd edition. Pyrmont, NSW: Lawbook Co.

Rostosky, Sharon S., Whitney W. Black, Erin D. Riggle, and Dani Rosenkrantz. 2015. "Positive Aspects of Being a Heterosexual Ally to Lesbian, Gay, Bisexual and Transgender (LGBT) People." *American Journal of Orthopsychiatry,* 85, 4: 331.

Roth-Douquet, Kathy, and Frank Schaeffer. 2006. AWOL: *The Unexcused Absence of America's Upper Classes from Military Service — And How it Hurts Our Country.* Harper Collins.

Rush, Michael, and Marie Keenan. 2014. "The Social Politics of Social Work: Anti-Oppressive Social Work Dilemmas in Twenty-First-Century Welfare Regimes." *British Journal of Social Work,* 44, 6: 1436–1453.

Ryan, Caitlin, and Ian Rivers. 2003. "Lesbian, Gay, Bisexual and Transgender Youth: Victimization and Its Correlates in the USA and UK." *Culture, Health & Sexuality,* 5, 2: 103–119.

Ryan, Thomas (ed.). 2014. *Animals in Social Work: Why and How They Matter.* Palgrave Macmillan.

Ryan, William. 1976. *Blaming the Victim.* New York: Vintage.

Rydgren, Jens. 2005. *Movements of Exclusion: Radical Right-Wing Populism in the Western World.* Nova Publishers.

Sakamoto, Izumi, and Ronald O. Pitner. 2005. "Use of Critical Consciousness in Anti-Oppressive Social Work Practice: Disentangling Power Dynamics at Personal and Structural Levels." *British Journal of Social Work,* 35, 4: 435–452.

Sandberg, Jorgen, and Mats Alvesson. 2011. "Ways of Constructing Research Questions: Gap-Spotting or Problematization?" *Organization,* 18, 1: 23–44. doi: 10.1177/1350508410372151.

Sandberg, Linda, and Aina Tollefsen. 2010. "Talking about Fear of Violence in Public Space: Female and Male Narratives about Threatening Situations in Umea, Sweden." *Social and Cultural Geography,* 11, 1: 1–15.

Sandor, Danny. 1994. "The Thickening Blue Wedge in Juvenile Justice." In C. Alder and J. Wundersitz (eds.), *Family Conferencing and Juvenile Justice: The Way Forward or Misplaced Optimism?* Canberra: Australian Institute of Criminology.

Saunders, Bernadette J. 2013. "Ending the Physical Punishment of Children by Parents in the English-Speaking World: The Impact of Language, Tradition and Law." *The International Journal of Children's Rights,* 21, 2: 278–304.

Sayce, Liz. 2000. *From Psychiatric Patient to Citizen.* New York: St. Martin's Press.

Scheper-Hughes, Nancy. 2013. "No Magic Bullets." *On Violence,* 1, 4.

Schwartz, Marie Jenkins. 2013. "Child Slaves in the Modern World." *Slavery & Abolition,* 34, 4: 680–681.

Schwartz, Martin D. 2005. "The Past and Future of Violence Against Women." *Journal of Interpersonal Violence*, 21, 1: 7–11.

Scott, John. 2000. "Class and Stratification." In G. Payne (Ed.), *Social Divisions*. Hampshire: Palgrave

____. 2003. "Competition Paper. Prostitution and Public Health in New South Wales." *Culture, Health & Sexuality*, 5, 3: 277–293.

SCRGSP. 2014. "Overcoming Indigenous Disadvantage: Key Indicators 2014." Productivity Commission: Steering Committee for the Review of Government Service Provision, Commonwealth of Australia. <http://www.pc.gov.au/research/recurring/overcoming-indigenous-disadvantage/key-indicators-2014/key-indicators-2014-report.pdf>.

Seidler, Katie. 2010. *Crime, Culture and Violence: Understanding How Masculinity and Identity Shapes Offending*. Bowen Hills, Qld: Australian Academic Press.

Sen, Gita, and Caren Grown. 2013. *Development Crises and Alternative Visions: Third World Women's Perspectives*. Routledge.

Senate Hansard. 2007. *Commonwealth, Senate Official Hansard*, 8, 8 August. <http://parlinfo.aph.gov.au/parlInfo/download/chamber/hansards/2007-08-07/toc_pdf/5596-3.pdf; fileType=application%2Fpdf#search=%22chamber/hansards/2007-08-07/0000%22> viewed 19 May 2015.

Serious Crime Act (UK). 2015. <http://www.legislation.gov.uk/ukpga/2015/9/pdfs/ukpga_20150009_en.pdf>.

Sewpaul, Vishanthie, Ingrid Østhus, and Christopher Mhone. 2013. "Power and Participation in Community Work Research and Practice." *Participation in Community Work: International Perspectives*, 107.

Shakespeare, Tom. 2004. "Disablism Ain't the Same as Racism." Ouch! It's a Disability Thing. BBC Online, September 6. <http://www.bbc.co.uk/ouch/opinion/disablism_aint_the_same_as_racism.shtml> retrieved 25 Aug. 2016.

Shalev, I., T.E. Moffitt, K. Sugden, B. Williams, et al.. 2013. "Exposure to Violence during Childhood Is Associated with Telomere Erosion from 5 to 10 Years of Age: A Longitudinal Study." *Molecular Psychiatry*, 18, 5: 576–581.

Sharp, Gemma, Julie Mattiske, and Kirsten I. Vale. 2016. "Motivations, Expectations, and Experiences of Labiaplasty: A Qualitative Study." *Aesthetic Surgery Journal*, 36, 8: 920–928.

Shepherd, Laura J. 2007. "'Victims, Perpetrators and Actors' Revisited: Exploring the Potential for a Feminist Reconceptualisation of (International) Security and (Gender) Violence." *The British Journal of Politics & International Relations*, 9, 2: 239–256.

____. 2009. "Gender, Violence and Global Politics: Contemporary Debates in Feminist Security Studies." *Political Studies Review*, 7, 2: 208–219.

Sherry, Mark. 2016. *Disability Hate Crimes: Does Anyone Really Hate Disabled People?* Routledge.

Shiva, Vandana. 2005. *Earth Democracy: Justice, Sustainability and Peace*. London: Zed Books.

Shonkoff, Jack P., and Deborah A. Phillips (eds.). 2000. *From Neurons to Neighborhoods: The Science of Early Childhood Development*. National Academies Press.

Shonkoff, Jack P., Andrew S. Garner, Benjamin S. Siegel, Mary I. Dobbins, et al. 2012. "The Lifelong Effects of Early Childhood Adversity and Toxic Stress." *Pediatrics*, 129, 1: e232-e246.

Sifris, Ronli. 2010. "Conceptualising Involuntary Sterilisation as 'Severe Pain or Suffering' for the Purposes of Torture Discourse." *Netherlands Quarterly of Human Rights*, 28, 4: 523–547.

Sinclair, Raven. 2007. "Identity Lost and Found: Lessons from the Sixties Scoop." *First Peoples Child & Family Review*, 3, 1: 65–82.

Sköld, Johanna, and Shurlee Swain (eds.). 2015. *Apologies and the Legacy of Abuse of Children in "Care": International Perspectives.* Springer.

Smith, Dorothy E. 2003. "Resisting Institutional Capture as a Research Practice." In B. Glassner and R. Hertz (eds.), *Our Studies, Ourselves: Sociologists' Lives and Work.* New York: Oxford University Press.

Smith, Jane M., Amanda Williams, and Frank Mullane. 2014. "The Problem of Domestic Abuse and Homicide." In J. Monckton-Smith, A. Williams, and F. Mullane (eds.), *Domestic Abuse, Homicide and Gender: Strategies for Policy and Practice.* Palgrave Macmillan UK.

Smith, Kerry. 2016. "Bangladesh: Editor of Only LGBTI Magazine Murdered." *Green Left Weekly*, 1093: 15.

South African Government. 2016. "The First Decade of Freedom." <http://www.gov.za/about-sa/history#decade_freedom> retrieved 9 August 2016.

Staggenborg, Suzanne. 2015. *Social Movements.* Oxford University Press.

Stanko, Elizabeth A. 2003. "Introduction: Conceptualising the Meanings of Violence." In E.A. Stanko (ed.), *The Meanings of Violence.* London: Routledge.

Statistics Canada. 2015. *Disability in Canada: Initial Findings from the Canadian Survey on Disability.* <http://www.statcan.gc.ca/pub/89-654-x/89-654-x2013002-eng.htm>.

Staub, Ervin. 1989. *The Roots of Evil: The Origins of Genocide and Other Group Violence.* Cambridge: Cambridge University Press.

Stokes, Geoffrey. 1997. *The Politics of Identity in Australia.* Cambridge: Cambridge University Press.

Strandh, Mattias, Anthony Winefield, Karina Nilsson, and Anne Hammarström. 2014. "Unemployment and Mental Health Scarring During the Life Course." *The European Journal of Public Health*, 24, 3: 440–445.

Straus, Murray. A. 2001. *Beating the Devil Out of Them: Corporal Punishment in American Families and its Effects on Children.* Transaction Publishers.

Strier, Roni, and Sharon Binyamin. 2014. "Introducing Anti-Oppressive Social Work Practices in Public Services: Rhetoric to Practice." *British Journal of Social Work*, 44, 8: 2095–2112.

Stroman, Duane F. 2003. *The Disability Rights Movement: From Deinstitutionalization to Self-Determination.* Universty Press of America.

Swain, John, and Sally French. 2000. "Towards an Affirmation Model of Disability." *Disability & Society*, 15, 4: 569–582.

Syed, Jawad. 2016. "Targeted Killings in Bangladesh: Diversity at Stake." *The Huffington Post*, April 28. <http://www.huffingtonpost.co.uk/jawad-syed/targeted-killings-in-bang_b_9789716.html>.

Tabili, Laura. 2003. "Race is a Relationship, and Not a Thing." *Journal of Social History*, 37, 1: 125–130.

Talusan, Meredith. 2015. "Being Transgender in a Transphobic Society Leads to Moments of Sheer Desperation." *The Guardian*, 2 April. <https://www.theguardian.com/commentisfree/2015/apr/02/being-transgender-in-a-transphobic-society-leads-to-moments-of-sheer-desperation>.

Tappis, Hannah, Jeffery Freeman, Nancy Glass, and Shannon Doocy. 2016. "Effectiveness of Interventions, Programs and Strategies for Gender-Based Violence Prevention in Refugee Populations: An Integrative Review." PLOS *Currents: Disasters*, 8. <https://www.ncbi.nlm.nih.gov/pmc/articles/PMC4865365/?report=classic>.

Tarrow, Sidney G., and J. Tollefson. 1994. *Power in Movement: Social Movements, Collective Action and Politics*. Cambridge: Cambridge University Press.

Taylor, Mark Patrick. 2012. "Lead Poisoning of Port Pirie Children: A Long History of Looking the Other Way." *The Conversation*. <http://theconversation.com/lead-poisoning-of-port-pirie-children-a-long-history-of-looking-the-other-way-8296>.

Taylor, Nik, and Heather Fraser. Forthcoming 2018. *Rescuing Me, Rescuing You: Companion Animals and Domestic Violence*. London: Palgrave.

Taylor, Nik, Heather Fraser, Tania Signal, and Kathy Prentice. 2016. "Social Work, Animal-Assisted Therapies and Ethical Considerations: A Programme Example from Central Queensland, Australia." *British Journal of Social Work*, 46, 1: 135–152.

Taylor, Tristan. 2016. "Eradicating Poverty, Resource Allocation, and the Environment." *International Journal of Applied Philosophy*, 30, 1: 27–42.

Taylor-Robinson, David, Margaret Whitehead, and Ben Barr. 2014. "Great Leap Backwards." *BMJ*, 349: g7350.

Tew, Jerry. 2006. "Understanding Power and Powerlessness: Towards a Framework for Emancipatory Practice in Social Work." *Journal of Social Work*, 6, 1: 33–51.

Thompson, Neil. 1997. "Children, Death and Ageism." *Child & Family Social Work*, 2, 1: 59–65.

Tilly, Charles, and Sidney G. Tarrow. 2015. *Contentious Politics*. Oxford University Press.

Tomei, Jenna L. 2016. "The Gay Panic Defense: Legal Defense Strategy or Reinforcement of Homophobia in Court?" PhD dissertation, Sam Houston State University.

Tomsen, Stephen. 2003. "'A Gross Overreaction': Violence, Honour and the Sanctified Heterosexual Male Body." In Stephen Tomsen and Mike Donaldson (eds.), *Male Trouble: Looking at Australian Masculinities*. Victoria: Pluto Press.

Tomsen, Stephen, Ross Homel, and Jenny Thommeny. 1991. "The Causes of Public Violence: Situational versus Other Factors in Drinking-Related Assaults." In D. Chappell, P. Grabosky and H. Strang (eds.), *Australian Violence: Contemporary Perspectives*. Canberra: Australian Institute of Criminology.

Tyson, Jemma, and Nathan Hall. 2016. "Medicalising 'Hatred': Exploring the Sense and Sensitivities of Classifying the Motivations for Hate Crime as Mental Disorder." In Jane Winstone (ed.), *Mental Health, Crime and Criminal Justice: Responses and Reforms*. Palgrave Macmillan UK.

U.N. Women National Committee Australia. 2016. "Eliminating Violence against Women – It's Everyone's Responsibility." <https://unwomen.org.au/our-work/focus-areas/eliminating-violence-against-women/>.

United Nations Women. 2012a. "Forms of Violence Against Women." Virtual Knowledge Centre to End Violence Against Women and Girls. <http://www.endvawnow.org/en/articles/296-forms-of-violence-against-women-.html>.

____. 2012b. "Campaigns for Behaviour Change." Virtual Knowledge Centre to End Violence against Women and Girls. <http://goo.gl/zYvSp>.

United Nations Convention on the Rights of the Child. 1989. <https://www.humanrights. gov.au/convention-rights-child> viewed 10 February 2016.

UPLIFT. 2015. "The Dalai Lama on the Reality of War." <http://upliftconnect.com/ reality-of-war/>.

van Doore, Kathryn E. 2016. "Paper Orphans: Exploring Child Trafficking for the Purpose of Orphanages." *The International Journal of Children's Rights*, 24, 2: 378–407.

Veenema, Tener, Thornton Goodwin, P. Clifton and Andrew Corley. 2015. "The Public Health Crisis of Child Sexual Abuse in Low and Middle Income Countries: An Integrative Review of the Literature." *International Journal of Nursing Studies*, 52, 4: 864–881.

Vera-Sanso, Penny. 2012. "Gender, Poverty and Old-Age Livelihoods in Urban South India in an Era of Globalisation." *Oxford Development Studies*, 40, 3: 324–340.

VicHealth. 2014. *Australians' Attitudes to Violence Against Women. Findings from the 2013 National Community Attitudes Towards Violence Against Women Survey (NCAS)*. Victorian Health Promotion Foundation, Melbourne, Australia

Victor, Christina. R. 2013. *Old Age in Modern Society: A Textbook of Social Gerontology*. Springer.

Vlais, Rodney. 2014. "Domestic Violence Perpetrator Programs: Education, Therapy, Support, Accountability 'or' Struggle?" No to Violence: Male Family Violence Prevention Association. <https://graddipfdr20161.pbworks.com/f/Domestic Violence Perpetrator Programs.pdf>.

Wadiwel, Dinesh. 2015. *The War Against Animals*. Brill.

Wahlström, Mattias. 2011. "Taking Control or Losing Control? Activist Narratives of Provocation and Collective Violence." *Social Movement Studies*, 10, 4: 367–385.

Walby, Sylvia. 2012. "Violence and Society: Introduction to an Emerging Field of Sociology." *Current Sociology*, 61, 2: 95–111. <http://csi.sagepub.com/content/early/2012/09/ 12/0011392112456478>.

Walton, Gerald. 2011. "Spinning Our Wheels: Reconceptualizing Bullying Beyond Behaviour-Focused Approaches." *Discourse: Studies in the Cultural Politics of Education*, 32, 1: 131–144.

Waring, Marilyn. J. 1988. *Counting for Nothing: What Men Value and What Women Are Worth*. Allen & Unwin.

Warriner, Katrina, Craig T. Nagoshi, and Julie L. Nagoshi. 2013. "Correlates of Homophobia, Transphobia, and Internalized Homophobia in Gay or Lesbian and Heterosexual Samples." *Journal of Homosexuality*, 60, 9: 1297–1314.

Weiss, Thomas, G. 2016. *What's Wrong with the United Nations and How to Fix it*. John Wiley & Sons.

Wendt, Sarah, Michelle R. Tuckey, and Brenton Prosser. 2011. "Thriving, Not Just Surviving, in Emotionally Demanding Fields of Practice." *Health and Social Care in the Community*, 19, 3: 317–325.

West, Candice, and Don H. Zimmerman. 1987. "Doing Gender." *Gender and Society*, 1, 2: 125–151.

White, Rob, and Daphne Habibis. 2005. *Crime and Society*. South Melbourne: Oxford

University Press.

White, Rob, and Santina Perrone. 2005. *Crime and Social Control.* South Melbourne: Oxford University Press.

White, Sarah. C. 2002. "From the Politics of Poverty to the Politics of Identity? Child Rights and Working Children in Bangladesh." *Journal of International Development,* 14, 6: 725–735.

Whitehead, Antony. 2005. "Man to Man Violence: How Masculinity May Work as a Dynamic Risk Factor." *Howard Journal,* 44, 4: 411–422.

Whitlock, Kay. 2004. "Our Enemies, Ourselves: Why Antiviolence Movements Must Relplace the Dualism of 'Us and Them' with an Ethic of Interdependence." In E.A. Castelli and J.R. Jakobsen (eds.), *Interventions: Activists and Academics Respond to Violence.* Gordonsville, VA: Palgrave Macmillan.

WHO (World Health Organisation). 2002. *World Report on Violence And Health: Summary.* Geneva: World Health Organisation.

____. 2008. *Eliminating Female Genital Mutilation: An Interagency Statement: UNAIDS, UNDP, UNECA, UNESCO, UNFPA, UNHCHR, UNHCR, UNICEF, UNIFEM, WHO.* Geneva.

____. 2010a. *Policy Approaches to Engaging Men and Boys in Achieving Gender Equality and Health Equity.* Geneva.

____. 2010b. "Childhood Lead Poisoning, 2010." Geneva.

____. 2013. "Global and Regional Estimates of Violence Against Women: Prevalence and Health Effects of Intimate Partner Violence and Non-Partner Sexual Violence." <http://apps.who.int/iris/bitstream/10665/85239/1/9789241564625_eng.pdf>.

____. 2016a. "Violence." <http://www.who.int/topics/violence/en/>. (ch 3)

____. 2016b. "Female Genital Mutilation: Fact Sheet." <http://www.who.int/mediacentre/factsheets/fs241/en/>. (ch 5)

Willig, Carla. 2001. *Introducing Qualitative Research in Psychology: Adventures in Theory and Method.* Berkshire: Open University Press.

Wilson, Monica. 2003. "Perpetrator Programmes for Male Domestic Violence Offenders: What Do We Know about Effectiveness?" Briefing Paper: Towards Effective Practice, Criminal Justice Social Work Development Centre for Scotland.

Wodak, Alex. 2015. "The Failure of Drug Prohibition and the Future of Drug Law Reform in Australia." *Australian Prescriber,* 38, 5: 148.

World Bank. 2012. *The World Development Report 2012: Gender Equality and Development — Overview.* Washington, DC: World Bank. <http://www.gsdrc.org/go/display&type=Document&id=4299>.

Worrall, Anne. 1997. *Punishment in the Community: The Future of Criminal Justice.* London: Longman.

Young, Iris Marion. 2006. "Responsibility and Global Justice: A Social Connection Model." *Social Philosophy and Policy,* 23: 102–130.

____. 2009. "Five Faces of Oppression." In George Henderson and Marvin Waterstone (eds.), *Geographic Thought: A Praxis Perspective.* London: Routlege.

____. 2011. *Responsibility for Justice.* New York: Oxford University Press.

Zack, Naomi. 2006. *Thinking about Race,* 2nd edition. California: Thomson Wadsworth.

Zevallos, Zuleyka. 2003. "'That's My Australian Side': The Ethnicity, Gender and Sexuality of Young Australian Women of South and Central American Origin." *Journal of Sociology,* 39, 1: 81–98.

INDEX